A

FORCE

FOR

NATURE

A

FORCE

FOR

NATURE

THE STORY OF NRDC AND
THE FIGHT TO SAVE OUR PLANET

John H. Adams & Patricia Adams

with George Black

Foreword by Robert Redford

CHRONICLE BOOKS
SAN FRANCISCO

Library of Congress Cataloging-in-Publication Data is available.

ISBN: 978-0-8118-7793-0

Manufactured in the United States of America

Designed by ALLISON WEINER

10 9 8 7 6 5 4 3 2

Chronicle Books LLC
680 Second Street
San Francisco, California 94107

www.chroniclebooks.com

Table of Contents

Foreword

Why NRDC? And why John Adams? Of all the superb environmental organizations that have grown up over the past forty years, why did I choose to spend most of my adult life associated with this one?

When I was a kid in California, I grabbed every opportunity I could to escape to unspoiled wild places. Those experiences exposed me to all the majesty of the natural world, but at a time when the threats to it seemed to be growing exponentially. We had few environmental laws to speak of; even calling yourself an environmentalist led most people to write you off as some kind of crazed extremist. But John Adams, a man I'd never met, was figuring out some answers. If there were no laws, make them—and then enforce them. If there were no lawyers, find them, train them, and set them loose in the courtroom. If environmentalism was seen as a fringe issue, take it into the mainstream. If environmentalists were condemned as naysayers, show that they had real, practical solutions.

In January 1970 John and a group of like-minded lawyers set up an organization that they called the Natural Resources Defense Council, or NRDC. Forty years later many people (myself included) regard it as possibly the most effective environmental organization on the planet.

I first met John in 1973. Lots of organizations were springing up around this time. I worked with many of them and admired what they were doing, but when I met with John it was clear that NRDC had a unique concept, a power. They could go to court.

The tiny organization had already begun to prove that it could defeat the worst corporate polluters. At the same time, NRDC was infinitely pragmatic: the message was, work with us to design solutions and we'll do all we can to find common ground; oppose us and we will see you in court—and more often than not we will win.

I joined John's board in 1974. Part of his genius was to see that protecting our environment would take generations, so he set about creating an organization for the long haul. Start with the smartest lawyers you could find and steadily add the best scientists, economists, communicators, fundraisers, administrators. Remain unswervingly loyal to these people, and they would repay you in kind. NRDC is full of people who have been there for twenty or thirty years or more. Can any other organization make that kind of claim?

To me, membership is a vital key to NRDC's phenomenal success. John and his colleagues have helped draft many of the nation's most important environmental laws; they have won landmark cases all the way to the U.S. Supreme Court. But lasting social change comes ultimately from the grass roots, and NRDC has built a community of 1.2 million members and online activists. That is real power.

But you never rest on your laurels. The biggest challenge of our generation is to fight global warming, and it involves standing up to the most powerful corporate and political adversaries. To NRDC, that's the whole point of building an organization for the long haul. There will be endless battles and frequent reversals of fortune. But in the end, you can outfight and outlast your enemies, and you can win.

So, John, my friend, here's to the next forty years.

—Robert Redford

We dedicate this book to NRDC's extended family, to our children, Kate, John Hamilton, and Ramsay, and our nephews, Tom and McCrea Burnham, and to our grandchildren who hold the future.

We are indebted to our founding chairman, Stephen Duggan, and his wife, Beatrice Abbott Duggan, for their warmth and commitment in building a strong foundation for NRDC. Whitney North Seymour Jr. created a model for NRDC that we have followed ever since. Bill DeWind led us into the international arena. Fritz Schwarz guided us through the transition to new leadership under Frances Beinecke. Our fourth chairman, Dan Tishman, has kept us secure through the recent economic crisis.

The intellectual leadership of Gus Speth, Ed Strohbehn, John Bryson, Dick Ayres, Tom Stoel, and Dick Hall in the new field of public interest law set the standard for our work. Founding board members David Sive, Jim Marshall, Adele Auchincloss, George Woodwell, Boris Bittker, Bob Gilmore, John Oakes, John Robinson, and Larry Rockefeller were mentors and friends.

Simpson, Thacher, and Bartlett has always given us superb pro bono representation, from Stephen Duggan to Dick Beattie, Tom Cashel, Chuck Koob, Sarah Cogan, and Pete Ruegger.

Countless people have made NRDC a great place to live and work. Pattie Sullivan has played a key role for nearly all the forty years of our story. Judy Keefer, our chief financial officer, and Laurie Alemian-Derian, our comptroller for many years, made us a much more professional organization. Our development team, led by Jack Murray and including Robert Ferguson, Priscilla Bayley, Abby Schaefer, Jennifer Chapin, and Denise Schlener, accomplished miracles. Linda Lopez and Stephen Mills made our membership program a great success.

Many others have been critical in supporting NRDC's work, including Bob Allen, Ned Ames, Peggy Ayres, Bill Beinecke, Sally and Martin Brown, Anna Scott Carter, Graydon Carter, Ann Clark, Jim Compton, Larry Condon, Sheryl Crow, Joan Davidson, Patrick Dollard, the Edgerton family, the Favrot family, Michael Fisher, Bill Haney, Cindy Horn, Ray and Beth Huger, Burks Lapham, Elizabeth McCormack, Barnabas McHenry, Scott McVay, Sam Rose, Ed Stack, Fred Stanback, the Wallace Family, and Julie Walters.

Members of the Green Group have been our partners in the tireless effort to protect the environment, particularly our colleagues at the Open Space Institute, led by Kim Elliman and Joe Martens and assisted by Susan Barbarisi; Gene Karpinski, president of the League of Conservation Voters; George Woodwell of the Woods Hole Research Center; Jim Moorman, former head of the Sierra Club Legal Defense Fund; Rodger Schlickeisen of Defenders of Wildlife; Bill Meadows of the Wilderness Society; and our colleagues at Environmental Defense and the Sierra Club. We remember three friends who are no longer with us: Rick Sutherland, Peter Berle, and Jay Hair. Thanks also to Duke University for supporting our work over the years. And for the long time encouragement of our author friends, Jean Marzollo and Irene O'Garden.

The support of Chronicle Books chairman Nion McEvoy and editors Sarah Malarkey and Jennifer Kong is greatly appreciated.

We conducted more than 150 interviews for this book. By necessity, this involved some tough editorial decisions, and many stories had to be edited out that were just as important as those that remained. All of these stories will be permanently preserved in our archives.

Finally, our thanks to our friend, advisor, and supporter Ann Roach, who played a special role in the creation of this book, and to George Black, who worked tirelessly with us to shape NRDC's many stories into a book we hope you will find rewarding.

—John and Patricia Adams
BEAVERKILL, NEW YORK, APRIL 2010

First Decade

1970–1980

Gathering Forces

I sat on a bench in Battery Park in lower Manhattan, eating a liverwurst sandwich. As the Hudson River flowed by, I idly watched lumps of raw sewage float right in front of me. It was outrageous to me that this could be happening in the greatest city in the world. My parents had come here from Ireland in the 1920s in search of a new life, and I had been born here. The city had been good to me; I had worked in a Wall Street law firm and after that had been in the U.S. attorney's office for four years.

It was 1969, and concern about pollution was building across the country. January had brought the massive Santa Barbara oil spill, just off the coast of California. In June, an oil and garbage slick on the Cuyahoga River in Ohio had caught fire. David Brower, the outspoken head of the Sierra Club, the country's oldest and best-known conservation group, had just left the organization to found Friends of the Earth after years of battling to block dams on the Colorado River. The most talked about of his "Grand Canyon Battle Ads" had asked, "Should We Also Flood the Sistine Chapel so Tourists Can Get Nearer the Ceiling?"

But I wasn't thinking about the raw sewage in the Hudson as a "cause." There was no strong professional avenue at that time for someone who wanted to address pollution issues, and what I was looking for was a new direction for my career. I knew I was ready to leave my job. I'd worked with U.S. Attorney Robert Morgenthau in the Southern District of New York, and after that I'd been special attorney with the Joint Strike Force on Organized Crime and Racketeering. I loved being in court, thinking on my feet, the daily interaction with a multitude of people. However, it was a job most people do for only a few years, and I was ready to move on.

The problem was, where was I going to find work as exciting and alive as being an assistant U.S. attorney? The freedom I felt there, and the collegiality I'd found with a group of brilliant, like-minded colleagues, would be hard to duplicate.

Expecting our third child and living in a one-bedroom apartment in Greenwich Village, Patricia and I were also looking for an alternative to life in the city. If our young children—Kate, who was five, and two-year-old John Hamilton—slept by an open window in our apartment, they would wake with soot on their foreheads. Patricia read that a New Yorker breathed as much poison each day as someone who smoked a pack of cigarettes. She said, "It's one thing for me to choose to breathe such air—but what about our children?" One day I saw an advertisement on the back of the city buses, just above the diesel exhaust pipe, a picture of beautiful, snowcapped mountains. The caption read, "Take a deep breath—and then fly Swiss Air to the Alps."

We knew the Swiss Alps weren't the answer, but we did think about moving upstate, where we had bought an old farmhouse on the banks of the Beaverkill River in the Catskills. I had grown up just a few miles away, on a small farm in Callicoon Center, with cows and chickens and surrounded by miles of open woodland and fields. There was a strong "back to the land" movement in the late 1960s, and we briefly considered trying farm life. But in the end we couldn't convince ourselves to leave the city. Patricia was still in graduate school at the City University of New York, and I couldn't imagine practicing small-town law.

One thing we both knew, although we didn't put it in specific terms, was that we wanted a life of public service. I had put myself through college at Michigan State and then law school at Duke by working summers for the company that was building tunnels to bring drinking water from the Catskill reservoirs to New York City. Unions and labor issues were very important to me. Patricia, meanwhile, had grown up in the southern Appalachians, where she spent lots of time camping with her father, who was a forester and Boy Scout leader, so wilderness was important to her. We talked about the various political causes that were roiling the country at the time—the civil rights struggle, labor disputes, the Vietnam War, the women's movement—but none seemed to provide the right professional "fit" in terms of our backgrounds.

As we considered our options, I couldn't get images like the raw sewage in the Hudson out of my mind. Some close friends from Duke Law School, Jim Moorman and his wife, Brenda, used to visit us in Beaverkill, and over plates of spaghetti and cheap red wine, with interruptions to put children to bed, we would have passionate discussions about environmental issues. One night the conversation turned to the cutting of redwoods in California. Another friend, who had a forestry degree from North Carolina State, argued that the best way to manage our forests was by clear-cutting and harvesting old-growth trees. Jim was adamant that this was sacrilege—destroying two-thousand-year-old trees to make picnic tables for suburbia! These early discussions were emblematic of the confrontations we would have in the future over competing visions of society's relationship to our natural environment.

Jim had just started work in Washington for the Center for Law and Social Policy, which was founded as a public interest law firm in August 1969 by Charles Halpern, with the assistance of former Supreme Court Justice Arthur Goldberg. Public interest law was a new idea, and the initial focus was on women's rights and health care for the poor—but environmental protection was also on Jim's agenda. He invited me to come with him to a seminar about Alaska, and I was horrified by what I learned there. In 1968 the Atlantic Richfield

Company and Humble Oil (which later became Exxon) had discovered huge deposits of oil at Prudhoe Bay, and plans were under way to build a pipeline that would cut across hundreds of miles of the wildest and most pristine landscape in the United States, ending up at Valdez, on Prince William Sound.

Urban pollution, dead rivers, clear-cut forests, destroyed canyons, a pipeline through Alaska—as our conversations continued, all these things came together in my mind until they reached a kind of critical mass. And in Jim's Center for Law and Social Policy, I had my first glimmer of what we might do about the problem.

At about the same time, similar thoughts were going through the heads of a group of law students from Yale—Gus Speth, Dick Ayres, John Bryson, and Ed Strohbehn—and a friend of theirs from Harvard Law School, a former Rhodes Scholar named Tom Stoel. All five had grown up in a relatively rural America—Ayres, Bryson, and Stoel are natives of the Pacific Northwest—and as children they had hiked, camped, hunted, and fished. They didn't call themselves "environmentalists"; the word didn't exist then in the sense that it does today. Instead, people thought of themselves as "conservationists" or "nature lovers." But like Patricia and me, the five had felt assaulted by the pollution they saw in the cities of the Northeast—the dirty air and the foaming rivers—while attending college. As products of the 1960s, the Vietnam era, they had seen how their own generation could change the world. Feeling empowered by their experiences in college and law school, they were convinced that they could make a difference.

One day in 1969, Gus Speth, a leader of the Yale group, was reading the *New York Times* when he saw an article about the NAACP Legal Defense Fund; on the opposite page was an article on the environment. The idea came to him in a flash: why not an NAACP-style legal defense fund for the environment?

Gus, Dick, John, Ed, and Tom decided that they would establish a law firm to represent victims of pollution. They were determined not to be captured by traditional law firms but to do something different with their law degrees. They felt the big corporations were getting away with murder. So they would sue the bastards! (For something—even if they weren't yet sure for what.)

Gus got in touch with David Sive, one of the few lawyers who practiced environmental law, to ask for advice. David was a generation older than Gus; his firm, Weiner, Neuberger, and Sive, represented private clients but used a portion of the fees to do pro bono work for environmental causes. At the time, David was representing the Sierra Club, which was opposing plans for a Hudson River Expressway between Albany and New York City. He told Gus that the Ford Foundation was looking for ways to fund legal action on the environment. Concerns about pollution were beginning to stir in Washington, both in Congress and in the Nixon administration, and a new law was being drafted that would eventually come into force on the first day of 1970—the National Environmental Policy Act, better known as NEPA. Someone was going to have to make sure that NEPA was properly enforced.

The foundation agreed to send someone up to Yale to meet with Gus Speth and his fellow students. Gus realized that they had no faculty advisors and needed someone who would give the group legitimacy in Ford's eyes. Two professors responded to his appeal for help: Charles Reich, who was writing the future bestseller, *The Greening of America*, and Boris Bittker, the Sterling Professor of Law and one of the most renowned tax law professors in America. (Both men would become early board members of NRDC.) Bittker said later that he knew the students hoped his "gray hair and reputation in the tax field might be sufficient endorsement for the Ford Foundation to take them more seriously than it would otherwise."

Even with these two advisors, Gus says, the foundation was uneasy at the prospect of funding these young "whippersnappers." Ford suggested that the Yale group join another organization that had already been formed, a very liberal group that was focusing on urban issues. Tom Stoel met with the group and called Gus as soon as the meeting was over. "These folks are going down a rat hole," he told him. "We don't want to be any part of them." He was right; the organization that Ford had recommended lasted only a short time, and Gus's group found itself still looking for the right home.

David Sive was also the link that eventually connected me to the third of the gathering forces that would result in the creation of NRDC. This was the fight to save Storm King Mountain in the Hudson Highlands, an effort that had been under way for several years and had very different—and quite specific—origins.

In 1962 Consolidated Edison had proposed building a pump storage power-generating plant on Storm King, a mountain celebrated by the Hudson River School painters of the nineteenth century and much loved by New York residents. The project involved cutting away part of the mountain, constructing a huge complex of turbines, transformers, and generators, and stringing high-tension wires across the river. Con Edison's plan was to pump millions of gallons of water during off-peak hours through a two-mile pipe from the Hudson River into the town of Cornwall's reservoir, which lay behind Storm King. During times of peak power generation, the giant utility would release the water through a forty-foot-wide tunnel inside the mountain to turn the plant's turbines. The water would then empty back into the Hudson.

One woman was particularly disturbed by what was happening. In March 1964, in a letter to the *New York Times*, Beatrice Abbott wrote, "If Consolidated Edison is not immediately halted, irrevocable damage will be done to one of the outstanding landmarks of the East on the glorious Hudson River."

In the beginning, she was a lone voice crying in the wilderness, even signing her maiden name to the letter to protect the reputation of her husband, Stephen Duggan, a partner at the white-shoe Wall Street law firm Simpson, Thacher, and Bartlett. But the Duggans learned that one or two individuals could do nothing in the face of Con Edison, and along with other concerned neighbors, they formed the Scenic Hudson Preservation Conference, which launched a lawsuit to protect Storm King. This was something entirely new: a major public utility being challenged by a small group of concerned citizens. It overturned the long-standing perception that individuals—homeowners, farmers, private citizens—could do nothing to "stand in the way of progress."

The lawsuit succeeded in stalling the plant, but it came at a high price. Scenic Hudson was soon looking at legal expenses and other costs that amounted to a quarter of a million dollars. And this was just the beginning. There was an important lesson here: environmental litigation would be expensive, and against a powerful adversary like Con Edison, it would require digging in for years, perhaps even decades.

Scenic Hudson considered turning itself into a national organization but rejected the idea after lengthy discussion. Instead, Sive, Duggan, and another lawyer, Whitney North Seymour, decided to form a separate nonprofit organization with a broader agenda. Like my old friend Jim Moorman, and like Gus Speth's group at Yale, they were conscious of being part of an emerging generation of public interest lawyers who would fight for the expansion of civil rights and the rights of women, children, and the poor. And one fundamental right of all citizens was the right to a clean environment: the air they breathed, the water they drank, and the open land they cherished. All were under assault by corporate interests, and all needed protection. So Sive, Duggan, and Seymour would create a public interest law firm dedicated to protecting the environment. They called it the Natural Resources Defense League, and its model would be the NAACP.

Seymour became the head of the new group. But then he was appointed U.S. attorney for the District Court for the Southern District of New York, where I had been working. He would take up his new post on January 1, 1970, and that meant he could no longer be involved with any kind of advocacy group. The new Natural Resources Defense League urgently needed a director, and a mutual friend suggested to Seymour that he give me a call. We met, we got on well, and he arranged for me to see Stephen Duggan.

I waited on a couch in the reception area at Simpson, Thacher, and Bartlett. I would get to know that couch well, since it was later donated to NRDC along with a lot of other office furniture. It's still in my office today. As I sat there, I thought of the three years I had worked at Cadwalader, Wickersham, and Taft at 14 Wall Street. I didn't know the Yale students yet, but like them, I was determined not to practice corporate law. I had made good friends at the law firm, but I hated the work and managed to survive by starting a softball team and taking on legal aid cases.

Within five minutes of walking into Mr. Duggan's office (I always called him Mr. Duggan, and he called me Mr. John), I knew this was a man I really liked. We talked for over an hour, and when I left I had the job—although it was a job that came with no staff and no office. On top of that, I had to raise the money for my own salary—a princely $25,000.

In retrospect, I am amazed that, without a second thought, I left a secure professional position for an *idea* of a job, with another child on the way and Patricia still in school. But we both felt that this was the chance of a lifetime, an opportunity to do something for a cause that we instinctively believed in.

There was another reason I was ready to take on this radical idea of being a lawyer fighting for the environment. I loved litigation. I have a competitive personality, and I had been a litigator for seven years. It felt right.

One of our first tasks was to decide what the new organization should be called. Natural Resources Defense League was long and cumbersome, but could we come up with anything better? As Mr. Duggan and I sat in the cab on our way to filing the papers of incorporation, we still had not come up with an alternative, other than to change *League* to

Council, which for some reason sounded better. In the end I decided that I liked the rest of the name well enough because it described our goals and our purpose—to *defend* the world's natural resources. So NRDC we became, and NRDC we remain.

Our second son, Ramsay, was born on December 31, 1969. The very next day, the new National Environmental Protection Act, NEPA, came into force—the law that would be the cornerstone of the slew of environmental laws that would follow. And the day after that, January 2, 1970, I started work at NRDC.

A colleague at the U.S. attorney's office, John Robinson, asked if there was anything he could do to help.

"Sure," I said. "I need an office."

John talked to his cousin, William Beinecke, chair of the S&H Corporation, the company that created Green Stamps. Bill found me a spare room at the S&H building in Midtown Manhattan. Neither of us suspected at the time that Bill's daughter, Frances, then a student, would later play such a large role in the history of NRDC.

After that, I met with Mr. Duggan every week at his club, the Downtown Association. He would order a martini and spend the first ten minutes asking about my family. Then we would talk about how to get people involved in NRDC, and how to organize the founding conference that we planned to hold in March.

Mr. Duggan gave me entrée to influential people I would never otherwise have met, people such as Adele Auchincloss, the president of the Park Association in New York and the wife of the lawyer and writer Louis Auchincloss, and Robert Gilmore, a Quaker who had helped with the Storm King fight and headed the Gilmore Foundation, whose mission was to promote world peace. At about this time, I also met James Marshall, one of three brothers (the others being Bob and George) who had done pioneering work with the Wilderness Society in the 1930s. Jim was a prominent New York lawyer, a man of vision, way ahead of his time, and had worked with the United Nations for many years and wanted to lay the groundwork for the United States to become a world leader in environmental protection. NRDC's job, Jim said with his typical eloquence, was to help launch a great world movement that would enable people to understand their relationship to the environment and the natural resources it provided. That meant hiring the best people we could find.

Then I met the "best" people: Gus Speth and his friends from Yale. It was the Ford Foundation that brought us together. When I went to the foundation to ask for start-up funding, they said that they would consider the idea, but only if we would join forces with the like-minded Yale group. We got together a number of times—Gus, Ed, Dick, Tom, John, and I—often at night in our apartment, brainstorming into the wee hours with the help of a little scotch. Nothing definite came of these initial talks, but the dynamic, the same kind of intellectual firepower and collegial exchange of ideas, reminded me of what I had enjoyed at the U.S. attorney's office. The relationship was full of promise, even though they were of the "don't trust anyone over thirty" generation, and I had reached the ripe age of thirty-four.

On March 19, we held our founding conference. Patricia and I made arrangements to be away from our children, including our son Ramsay, who was still nursing. We drove to Princeton, New Jersey, clean and pressed and excited, yet nervous and not knowing what to expect. We had put together a stellar lineup of speakers: the legendary David Brower, head of the newly created Friends of the Earth; New York Congressman Richard Ottinger; Princeton biologist Dr. Robert Faulk; John Oakes, editor of the New York Times editorial page; and theater critic Brooks Atkinson. Almost a hundred people attended, including wealthy donors from New York, friends from law school, and neighbors from upstate New York. Dick Hall, a close friend and colleague from the U.S. attorney's office, and his wife Mary came, and Dick soon joined our team.

I have always believed that including your friends is essential in building any organization. Some of them helped fund NRDC—and continue to do so—but much more important was the support and comfort they provided. It's hard to convey how precarious our new enterprise felt for those first few years, and those friendships were what kept us going when times were hard, as they often were.

Several members of the Yale group came to Princeton that day, and so did a third-year student at Columbia Law School named David Hawkins. David had left law school for two years because he could not see a way to practice law that was tolerable to him. During that absence, he taught mathematics in a New York school and spent summers with his wife, Betsy, in a cabin on an island in Nova Scotia. Watching the summers unfold in a pristine wilderness made him more aware of the smog and pollution in New York and convinced him that his purpose in life was to work for the environment. When he went back to Columbia, he could find almost no environmental law courses, but a professor told him about our conference. He decided to come, his main purpose being to lobby John Oakes to have the *New York Times* demand that Fifth Avenue be closed for the first Earth Day, which was scheduled to take place in April.

David asked Dick Ayres how he could get a job with NRDC.

"Are you kidding?" Dick responded. "We don't even have money for our own salaries yet."

That was just the beginning of our relationship with one of the most important figures in NRDC's history. David did eventually get that job, and he is still with us today, almost forty years later, as head of our climate center.

We had an organization, a name, a purpose, an office, and a group of friends and supporters. What we needed now was money.

Gordon Harrison and Ned Ames of the Ford Foundation had informally promised us $350,000 a year for three years, but only if we could work out an agreement with the Yale group. This did not come easily. The Yale law students were young and brash, outraged at what they saw as the crimes of corporate America and very suspicious of anyone from Wall Street. "I don't know if we can survive these guys," I often said to Patricia. "They can be such a pain in the ass. And if anyone refers to Mr. Duggan again as grandpa . . ."

However, Gus Speth had the foresight to see what we could accomplish as a single organization, and he was anxious for us to join forces. In March 1970, we assured the Ford Foundation that we would do just that. We had succeeded in uniting two very different groups and styles—the aggressive initiative of the Yale group and the seasoned experience of "establishment" lawyers and old-style conservationists. Together we would bring about change within the system. I thought of what we were doing as "responsible militancy."

Now another problem arose, and it was the most serious of all. We might be lawyers, but were we legal? We were already incorporated in New York as a public interest law firm, and our license to practice law in the state was the first granted to a not-for-profit organization. But in May, before Ford had made its decision to fund us, the Internal Revenue Service told us that, as a nonprofit, we would not be able to litigate— and that was the only reason Ford was interested in supporting us, not to mention being the entire purpose of our existence. Citizens needed to be able to go to court to protect their rights to clean air and clean water, just as they could do to protect their civil rights.

The IRS accepted that we were a charity, which meant that the donations we received were tax deductible. Educating the public about the environment was fine, but if we wanted to go to court we had to come back for a supplemental ruling. There seemed little chance that the IRS would rule in our favor, since it argued that litigation by a nonprofit was a coercive activity, like picketing or holding demonstrations. It felt like being shot in the knees.

The IRS's stance had a lot to do with the political turmoil of the times. The chaos of the 1968 Democratic Convention in Chicago was still fresh in everyone's memory. People like Abbie Hoffman and the Yippies were regularly in the streets and in the news, protests against the war in Vietnam seemed constant, and sit-ins were under way in

campuses across the country. The Nixon administration felt belea-
guered. My own view is that the president himself lumped all these
activities together as one big liberal threat—which he once said showed
"weakness in the American character"—and that environmental advocacy
was something he wanted to curb along with antiwar activism. During
the Watergate hearings, investigators found a memo to Nixon from a
White House aide, Tom Charles Huston, about the need for the IRS to
"take a close look at left-wing organizations which are operating with
tax-exempt funds." Huston singled out Ford Foundation support for
such groups as a particular concern. Nixon himself scrawled a note in
the margin: "Good. But I want action. Have Huston follow up hard on
this." Whether or not NRDC was actually on Nixon's blacklist, we might
as well have been.

This was paradoxical, to say the least, because even as the administration drew the line against environmental litigation, Congress was
passing a series of historical environmental laws, starting with NEPA,
with strong bipartisan support and big majorities. Nixon, I think,
bowed to the necessity of these laws as one way of getting liberal
critics off his back. The mood in Washington had been transformed in
just a few short years. As recently as 1965, Senator Gaylord Nelson had
failed to find a single cosponsor for a bill to outlaw DDT. During the
1969–70 congressional session, a staggering eight thousand environmental bills were introduced.

The first of the new laws, NEPA, which passed in 1969 and went
into force on January 1, 1970, required that every new federal action that
significantly affected the environment had to be the subject of a detailed
environmental impact statement. This statement had to include an analysis of possible alternatives to the proposed action. Next came the Clean
Air Act (technically the Clean Air Amendments of 1970), which required
the newly created Environmental Protection Agency (EPA) to set air quality standards that would protect human health and welfare, and then
to demand a detailed plan from every state showing how it intended to
comply. Third, two years later, it was the turn of the Federal Water Pollution

MEMORANDUM   THE PRESIDENT HAS SEEN.

THE WHITE HOUSE

WASHINGTON

① good —
② But I want
action —
Have Huston follow
up hard on this —
(You of course should super—

MEMORANDUM TO THE PRESIDENT

FROM: TOM CHARLES HUSTON

JUNE 18, 1969

Some weeks ago, the Committee of Six recommended that we
explore the possibility of getting the IRS to take a close
look at the activities of left-wing organizations which are
operating with tax-exempt funds. You approved our recommendation

After some delay, Dr. Burns and I have finally had an
opportunity to discuss the matter with Randolph Thrower, and
while I am afraid he does not fully appreciate the extent of
our concern, he has indicated that he will have his people
look into the matter. In order to give them a gentle nudge,
I have sent over some background material on some of the more
conspicuously offensive groups with which I am familiar. I
intend to keep on top of the situation to see if any positive
action is taken since several of the groups appear to be
rather flagrantly in violation of existing IRS regulations.

Thrower is discussing the possibility of appointing an
advisory committee to recommend new guidelines for tax exempt
groups. He had a list of five people whom he was considering
for chairman. Dr. Burns and I agree that none of the five
appear to be the type of people we need for this task, and

MEMO TO PRESIDENT NIXON CONCERNING TAX EXEMPT
STATUS OF ACTIVIST ORGANIZATIONS, JUNE 18, 1969

we are submitting some names of our own for his consideration.
I think it is vital that we put the brakes on some of these
foundations which are busy financing leftwing causes with
the tax payer's money. Certainly we ought to act in time
to keep the Ford Foundation from again financing Carl Stokes'
mayoralty campaign in Cleveland.

Huston

Amendments of 1972, commonly known as the Clean Water Act, which set a national goal of "zero discharge" of waterborne pollutants by 1985 and created a nationwide system of permits for any effluents released until that goal was met.

The new laws were written in a creative ferment that was inseparable from the larger political mood in the country. The offices of the Senate Subcommittee on Air and Water Pollution were right across the hall from those of the Foreign Relations Committee, and antiwar demonstrators milled around in the corridors and camped out in members' personal offices. Senator Ed Muskie, Democrat from Maine, who chaired the subcommittee and would become a great friend and supporter of NRDC, hosted virtual teach-ins in his office, discussing environmental issues with fellow senators and staffers, who called them "Ed's seminars."

The new laws were also immensely detailed and technical, and the task of enforcing them fell to the EPA. Over time, the EPA would grow to become the second largest bureaucracy in the federal government, exceeded only by the military. Then, it was a new, inexperienced, and underfunded agency that would have to go up against powerful federal monoliths like the Atomic Energy Commission and the U.S. Army Corps of Engineers, both massive polluters that had always considered themselves to be above the law.

Most important from our point of view, both the Clean Air Act and the Clean Water Act encouraged ordinary citizens to bring suit against polluters—a provision Congress insisted on in part because it knew that the EPA's task of regulation and enforcement would be impossible without the support and, when necessary, the criticism of citizens who would stand up and address its failings. Citizens were not to be viewed as "nuisances or troublemakers," as a federal court put it later, but "welcome participants" in the enforcement of the law. Clearly, if we were planning to litigate, we needed to be able to do so at the federal level, not only to give substance to the citizen suit provisions but to help the EPA do its job. In the words of Ralph Cavanagh, who joined NRDC in 1980 and remains there today as our resident expert on utilities, "States are where you go to swat mosquitoes, and Washington is where you go to drain the swamp."

Our fight with the IRS became the test case for the whole generation of public interest lawyers who had emerged in the late 1960s and were now ready to litigate. It was a highly technical dispute, and we needed expert legal representation by a firm that specialized in tax law. Mr. Duggan introduced me to Mortimer Caplin, a former IRS commissioner and founder of a law firm in Washington, DC. He assigned our case to Tom Troyer, a specialist in charitable tax law. We hoped privately that Caplin and Drysdale would take us on pro bono, but that didn't happen, and our legal bills began to pile up.

Most of the members of the Yale group had been in Washington in early 1970 and were ready to open an office there, even without funding. Gus Speth, Ed Strohbehn, and Tom Stoel had all been working at the Supreme Court. Gus had been clerking for Justice Hugo L. Black, Ed for Justice John M. Harlan, and Tom for Chief Justice Earl Warren. John Bryson had been clerking with the District Court for the District of Columbia. And Dick Ayres was heading the plea bargaining project at the Vera Institute for Justice in New York. But it was important for us to stick together in readiness for the fight, so they all moved to New York, where they lived with friends or in sublets, or slept in our tiny Greenwich Village apartment. Patricia said she would remain at our farmhouse in the Catskills until October so we could use the apartment as a place to meet and work.

The NRDC staff at this point consisted of two people: myself and a volunteer secretary. Gus and his wife, Cameron, had a new baby girl. Dick was taking his turn to put his wife, Margaret, through law school. John, Ed, and Tom were done with their clerkships. No one had any money. Everyone was taking a big risk. We lived in a state of permanent, intense anxiety. Every day we waited for a decision from the IRS, or a call from Tom Troyer, or word from the Ford Foundation that it had decided to pull out.

Troyer initially felt that we would not have a problem because we were like the ACLU and the NAACP, charities that had litigated for years without endangering their tax-exempt status. But the IRS was clearly not disposed to grant that privilege to an environmental group. The agency's New York office had forwarded our proposal to Washington; from there it went to the IRS's chief counsel for "further study." We were bogged down in the bureaucracy.

Troyer advised us to enlist the support of other not-for-profit organizations and national legal figures, law professors, and well-known advocates. The Yale group wrote speeches and press releases, and went to Capitol Hill to meet with senators from their home states. The connections that John, Tom, and Dick had in the Pacific Northwest paid off handsomely when they gained a sympathetic ear from Senators Bob Packwood, Republican from Oregon, and Henry "Scoop" Jackson, Democrat from Washington.

Meanwhile I shuttled back and forth between New York and Washington for meetings with Troyer. On one of those trips, he arranged a personal meeting for us with IRS Commissioner Randolph Thrower. Troyer argued that private litigation helped the government do its work and that actions by citizens to enforce the nation's laws were a public and charitable benefit. I felt that we had made a strong case, but Thrower remained noncommittal.

It was an arduous fight, and the stress was constant, but we did have one incalculable asset. The forces that had come together to create NRDC gave us great connections: people of means—many of whom were longtime conservationists—from Wall Street law firms and elite law schools. As we searched for support, perhaps the single most important contact we made came through a young man who had been working in Harlem and had come to NRDC that summer as an intern. His name was Laurance Rockefeller, and he introduced us to his father, Laurance S. Rockefeller Sr. We met at the family offices at Rockefeller Center in New York, and Larry's father could not have been more sympathetic. As we sat there, he picked up the phone and called Russell Train, a fellow supporter of the World Wildlife Fund and the newly appointed chair of the new Council for Environmental Quality, which had been created in the White House as part of NEPA to oversee the environmental work of various federal agencies and report to the president.

"Russ, isn't there anything you can do for these folks?" Rockefeller asked.

Within a week, Train wrote to IRS Commissioner Thrower, saying that in his view private litigation of the kind we aimed to do was "an important environmental protection technique supplementing and reinforcing government environmental programs."

As the battle went on, the meter continued to run on our legal bills. When they reached $100,000, someone said to me, "We can't survive this. A hundred thousand dollars and we're not out of the woods yet. We may never be. "

"It doesn't make any difference what we owe," I reasoned. "If we don't get our tax-exempt status, we can't pay anything. So we have to go forward."

It was a painful summer, and the tension took its toll on our personal lives. The Yale group called it their "Babylonian exile." In September,

Stephen Duggan and Tom Troyer went to the Ford Foundation and explained the bind we were in. Ford kept us alive with an emergency grant of $100,000, which enabled us to pay our rent and bare-bones salaries. But that was immediately followed by yet another delay, when the IRS announced a sixty-day moratorium on issuing any rulings for groups that litigated. During that time, the agency said it would determine a set of standards for anyone who claimed to act on behalf of the public interest. This meant that the new public interest lawyers like NRDC were no longer the only ones in jeopardy; now it was possible that even established organizations such as the NAACP Legal Defense Fund and the ACLU might no longer be able to litigate without losing their tax-free status.

The entire nonprofit community rallied to our cause. Newspapers across the country wrote editorials criticizing the IRS's actions as "ominous" and "specious." Senators Packwood and Jackson gave speeches attacking the agency for standing in the way of Americans doing their civic duty. Senator Gaylord Nelson, Democrat from Wisconsin, who in later years would become head of the Wilderness Society, announced hearings and called Commissioner Randolph Thrower as the first witness.

Then, on the eve of Thrower's scheduled testimony, the IRS abruptly capitulated. In a statement issued on November 12, it announced that a public interest law firm could litigate "to present a position on behalf of the public at large on matters of the public interest." I was invited to Washington to collect the ruling in person, and that night we held a great celebration.

Things happened quickly after that. Caplin and Drysdale agreed to a modest reduction in our bill; the Ford Foundation paid that bill for us and gave us the three-year grant it had promised (the foundation later extended it for ten years). It had been a year of incredible stress. I had left a secure job and had no money. I had spent months negotiating with the young toughs from Yale. The IRS had almost destroyed us. But we were free at last to go about our business as the country's first environmental law firm. All we needed was cases—and clients.

Here to Stay

The Environmental Protection Agency was new, the rules were new, and we were new. We had been present at the creation of the nation's first environmental laws, and we intended to help write and enforce the rules—a top-down style of work to make the government do its job. The year we had spent fighting the IRS had sharpened our zeal as well as given us some time to think. The challenge for me was to figure out how to lead our group so we could take the best advantage of the new opportunities.

The model I wanted to follow was the one I'd known at the U.S. attorney's office: a group of lawyers of roughly the same age and experience, operating collegially. From the very start, we worked as a team, making decisions collectively about everything from who should sit at the reception desk to whose job it was to order water for the cooler. The core of our work was the National Environmental Policy Act, the bedrock law that established the principle that planning should come before action. The importance of NEPA cannot be overstated. We spent hundreds of hours researching matters related to the act. We wrote papers, attended hearings, monitored regulations, and brought a score of the earliest NEPA-related lawsuits. You might almost say we "owned" NEPA.

As Dick Ayres said, "From the beginning we had to persuade government officials that we knew as much as they did and we weren't going away. Someone at the EPA once joked that we were like the American Revolutionaries—behind every tree."

In addition to the NEPA work, which was overseen by Tom Stoel and Ed Strohbehn, we established a rough division of labor that assigned cases related to water to Gus Speth, the Clear Air Act to Dick Ayres, and the protection of lands and forests to John Bryson. By this time, Dick Hall had joined us, and he tackled the issue of strip-mining in Tennessee, our first litigation case. We also used part of the Ford Foundation grant to set up shop in Washington, which the Yale group had always seen as the center of the action, sharing a rabbit warren of small offices and dark hallways with the Center for Law and Social Policy in an old, converted brownstone near Dupont Circle. "We used the attic floor," Ed Strohbehn remembers. "It was not designed for human use. The person in the middle of the room could stand upright, but if you moved around, you had to hunch under the sloping roof."

One of our earliest board members, George Woodwell, was instrumental in sharpening our identity and our role. George, a native of Maine, was a scientist at the Brookhaven National Laboratory in Long Island, where he had been a pioneer in the effort to ban DDT. He was—and still is—a man of great passion, who believes that catastrophic consequences await us if we fail to use our natural resources responsibly. Starting in the 1970s, he was one of the first scientists to raise the alarm about fossil fuel emissions and global warming.

Gus Speth called George in 1970 and asked him to join our board. George protested that he should stay with the Environmental Defense Fund, a more science-oriented group that he had helped found three years earlier. But Gus would not take no for an answer, and we elected George to our board despite his reservations. Before the next board meeting, I called him up and insisted, "George, you have to come! We need a quorum!"

George made us understand more clearly how our new brand of environmentalism differed from (and complemented) the conservation movement that preceded us. Conservation was an idea that emerged in the late 1800s, driven initially by visionary lovers of wilderness like Henry David Thoreau and John Muir, who founded the Sierra Club in San Francisco in 1892. Over time, a second generation of pioneers, men like Teddy Roosevelt and Gifford Pinchot, had added a more pragmatic strand of conservationism that gave birth to the national parks system and the U.S. Forest Service. A variety of not-for-profit groups had embraced these ideals, beginning with the Sierra Club and expanding to include the Audubon Society (established in 1905), the Wilderness Society (founded in 1935 by a group that included Jim Marshall and his brothers), the National Wildlife Federation (1936), and many others. All were centered on the need to preserve wild places and wild creatures.

Our concept of environmentalism, by contrast, had grown out of the shocks of the 1960s—the oil spills, the burning rivers, the smog and the sewage, the fresh insights that scientists such as Rachel Carson had given us about the risks that new synthetic chemicals like DDT posed to the natural world and to human health. Our aim was to develop strategies based on law and science that would protect the environment as a whole. The older groups welcomed the new approach that we brought, I think. Over time a kind of loose ideological coalition developed, and we would often work together in various combinations on particular issues and cases.

This convergence of law and science was central to George Woodwell's vision of how we should operate. The Environmental Defense Fund had started off as a group of scientists and later found that it needed to add legal skills to the mix. We did the reverse, starting with nothing but lawyers, but in 1973 we began to hire our first staff scientists. The basic model for all our future litigation was set: identify the most egregious cases of abuse, those on which court rulings could set important legal precedents; make a thorough, scientific analysis of the environmental harm being done; develop scientifically feasible remedies to the problem; and stick with the case for as long as it takes to uphold, or if necessary expand, the law. By January 1974, we were involved in more than fifty ongoing legal actions, and dozens of other lawsuits and administrative proceedings had been closed, most of them ending in victories for NRDC.

With the pace of litigation increasing at such an incredible rate, our limited administrative and management skills became glaringly apparent. Even though we had the crucial support of the Ford Foundation, and the battle with the IRS was behind us, we still lived constantly on a knife edge, full of energy and a sense of adventure, but equally filled with trepidation about the precariousness of our situation. We could no longer afford to go on making collective decisions about every bill that needed to be paid, or keep our financial records in a shoebox. That was where Pattie Sullivan came in.

Once again, our high-level connections came into play. I had a call one day from Ashton Hawkins, a great lawyer and patron of the arts who had been an associate of mine at Cadwalader, Wickersham, and Taft and later became general counsel at the Metropolitan Museum of Art. Hawkins said he had a young woman to recommend. She had an excellent head for business and lots of influential friends, and he thought she would fit right in with us.

I have to admit that it was not exactly love at first sight. I had a hard time getting past the aristocratic Cambridge accent—this was one of the celebrated Boston Sullivans, fresh from a traditional Catholic upbringing followed by Radcliffe and a stint in banking. But once I got past first impressions, it became clear that I was dealing with a person of tremendous dignity and integrity, and great practical instincts, yet at the same time someone who could go head-to-head with the smartest brains and sharpest tongues in the organization. Looking back, I can't think of a single person who has been more important to NRDC's forty-year history.

Pattie quickly knocked us into shape: there were more professional management systems; quarterly board meetings at the Harvard Club; weekly visits from Mr. Duggan to inspect the books; elegant dinner parties at Adele Auchincloss's Fifth Avenue apartment to introduce us to new supporters; weekly meetings with me to review lists of potential donors, which I carried around in my wallet. Although some foundations, such as the Rockefeller Family Fund, the J. M. Kaplan Fund, and the Beinecke Foundation, were willing to take a chance on funding a group of brash young lawyers going up against the government, our financial situation was never easy. After the Ford Foundation agreed to support us, Mr. Duggan wrote a personal letter to Henry Ford himself asking for an individual donation. He wrote back that he did not approve of litigation and would not give any money to lawyers; a lot of people felt the same way.

The end of the year was always our worst moment, and as 1973 drew to a close, we were facing a budget deficit of $170,000 with a growing staff and an urgent need for new offices. I spent the week between Christmas and New Year's working the phones, or tramping the freezing streets with Pattie Sullivan, hoping desperately that a last-minute grant would come through, or that a board member would agree to plug the gap and put us in the black by January 1.

We built up a loyal yet relatively small group of donors, but from the beginning I was convinced that we also needed members. This was not just for financial reasons; it seemed a reflection of the kind of organization we wanted to be. NRDC was there to represent the environment and its constituency. We were setting out to protect the air, the water, the land, and public health, and we supported the people who cared about those things. When we filed papers in court, we were doing so on behalf of Mr. Jones or Ms. Smith, who liked to hike or fish or simply breathe the air. If we were representing these people's interests, it seemed logical to me that we should also enlist them as our members.

The idea of becoming a membership organization turned out to be a serious bone of contention, and I suppose this reflected a certain amount of elitism within NRDC. For one thing, it meant establishing a system of direct mail, which many people on the staff and board saw as being "beneath" our high standards. They also worried about the impact on our fragile finances: How much would these mailings cost? Would we get our money back? Or the much-repeated protest, "We should use that money to hire another lawyer."

Henry Ford II
Chairman of the Board

Ford Motor Company
The American Road
Dearborn, Michigan 48121

March 2, 1970

Mr. Stephen P. Duggan, Jr.
Chairman
Natural Resources Defense Council, Inc.
36 West 44th Street
New York, New York 10036

Dear Mr. Duggan:

       Thank you for your letter inviting
me to help launch the activities of the Natural
Resources Defense Council.

       I agree that the conservation of our
natural environment and resources is an urgent
problem. In my opinion, however, litigation
should play a limited role in the search for
solutions. It seems to me that the judicial
process is not the best way to establish public
policy in this extremely complex area and that
legislative and administrative processes are
generally better suited to this task.

       For this reason, although I appreciate
your thinking of me, I must decline your invitation.

Very Sincerely,

Henry Ford

LETTER FROM HENRY FORD II DECLINING INVITATION TO
NRDC'S FOUNDING CONFERENCE, MARCH 2, 1970

But I stuck to my guns, and Pattie Sullivan, as pragmatic and humorous as always, backed me up. Her view in those early days of the unfamiliar world of direct mail: "It's like the whorehouse in the base-ment . . . as long as it's bringing in the cash."

Harold Oram, who had helped us from the start with our fund-raising efforts, provided advice on direct mail as well as lists of peo-ple who might be interested in membership, and by 1974, our first 18,000 members had signed up. It was the first step on a forty-year path that would eventually build a community of 1.2 million members and online activists.

In the meantime, even as we embarked on the first wave of NEPA law-suits and cases under the Clean Air Act, we had unfinished business in the shape of Storm King.

The case had been a vital part of our history, and it was also a landmark for the whole environmental movement—for a number of reasons. Not only did it involve the protection of a national treasure, the Hudson River, which flowed past West Point, Manhattan, and the Statue of Liberty. It was also the direct forerunner of NEPA, establishing for the first time the right of ordinary citizens to bring suit to protect the environment, even if their direct, personal economic interests were not involved. In 1965 the U.S. Court of Appeals for the Second Circuit had ruled that caring about the river for aesthetic or recreational rea-sons was enough for a citizen to be heard in court—to have *standing*, in legal parlance.

Our client by this time was not Scenic Hudson, whose primary focus was protecting the scenic heritage of this part of the river, but the Hudson River Fishermen's Association, whose members were sick of eating fish that tasted like diesel oil and wanted to shield the fish from mass destruction by the string of four power plants that lined a twenty-mile stretch of the Hudson north of New York City and drew in huge amounts of the river's flow to cool the machinery. This included Consolidated Edison's nuclear power plant at Indian Point, near the town of Peekskill, which had been in operation since 1962.

The fishermen were led by a combative, "take no prisoners" kind of advocate, Robert Boyle, a writer for *Sports Illustrated*. His concern about the river had begun when, on his train commute to New York City from the Hudson Valley, he regularly saw waste oil from the diesel yards at Croton Point pour through a three-foot-wide pipe into the river. Farther down the line, he could tell what paint was being used at the Tarrytown General Motors Factory by the green or red color of the water along the shore. Bob was a believer in the adage "The pen is mightier than the sword," and he became a muckraker for the Hudson with his articles about pollution in the river. In 1965 a fellow sports fisherman, Professor Dominick Pirone, was shown photos of dead striped bass piled twelve feet high at a Con Edison dump. While fishing, Bob had seen thousands of dead fish on screens over the intake that sucked in water to cool the reactors at Indian Point. That same year, the Federal Power Commission had agreed with Con Edison's argument that the "allegations" about fishery impacts were "irrelevant." Bob wrote an article, "A Stink of Dead Stripers," for *Sports Illustrated* to show that these fish kills were proof that if a pump storage plant were built ten miles upstream from Indian Point, countless more fish would be needlessly slaughtered.

In his research for these articles, Bob learned two things: industry was despoiling the Hudson, and the government agencies charged with protecting the river were doing nothing about it. In his book *The Hudson River, A Natural and Unnatural History*, published in 1969, he described the cozy relationship between industry and the agencies.

> "Instead of acting as cops on the beat, as intended by Congress, these agencies actually embrace the industries they are supposed to police in the public interest . . . the same utilities and spokesmen invariably appear before them (and) a certain

friendship springs up over the course of time. By contrast, the opponents are strangers. One week they may be farmers, the next week a group of fishermen, and after that, ladies in silly hats. . . . Then, there has been a cozy flow of officials from government to industry. . . . One hand washes the other, but the dirty linen never gets aired. It's 'Hiya, Bill,' 'Hello Charlie, howza family?' between government and industry. Today's ravisher of a river may be tomorrow's employer."

Bob soon realized that words were not enough and in 1966 gathered a group of sports and commercial fishermen in his living room, where they formed the Hudson River Fishermen's Association. He met with Stephen and Beatrice Duggan ("Steve and Smoky" to their friends) and other Scenic Hudson advocates, but while he admired their concern for the scenic value of the river, that was not his main interest. He wanted to protect the fisheries. There was still no Clean Water Act in those days, so Bob reached back to obscure state and federal statutes from the nineteenth century that prohibited dumping anything other than municipal sewage in navigable waters without a permit—laws to which industries up and down the Hudson had never paid the slightest attention.

After the decision to allow construction of Storm King to go ahead, the Federal Power Commission was flooded with petitions to reopen the hearings, and the U.S. Court of Appeals for the Second Circuit agreed to do so. The Hudson River Fishermen joined with Scenic Hudson in this second round of hearings, which went on for over two years. The fishermen submitted thousands of pages of evidence showing how the proposed Storm King plant would harm fish. This included research done by biologist Dr. John Clark, who reported that close to 90 percent of striped bass eggs in the entire Hudson were concentrated in a seven-and-a-half-mile stretch of the river where Storm King is located. A pump storage plant would suck up these eggs as well as young fish.

Con Edison submitted another study that again "proved" Storm King would have minimal impact on fish. Additional delays and hearings continued with no resolution until 1972, when the fishermen asked NRDC to represent them.

We gave the case to Angus Macbeth, a former Carnegie Teaching Fellow at Yale whom we'd hired a year earlier. Within a year, when Angus left on a Churchill Fellowship to study salmon fisheries, we passed the case on to Sarah Chasis, NRDC's first full-time female lawyer.

Sarah came from a distinguished family. Her parents were both prominent doctors at New York University. One of her aunts had been a B-17 pilot during World War II and used to enjoy buzzing the family's hometown of Oxford, New York. Sarah had planned to become a doctor and had been premed as an undergraduate. But a summer job in a marine biology lab, as well as a study she had conducted about oil pollution in New York Harbor, convinced her that she wanted to do environmental law. Now, fresh out of New York University Law School, where she had won the Founders Day Award for overall academic excellence, she found herself representing Bob Boyle and the Hudson River Fishermen. It was her first case.

In the beginning, NRDC was a bit of a shock to her system. She had heard that it was a place where bright people were doing great work. What she encountered was a very male-dominated environment that also seemed a little off the wall. But Sarah became a close friend as well as a core member of NRDC. From the start, she was fiercely devoted to the organization's basic values of fairness and loyalty, and almost forty years later she is still with us, having become one of the nation's leading experts on oceans.

By 1973 Patricia and I had left our apartment in the city and begun renting a house in the small town of Garrison, New York, on the east side of the Hudson. Three years later, we bought a historic home in the town, which became the center of our environmental activity. Sarah and her soon-to-be-husband, Clay Hiles, would house-sit for us while we were away. You wouldn't exactly call the place a commune, more of an extended NRDC family home with lots of young people hanging out together, either newly married or looking to get married soon. Surrounding the house were big fields where we played softball games, and where little kids ran around. Frances Beinecke, whose father had given us our first office space, was interning with us now, and she was also a frequent visitor. Another was a young man named Paul Elston, a deputy commissioner of the New York State Department of Environmental Conservation. Before long, Frances told us that she and Paul were getting married.

Angus MacBeth had quickly realized the key to the Storm King case: the Hudson is not a conventional river, but a tidal fjord, and this had a critical impact on the extent of the fish kills. Bob Boyle had tried to make this point in a previous hearing, but the examiner had refused to let him testify on the ground that he was not an expert on tides.

It turned out that Con Edison's study of the consequences of fish passing by the plant's intake valves as the tide changed had one basic, astounding error. The utility said that the fish and larvae would pass the intake pipes only once. John Clark's study showed that during the spawning season in May, June, and July, because of the tides, the migratory fish eggs and larvae would pass by Storm King no fewer than *ten times* before reaching the safety of the lower river. This would increase the mortality rate from less than 3 percent, as predicted by Con Edison, to more than 35 percent. On the basis of these data, we argued that the decision to issue the license should be set aside and sent back to the Federal Power Commission for further review.

This didn't mean, however, that the battle for the river was over. The fish kills continued at other Con Edison plants, and we fought them with every tool at our disposal. First Angus and then Sarah spent hours making the same arguments in tedious, technical hearings before the Atomic Energy Commission. They went to court on behalf of the fishermen in several separate suits against the Army Corps of Engineers, with the expert help of a former colleague of mine from the U.S. attorney's office, Ross Sandler, who later joined the NRDC staff. They charged that the Corps of Engineers had granted permits for new construction at two conventional oil- and coal-fired plants on the Hudson without carrying out a study of the environmental impact, as they were compelled to do by NEPA. These were huge, powerful federal agencies that were not used to dealing with challenges from ordinary citizens or environmental lawyers.

The fight dragged on, and it became clear to all concerned that any final settlement would have to apply to all five power plants on this twenty-mile stretch of river (a fifth plant, Bowline Point, was built in 1974). Finally, in 1980, we got help from two of the same people who had been so important in our battle with the IRS ten years earlier. Laurance S. Rockefeller Sr. called me to offer his assistance. He said he was a friend of Charles Luce, the CEO of Consolidated Edison, and knew that Luce wanted to work out a settlement. Rockefeller, Ross Sandler, and I then met with Russell Train, who had been head of the President's Council on Environmental Quality under Nixon and then served from 1973 to 1977 as the head of the EPA. Ross took charge of the negotiations with Con Edison, and Train agreed to act as mediator.

In December 1980, NRDC, along with ten other environmental groups, reached a final agreement with Con Edison and other utility companies in what became known as the Hudson River Peace Treaty. Under the agreement, Con Edison abandoned its efforts to build the Storm King plant and donated the land for a state park. It also agreed to install devices on the intake screens at Indian Point to protect fish. In return, we dropped our demands for Con Edison to build six costly cooling towers.

The agreement also had much broader ramifications for the environmental movement, all of them positive. To my delight, Charles Luce became a strong supporter of NRDC. As part of the settlement, Con Edison set up the Hudson River Foundation with a $12 million grant to carry out extensive scientific research on the river's fisheries. The foundation's first director was Ross Sandler.

Meanwhile, Bob Boyle never slowed down. In 1982 the Hudson River Fishermen's Association turned into the Riverkeeper, which became one of the most effective environmental organizations in the United States. Its first director—also known as the riverkeeper—was John Cronin, a former commercial fisherman. A year after that, I received a call from Robert F. Kennedy Jr. Bobby, recently married and expecting his first child, had been arrested on drug charges and sentenced to several hundred hours of community service. He saw this as an opportunity to remake his life. Since he had spent much of his life on the water and was an avid fisherman, the Riverkeeper seemed like a perfect match. Bobby has since served for years on the staff or board of the organization, and Riverkeeper has joined an international alliance of more than a hundred riverkeepers and baykeepers. Bobby, who founded the alliance, remains its president, as well as a close friend, collaborator, and staff member of NRDC.

As We Live and Breathe

The end of 1970 was a heady time for us. Within a matter of weeks, we received our three-year grant from the Ford Foundation, the Environmental Protection Agency was established, and Congress passed the Clean Air Act. By January, we had set up NRDC's project on clean air. Dick Ayres took charge of the project, and he was joined by David Hawkins, the former high school math teacher who had come to our founding conference in Princeton looking for a job. Now we had the money to offer him a salary.

Dick Ayres saw the Clean Air Act as something revolutionary. "We believed that if we could make this real, if we could make this act live up to its promise, it could change the world!" It was obvious to everyone that the nation's air quality had degenerated to an unacceptable level, and that the health of every person, as well as plant and animal life, was threatened. Fossil-fuel power plants belched sulfur and nitrogen oxides into the air, as well as toxin-laden particles that we breathed deep into our lungs. Automobiles emitted carbon monoxide and lead and created ozone that was suffocating our cities. Smelters, refineries, chemical plants, and industrial facilities pumped out airborne pollutants such as arsenic, beryllium, asbestos, mercury, cadmium, benzene, and toxic hydrocarbons. Small children, with underdeveloped immune systems and proportionately larger lungs than adults, were at special risk.

The father of the Clean Air Act was Senator Edmund S. Muskie of Maine. Known in Congress as Mr. Environment, Muskie was also the front-runner for the Democratic Party's 1972 presidential nomination. Without him, the great environmental changes of the 1970s would never have happened. He liked to quote James Harrington, the seventeenth-century English political theorist, who said that laws were "words and paper without the hands and swords of men." When it came to clean air and clean water, Muskie's approach was simple: "We must find out what the public health needs are, and make our decisions based on that." This was a whole new approach to governing, to making change happen. At the time, it enjoyed bipartisan support.

In 1970 Congress recognized that the problem of setting clean air standards could not be left to individual states. The federal government has a responsibility for the general welfare, and that means fundamental things like guaranteeing healthy air.

The Clean Air Act Amendments of 1970 gave the new EPA authority to regulate airborne pollutants from two sources: those from stationary sources like power plants, smelters, and incinerators and those from motor vehicles. The EPA also directed states to address the urban sprawl largely responsible for auto pollution. The regulations would be comprehensive, they would encourage the development of new technologies to reduce pollution, and they would be backed up with strong legal sanctions, with significant financial penalties against violators of $25,000 a day. In the absence of these, polluters would continue to enjoy an economic advantage from resistance and delay. Dirty plants meant cheaper electricity than competitors could offer, and lawyers' bills cost less than installing new pollution controls.

The EPA was given a mandatory deadline to set health-based air quality standards, and each state would then have to submit a comprehensive "implementation plan" to meet those standards. This meant, for example, that New Jersey and New York had to pass stricter laws to clean up their air than Nevada and Montana, because they were starting out with higher levels of pollution. Like the EPA, state governments were given very strict deadlines for compliance.

For the first time, the 1970 act provided for citizen suits against a polluter for violating the law or against the EPA for failing to carry out its responsibilities under the act. "Any person may commence a civil action on his own behalf," the law stated. The citizen suit was the idea of Senator Thomas Eagleton, Democrat from Missouri, later a candidate for vice president. Eagleton said that he did not want to pass a law that was ignored by polluters and government. Therefore, he proposed the novel idea of empowering ordinary citizens to invoke the power of the courts to hold polluters'—and the government's—feet to the fire.

Foot-dragging by polluters was only one of innumerable challenges. Imposing clean air norms was fiendishly difficult from both technical and legal points of view, and the young EPA was laboring under strict deadlines and was working with states whose commitment and expertise were often questionable. In addition, as our scientific understanding of air pollution increased, it became clear that pollution did not respect state lines any more than the wind did: sulfur oxides emitted by a coal-fired power plant in Ohio fell as acid rain on trees and lakes in upstate New York. The Clean Air Act did not provide the tools to deal with the kind of regional, interstate disputes that would arise as a result.

At first, NRDC's project on clean air concentrated on the enormously complex process of developing the state implementation plans. Advocating for stronger plans, the project acted as watchdog over both the EPA and the states. Dick hired two recent college graduates who read every one of the fifty state implementation plans to assess the level of compliance. They then summarized the highly critical conclusions in a dense, 180-page report, which was entered into the permanent congressional record as the only comprehensive analysis of how the new law was working. They also translated this labyrinth of technical requirements in two clean air manuals that we distributed to thousands of citizens and local groups across the country. Our work was soon recognized as authoritative, and NRDC was regarded as the most important voice representing the public interest in clean air.

———————

While playing this technical role in support of the Clean Air Act, we did not hesitate to take on the biggest and most powerful polluters in court. NRDC had begun life as a group of litigators, and, as Gus Speth put it, the Clean Air Act was "a litigator's dream."

We started with the nation's largest electric utility, the Tennessee Valley Authority (TVA). For decades the TVA had been almost literally above the law. From the moment of its creation by the Roosevelt administration in 1933, it had been insulated from intrusive political controls and judicial oversight. The TVA also had a highly positive public image for its achievements in bringing low-cost electricity and prosperity to impoverished rural areas in the southern Appalachians. In wartime, its power plants had driven the factories that produced materials critical to our national security. So almost by definition, the TVA represented the public interest, and it was rarely challenged either in the Tennessee Valley or in Washington.

Furthermore, the agency had a virtual monopoly on scientific data and expertise about the operation of its plants, since its lavish budget allowed it to hire the best scientists and engineers. A big reason for the low cost of the electricity generated by the TVA was its use of cheap, dirty, high-sulfur coal extracted by strip-mining. Even the pollution that the TVA created was depicted as a public good: TVA scientists claimed, for example, that its emissions of sulfur dioxide—more than two million tons a year, the worst in the country—increased soil fertility and yielded more bountiful harvests. By the mid-1970s, the TVA seemed impregnable.

The twelve coal-fired power plants operated by the TVA in Alabama, Kentucky, and Tennessee had been built between 1940 and

1968. Rather than committing extra resources to upgrade or phase out the older plants, the agency's strategy was to wait for a new generation of nuclear plants (it anticipated building seventeen) to replace them.

We filed suit against the TVA for the first time in 1971 to block plans to increase the use of coal from massive strip-mining in the Appalachians. We lost that suit. Then, in 1972, we filed another suit, this time to outlaw a stratagem that the TVA was employing—as were many other utilities—to evade installing the pollution controls required by the Clean Air Act: the building of so-called tall stacks.

Before 1970 there were only two industrial smokestacks more than five hundred feet high in the whole country. Soon after the passage of the Clean Air Act, the number soared to 180, many of them exceeding the limits of "good engineering practice." The claim made by the TVA and others was that these tall stacks would improve local air quality by dispersing pollution over a wide area. In fact, the tall stacks were a way of avoiding the cost of installing air pollution equipment or buying more expensive, higher-quality coal with a lower sulfur and ash content. It had long been clear that tall stacks did nothing to reduce the overall amount of airborne pollution—indeed, concern about "atmospheric loading" had been one of the main things prompting the act in the first place. Now, a new wave of scientific data also showed how emissions of sulfur dioxide and nitrogen oxides (later commonly known as SO_x and NO_x), once airborne, turned into even more toxic sulfuric and nitric acids, and could come to earth hundreds of miles away in the form of acid rain, with devastating effects. Nonetheless, the EPA had approved state clean air implementation plans that relied on tall stacks.

Our 1972 lawsuit against tall stacks was the first time an environmental organization had tackled the problem of acid rain. Some people have referred to acid rain (or, to be more accurate, acid *precipitation*, since it may also fall as snow, sleet, hail, fog, or dew) as a kind of "chemical leprosy." It kills fish, disrupts soil chemistry, destroys forests—especially conifer forests with naturally acidic soils—and eats away at limestone buildings, including such national monuments as the Lincoln

Memorial. Our national acid rain "hot spot" was the Ohio Valley, with effects that radiated outward as far as New England and the Southeast.

The court agreed with us that the Clean Air Act required the installation of pollution control equipment, not tall stacks, to achieve national air quality standards. Even so, the EPA adopted new regulations that fell short of the court's intent, so we asked Congress to codify the decision in federal law. This was a classic pattern of NRDC action, repeated countless times over the past four decades: first, Congress passes legislation; second, the EPA makes the rules for compliance; third, if the rules do not comply with the law, we take the EPA to court; fourth, if necessary, we go back to Congress to codify the correct interpretation of the law. This approach requires technical expertise, sophistication, and a great deal of dogged work.

By 1975, the TVA had done nothing to comply with national air quality standards, and the following year, the EPA issued a notice of violation. Ten of the TVA's twelve coal-fired plants had failed to meet federal standards for one or both of two "criteria pollutants"—sulfur dioxide and toxin-laden particulates, or soot. There was a standoff between the two government agencies, and we saw that the main hope for breaking the impasse was for us to step in, this time with a coalition of ten environmental and public health organizations from the Tennessee Valley. We filed suit in March 1977 and were later joined by one of three states affected, Alabama, as well as by the EPA. In response to our suit, the TVA made the audacious claim that it was exempt from the Clean Air Act because the law applied only to "persons"—and a federal agency was not a person.

Dick Ayres had an exchange with the judge that went to the heart of the matter: what did it mean to pursue the public interest, and who was most entitled to claim that they were doing so? We maintained that we represented the public interest. We weren't under the sway of any corporate or political interests; our client was the environment. The judge noted that the TVA and the EPA also claimed to represent the public interest. His job, he supposed, was to resolve these competing claims.

This was the real significance of the coalition we built to conduct the lawsuit. It included traditional conservation groups like the Tennessee Citizens for Wilderness Planning; public health organizations such as the Alabama Lung Association and the Tennessee Thoracic Society; and a number of grassroots groups representing the local purchasers of the energy that TVA produced. What NRDC was able to bring to the table was hard science about tall stacks, antipollution technology such as "scrubbers," and the sulfur content of coal. In other words, our coalition broke the TVA's monopoly of scientific data and directly challenged, for the first time, the agency's claim that it represented the best interests of its consumers. These people *were* its consumers.

The big breakthrough came in July 1977, when President Carter appointed David Freeman to the board of the TVA with a mandate to resolve the dispute. Freeman was a patient and dogged negotiator who was ready to work until three in the morning if that was what it took to reach an agreement. The negotiations were complex and difficult, and lasted for months, but as they went on, it became clear that all the parties wanted to reach a compromise and avoid an all-out courtroom war. In the end, the TVA agreed to cut its sulfur oxide emissions in half by switching to lower sulfur coal and installing scrubbers on two of its largest plants.

The final consent decree eliminated more than one million tons of airborne pollutants, a full 5 percent of the national total, establishing the largest sulfur dioxide cleanup program in United States history up to that time. It also reaffirmed the importance of citizen action as a spur to polluters and demonstrated that it was possible, in the end, to achieve major reductions in pollution through tough-minded citizen-suit litigation based on hard, scientific facts. This model is one we have believed in and adhered to ever since.

The battle with the TVA also showed that the Clean Air Act was far from a perfect document. There were loopholes that needed to be closed, and we played a major role in closing them. By now, thanks to the work of David Hawkins and Dick Ayres, we were the acknowledged leaders of the National Clean Air Coalition, and David and Dick were instrumental in drafting a set of amendments to the Clean Air Act that passed in August 1977. Two months later, David joined the Carter administration as the EPA's assistant administrator for air, noise, and radiation. The amendments stressed, first of all, that federal agencies, including the TVA, were subject to the Clean Air Act. They also left no doubt that tactics like tall stacks were unacceptable. Drawing in part on the new scientific understanding of acid rain, the act demanded the constant, continuous control of pollutants at their source.

The most important innovation in the 1977 amendments was the "prevention of significant deterioration" in previously clean areas. The strictest requirements were intended to protect the air quality of the Grand Canyon and other pristine national scenic treasures. To safeguard these areas, the law required pollution-control technologies to be installed in any new or significantly upgraded coal-fired power plants, oil refineries, and other large industrial facilities. The amendments also incorporated the concept of "offsets," which allowed corporations to trade off new sources of pollution against corresponding reductions in the emissions from their other plants, and even to negotiate such arrangements with other companies that owned plants in the same geographical area. Corporations could also bank credits for pollution reductions to be used as offsets in the future. This was the embryo of later "cap and trade" schemes that would be proposed for other pollutants, most notably the carbon emissions that contribute to global warming.

In the environmental world, even when you *do* win, it can take years to implement the court decisions, and David threw himself into the fight with renewed energy when he returned to NRDC after Carter lost his bid for reelection. The federal court might have ruled against tall stacks, but the system of offsets meant that many power plants continued to emit acid rain pollutants. Not until 1990 did Congress again amend the Clean Air Act to introduce the nation's first truly systematic acid rain control program. Even then, we had to be vigilant to the very last moment.

"We were down to the last forty-eight hours," David recalls. "Congressional staff were negotiating night and day on the precise language. . . . We wanted the criteria narrowly defined to close as many loopholes as possible. It was about ten o'clock on a Friday night when the other side dropped on us what they called 'a technical amendment.' We had less than an hour to respond to thirteen pages of corrections—such as 'strike line thirteen on page thirty-four.' Amid all this was a passage that had to do with the extension of compliance dates, which eventually became section 409 of the amendments. On first reading, it looked identical to the language already in the bill. So I read it again. This time, I noticed a semicolon inserted in a sentence of about forty-five words."

History can sometimes hinge on these tiny details. "That single semicolon completely changed the thrust of the paragraph—weakening the bill considerably. I called our congressional allies and said, 'You've got to nail this semicolon.' And they did."

Waters of Life

Our work on clean water during NRDC's first decade
directly paralleled our work on clean air. While Dick
Ayres and David Hawkins headed the project on clean air, Gus Speth and
Ed Strohbehn oversaw the project on clean water, which we set up right
after the passage of the Clean Water Act in 1972. The pattern was very
much the same: provide technical input into the EPA's writing of the
regulations for the enforcement of the act, adding biologists and other
scientific experts to our staff as we did so; hold the EPA to its commitments and especially to its deadlines; spend hours poring over the permits that the agency issued to industry, often analyzing the companies'
own records to determine whether they were in compliance with the
law; publish manuals to help ordinary citizens understand how the new
act was supposed to work, since we saw them as its essential watchdogs;
and then hit major polluters, including if necessary the most powerful
federal agencies, with lawsuits.

Even before passage of the Clean Water Act, we were engaged with
water-related issues. Gus and Ed had taken on an important case the
previous spring, and, like Bob Boyle and the Hudson River Fishermen,
they had reached back to the 1899 Refuse Act, the antiquated predecessor of the new law, which prohibited dumping in the nation's

NRDC STAFF RETREAT, MOHONK, NEW PALTZ, NEW YORK, 1975
Photo includes NRDC Founding Staff: Richard Ayres (2nd row, 2nd from the right); Angus Macbeth (back row, 5th from the left); Thomas Stoel, Jr. (back row, 10th from the left); John Adams (back row, 13th from the left); James Gustave Speth (back row, 15th from the left); Richard Hall (back row, 10th from the right)

Photo also includes: Patricia Sullivan (1st row, 5th from the left); Frances Beinecke (2nd row, 1st on the left); Sarah Chasis (2nd row, 2nd from the left); Patricia Adams (2nd row, 5th from the left), Tom Cochran with child on shoulders (back row, 11th from the right); Larry Rockefeller (back row, 5th from the right)

waterways. The case involved stream channelization—dredging and scouring riverbeds, straightening the natural flow of water and confining it between artificial banks, ostensibly for flood control or to benefit agriculture. This immensely destructive practice eroded riverbanks, altered landscapes, destroyed habitat, harmed fish and other wildlife, and sped up the flow of rivers, creating an increased risk of flooding downstream. In Gus's mind the whole thing was a gigantic boondoggle designed mainly to benefit local contractors.

The agency carrying out the scheme was the Soil Conservation Service (SCS), a division of the U.S. Department of Agriculture, which was planning channelization on a massive, nationwide scale. The initial plan was for four hundred projects that embraced 12,000 miles of streams; eventually a total of 175,000 miles would be affected. In the summer of 1971, we sent out thousands of information packets to newspapers and citizens' groups in the twenty states that would be worst affected, describing what was going on and urging them to write to their state SCS representatives. At the same time we mounted a lawsuit in the U.S. Court of Appeals for the Fourth Circuit, singling out the SCS's plan to reengineer sixty-six miles of Chicod Creek and its tributaries in the beautiful and productive ecosystem of streams and wetlands in the North Carolina low country. Tom Barlow, a former banker who subsequently became a full-time educator and lobbyist on wetlands issues, joined Gus on the stream channelization project, starting with the Chicod Creek case.

We argued that the U.S. Army Corps of Engineers had not issued a permit for the project, and invoking the National Environmental Policy Act, as we were doing routinely, we demanded a full assessment of the project's environmental impact. The court granted us a preliminary injunction and ordered the assessment. When that was found to be inadequate, it ordered the project to be halted. The Department of Agriculture realized that we were a force to be reckoned with, and just as important, the court acknowledged that we were a proper party to bring the lawsuit, since we were acting, in effect, as private attorneys general. It was the first time we had established our standing to act alone in court. We would still represent other organizations and continue to build coalitions for our legal actions, but now we had a precedent that allowed us to go to court on our own. This was vitally important.

We accomplished all this on the basis of the Refuse Act, a statute that was more than seventy years old. When the Clean Water Act was passed in 1972, we knew we had a much more potent weapon. The act had been thrashed out in Congress after huge amounts of research, rancorous debate, and some good, old-fashioned horse-trading. The final product, sweeping in its ambition, aimed to eliminate the discharge of all pollutants into our waterways by 1985, except for those that would be allowed under a rigorous permitting system. This would put an end to practices that had been routine since the start of the Industrial

Revolution. Like the Clean Air Act, the Clean Water Act was designed to force industry to use the best available technologies to reduce pollution, including in this case technology that would reclaim and reuse toxic chemicals. As a result, our waters would be made clean enough for aquatic life to thrive; for people, they would be considered "fishable and swimmable."

The act's overall purpose was set out boldly in the first sentence. It was nothing less than "to restore and maintain the chemical, physical, and biological integrity of the Nation's waters." This came to be known as the "Integrity Principle," and its author was George Woodwell, the Brookhaven scientist whom Gus Speth and I had successfully urged to join the NRDC board. The language came from an eloquent letter that George, who was serving as an advisor to the Senate Committee on Public Works, had written to Senator Ed Muskie in the summer of 1971.

In this letter, George stressed the vital importance of protecting "in water bodies worldwide the full array of living systems that have dominated these water bodies for all of the time of interest to man, performing the broad and vital service of maintaining a stable and congenial environment." In addition, he pointed out that "the waters of the earth are inextricably linked to the atmosphere, and problems of water pollution are also problems of air pollution." If our waters were contaminated with mercury or DDT, for example, it was because that mercury or DDT had fallen from the air in the first place. Like much of what George said, this comprehensive, integrated vision of what we needed to do to protect our environment was years ahead of its time.

———

Once the Clean Water Act was passed, we redoubled our efforts with the Corps of Engineers, broadening our focus to protect a vast, priceless natural resource to which the drafters of the law had given little thought—the nation's wetlands.

Wetlands were the poor stepchild of the act. Covering millions of acres, they had traditionally been regarded as useless swamps and bogs, obstacles to progress and economic development that needed to be eliminated. And they were being eliminated at the rate of several hundred thousand acres a year by being drained and filled—a process of destruction that was encouraged and subsidized by the federal government.

In the 1960s, however, scientific understanding of the immense ecological importance of wetlands had developed rapidly. By the early 1970s, we knew that they were critical to flood control and the filtration of clean water, and that they were a vital place of residence, breeding, and migration for countless forms of wildlife, especially amphibians and birds. We also learned that it was impossible to protect a river unless the smaller streams and water bodies that fed it were protected as well. All were part of a single, interconnected hydrologic system. Drain a wetland, or use it as a dump for pollutants, and a river or drinking water source miles away would feel the impact. Recognizing this, a handful of states, starting with Massachusetts, had begun to enact laws prohibiting the dredging and filling of wetlands. The challenge was to do the same at the federal level.

The critical provisions of the Clean Water Act in this regard were contained in Section 404, which empowered the secretary of the army, acting through the Army Corps of Engineers, to issue permits for the disposal of "dredge and fill" material at specified sites. The Corps chose to interpret this mandate as applying only to "navigable waters"—in other words, only the largest water bodies and not all "waters of the United States," as the act provided. The effect was to exclude a huge portion of the nation's wetlands from protection. The old guard at the Army Corps of Engineers was still calling the shots and intended to continue with business as usual. We decided it was time to sue Secretary of the Army Howard "Bo" Callaway and to persuade the courts that the intent of the law was for the Corps to exercise its jurisdiction over *all* water bodies.

NRDC v. Callaway was a landmark case. In March 1975, Judge Aubrey Robinson of the District Court for the District of Columbia ruled in our favor and found that the Corps of Engineers had acted unlawfully. He ordered the corps to work with the EPA to develop new regulations in three phases that would eventually apply to all rivers and streams and to all freshwater and tidal wetlands. The waters for which the corps was responsible were "not limited to the traditional tests of navigability," Judge Robinson said, an opinion he supported by citing not only the Clean Water Act but the Commerce Clause of the Constitution.

The Corps of Engineers did not go down without a fight. Immediately after the ruling, its senior officials went on the counterattack, abetted by President Ford's secretary of agriculture, Earl Butz, who traveled around the country trying to inflame public opinion against the Clean Water Act. Butz told farmers and ranchers that Judge Robinson's ruling would trample on their rights and that they would not be allowed to go about their basic daily activities without the permission of interfering bureaucrats from Washington. These were naked scare tactics, and we fought back hard. "With the outrageous threat that they are going to strictly police the plowing of fields and the construction of farm ponds across the nation," we said in a statement, "Corps officials are attempting to incite an uninformed backlash from citizens to help the Corps escape the environmental responsibilities Congress has given it."

Forced in the end to back down, the Corps of Engineers agreed to work with the EPA to develop the new regulations. The last step in the process was a direct parallel to our efforts to have the Clean Air Act fully enforced. In both cases, our litigation had pointed up serious loopholes in the law, and in 1977 Congress was obliged to amend the Clean Water Act. By a razor-thin margin of 50-49, the Senate affirmed that the jurisdiction of the Corps of Engineers did indeed extend to *all* waters. As a result, millions of acres of vital wetlands would be protected, and we cemented NRDC's reputation as the leading voice in the public interest community on the quality of the nation's water as well as its air.

Our work with the EPA in the early years of the Clean Water Act was, if anything, even more intense than it had been with the Clean Air Act. The rules that had to be drawn up were extremely complex, and we found ourselves offering expert comment about the application of the law to every kind of water body—rivers, streams, tributaries, lakes, wetlands, coastal waters, and estuaries—and to every kind of pollution, both "point source" (for example, where discharges flowed straight into a river from a factory or sewage plant) and "nonpoint source" (where waters might be polluted by nearby development, dumping, agricultural and other kinds of land use, or by runoff from stormwater drains). Where permits were to be granted for legal discharges, they had to be governed by carefully written guidelines, and we gave our input on these, too.

One of the biggest challenges was to help the EPA stand up to industries that were trying to undermine the intent of the new law, especially as it related to "the discharge of toxic pollutants in toxic amounts." The worst offenders were manufacturers of inorganic chemicals, although others, such as petroleum refiners, rubber processors, food processors, and iron and steel foundries, also joined the fight against the EPA. A dozen big corporations and trade associations, including DuPont, Union Carbide, the American Iron and Steel Institute, and the American Meat Institute, took the agency to court, arguing against uniform national standards for pollution control and demanding that the technical controls on pollutants should be determined at the level of each individual factory and each individual discharge. This would have meant the EPA issuing seventy-five thousand separate permits, which was obviously absurd. We came in on the side of the EPA, filing amicus or friend of the court briefs in a number of individual cases.

We used the stick as well as the carrot to strengthen the EPA's role. When the agency fell behind schedule, as was often the case, we took it to court—even though this meant suing the head of the EPA, Russell Train, who was a good friend to NRDC on many occasions. After the EPA missed fourteen separate deadlines for publishing the required regulations, reports, and guidelines, we brought the first citizen suit under the Clean Water Act. We followed up with others demanding uniform national standards for the control of toxics and a comprehensive list of the substances that were to be regulated.

The first such list produced by the EPA contained just nine chemicals and heavy metals, including mercury, cadmium, and DDT. Astonishingly, it omitted some of the most dangerous substances, such as lead, arsenic, chromium, zinc, asbestos, and numerous other known neurotoxins and carcinogens. We were especially concerned about herbicides and insecticides like aldrin/dieldrin, endrin, and toxaphene—a problem that would come to occupy a great deal of NRDC's attention over the years. Gus and Ed pointed out to the court that the EPA had not even drawn up proper selection criteria for which substances should be included on its list. At first the U.S. Court of Appeals for the District of Columbia ruled against us, saying that the EPA could always add new chemicals to the list later on. But we went back to court again, as the agency continued to drag its feet in the face of fierce resistance from industry.

We now had three active lawsuits going against the EPA, and in 1976 the court consolidated them into a single case before Judge Thomas J. Flannery. Over strenuous objections from industry groups, Flannery entered a landmark consent decree, signed by NRDC and the EPA, which gave us everything we had asked for and everything the Clean Water Act had intended—uniform standards that would apply to twenty-one different industry groups, each in its entirety, rather than to individual industrial plants, and a comprehensive regulatory program for a list of sixty-five named toxic pollutants, many of which were known or suspected carcinogens. Any release of one of these substances had to be controlled by the best available technologies, and discharges of some of the most dangerous chemicals, such as polychlorinated biphenyls (PCBs), were banned altogether. The Flannery Decree probably had a greater impact on how the EPA did business than any other single action, and agency staff told us later that the pressure from our litigation had given them both the motivation and the opportunity to do what they had always wanted. When industry appealed the Flannery Decree, the matter went back to Congress, which amended the law so that the regulations were shielded from further challenge.

That was not the end of the story, of course—stories like this never end. Judge Flannery had given the EPA until the end of 1979 to complete its list and ordered the pollutant control program to be in full operation by mid-1983. That did not happen. The EPA did not finish writing the regulations for the last of the sixty-five chemicals until 1987, and five years after that we filed yet another lawsuit to bring about a second generation of toxic water pollution controls. With industry inventing thousands of new synthetic chemicals each year, guarding against the release of toxics into the environment is a matter of eternal vigilance.

Even so, by the end of the 1970s, the nation's water had never been cleaner, and public support for the core principles of clean air and clean water was at an all-time high. The EPA was beginning to do its job, if not as thoroughly as we would have wished. Yet far too many corporate leaders continued to defy the demands of the Clean Water Act and pollute our rivers, whether or not they had an EPA permit for their activities. It was time for us to expand our focus.

The impetus came from a board member, Mike McIntosh, who had also been instrumental in the decision to open our West Coast office in Palo Alto in 1972. Mike had respected our work with federal agencies but was determined to find more ways to litigate. He was acutely aware of corporate failures, which he saw as a moral crime. So he urged us to focus on the citizen enforcement provisions of the Clean Water Act, which allowed any private individual to take a corporation to court. If we supported such actions and won in court, the company in question would have to pay to clean up the pollution at its site, as well as fines and legal fees.

Mike's family owned the A&P chain of supermarkets, and he was now head of the family foundation, which had a tradition of supporting liberal social causes. In 1982 funding from the McIntosh Foundation allowed us to set up NRDC's citizen enforcement project, the first head of which was attorney James Thornton. Over the succeeding decade, we would bring more than a hundred actions against corporate polluters in twenty-three states—more than the EPA and the Justice Department put together—and obtain millions of dollars in settlements for cleanups.

Does a Tree Have Standing?

Most people's view of the world is strongly colored by the environment in which they grew up. For me, it was a farm in the Catskills. For Patricia, it was the mountains and forests of the southern Appalachians in North Carolina. Her father, Walton Smith, chose to become a forester, over the objections of his parents who saw this as "life in a fire tower." As it turned out, his first job *was* mapping high peaks in the Nantahala National Forest in western North Carolina to find the best locations for fire towers. There, he met Patricia's mother, Annie Dee, whose family owned a mountain farm in the Nantahala.

Walton and Annie Dee built a log cabin on this land, and the family spent vacations there, sitting by an open fire, listening to stories of the mountains and of Walton's early days spent in the wilderness, measuring the big trees in what would become the Joyce Kilmer Memorial Forest. We still use that cabin as our regular family retreat, delighting in the unbounded vistas of blue, forested ridges stretching to the misty horizon. Walton worked for the U.S. Forest Service from 1934 to 1970, becoming a wood scientist at the Southeastern Forest Experiment Station in Asheville, North Carolina. He was once quoted in a book—Steve Lerner's 1998 *Eco-Pioneers*—as saying, "I love the Forest Service. I thought it was the best agency in the world and I thought everyone in the Forest Service wore a white hat." Patricia grew up sharing that view.

Little wonder, then, that we had a special concern for how the nation's forests were protected, or that this would be another central focus of NRDC's work from the beginning. In particular, we cared about the almost two hundred million acres of land in the national forest system, and the responsibility of the Forest Service to act in the spirit of the nation's new environmental laws.

The main threat was clear-cutting—the harvesting of all trees in a particular area, regardless of their size and condition—which destroys critical wildlife habitat and leaves behind bare soil prone to erosion, rutted access roads, naked white stumps, and burning slash piles. The building boom after World War II created a great demand for timber, and clear-cutting in the forests of the Pacific Northwest and the northern Rockies was rampant; by the early 1970s, the practice was spreading eastward.

In the summer of 1973, when the Forest Service proposed clear-cutting in the Monongahela National Forest in West Virginia—a beautiful expanse of almost a million acres, with seventy-five species of trees, numerous endangered and threatened species, and hundreds of miles of sparkling native trout streams—Larry Rockefeller decided to do some research. He found that no single law governed the management and protection of our forests. The Multiple-Use Sustained-Yield Act of 1960 set out some rather vague guidelines, stipulating only that Congress should pass laws ensuring that the national forests were managed for a variety of purposes including "outdoor recreation, range, timber, watershed, and wildlife and fish purposes." For more specific guidance, Larry had to go back to the Organic Act of 1897, which had established the U.S. Forest Service in the first place. The act maintained that the agency could only cut and sell "dead, mature, and large growth of trees . . . for the purpose of preserving the living and growing timber and promoting the younger growth on national forests." In addition, each tree that was to be cut had to be individually marked.

Logically enough, Larry wondered, "How can you clear-cut if you have to mark each tree?"

He spent that summer in the stacks of the New York Public Library, reading documents about the Organic Act and sneezing as the dust flew up off the old books. I asked Tom Barlow, who came to NRDC in 1973 and had been working with Gus Speth on stream channelization, to team up with Larry on this project. Tom researched the legislative history of the Organic Act, which went back to the Louisiana Purchase of 1803. After that date, all those lands that were not sold to farmers, given to land grant colleges, or otherwise designated became our first national forests. There was little regulation or management of these federal lands, and in the 1890s Congress saw that they were being ransacked for timber. Its response was the Organic Act, which became law during the presidency of William McKinley. The act was designed to improve and protect the national forests and secure reliable water flows, as well as furnish a continuous supply of timber for the citizens of the United States, all under the management of a new U.S. Forest Service. Tom concluded that Congress had known exactly what it was doing when it passed the act, and that its manifest intent was to make clear-cutting illegal.

Our old friend Jim Moorman took the same position. Jim was now head of the Sierra Club Legal Defense Fund, which had been set up by the venerable conservation group in 1971 with much the same purpose as NRDC—to use the strategies of public interest law to protect the environment. Jim was already well known to the Forest Service after a landmark suit brought by the Sierra Club, contesting the agency's decision to sell Mineral King Valley, part of the Sequoia National Forest, to Walt Disney Enterprises for development as a huge ski resort. The case had gone all the way to U.S. Supreme Court, where Disney and the Forest Service argued that the Sierra Club had no "standing" to become involved in the case, since it owned no property that was directly affected. The dispute over this critical question of law had powerful echoes of the celebrated Storm King case in 1965, where the judge had ruled in favor of Scenic Hudson on the grounds that the group's recreational and aesthetic interests in the river were enough to give its members standing. Even though the Supreme Court ruled against the Sierra Club in this case, it explained that if the group's members liked to hike in the Mineral King Valley, that was tantamount to having an economic interest in the place. Justice William O. Douglas filed a celebrated dissent, arguing that even this convoluted argument was unnecessary. In his view, Mineral King itself had to be thought of as the virtual client and the Sierra Club Legal Defense Fund as its representative. In effect, the trees themselves should have standing.

In 1973, on behalf of the fund and the West Virginia division of the Izaak Walton League of America, another long-established conservation group founded by anglers in the 1920s, Jim Moorman took the Forest Service to court, charging that it had violated the Organic Act by clear-cutting in the Monongahela. NRDC joined the suit as plaintiffs.

The Monongahela was one of a number of similar cases that we took during the early years. We went to court in California to stop clear-cutting by the Louisiana-Pacific Corporation on hillsides next to Redwood National Park, home to four of the six tallest trees in the world. We won that case. We also joined the Sierra Club in litigation to block clear-cutting in Alaska's Tongass, the largest of our national forests, the heart of the world's largest temperate rain forest, and home to vibrant populations of wolves, grizzlies, bald eagles, and salmon. This time, the prospective purchaser in what would have been the largest timber sale in history from a national forest backed out of the deal before the judge made a ruling.

But the Monongahela was the landmark case that changed federal law. In November 1973 the District Court for the Northern District of West Virginia ruled in our favor. The Forest Service appealed, but in 1975 the U.S. Court of Appeals for the Fourth Circuit upheld the original ruling. The Forest Service was furious and in a dramatic gesture shut down timber sales throughout the national forest system to force the hand of its friends in Congress. In Tom Barlow's view, "They would show these young whippersnappers who had power on Capitol Hill." To the agency's enormous surprise, it turned out that *we* did.

BOAT COMPANY TRIP, SOUTHEAST ALASKA, 1997
John and Patricia Adams

The key legislator was Senator Jennings Randolph, a veteran Democratic senator from West Virginia who was not known for any particular interest in environmental causes. But Randolph had been getting complaints about clear-cutting from his constituents. The Dietz family, who owned a local shoe business, reported that there were already over four hundred clear-cuts in the Monongahela, so Randolph invited himself along on a Forest Service tour to check out the charges. After a few hours of looking at maps and charts and being escorted through forests that had been cut selectively, Randolph was satisfied that the Forest Service had been acting correctly. Then the driver, a local man, suddenly took an unscheduled sharp turn down a small logging road—and arrived in the middle of a three-hundred-acre clear-cut. Randolph immediately decided something had to be done.

When he got back to Washington, he called Jim Moorman and asked him to draft a bill that would protect the national forests.

Jim asked, "Are you sure you want the Sierra Club's name on this?"

Jennings said, "Yes."

The bill was passed in 1976 as the National Forest Management Act (NFMA). It was not a perfect document, because it only restricted the practice of clear-cutting rather than prohibiting it outright; the Forest Service was given discretion to determine when clear-cutting was appropriate. Nonetheless, by including provisions that encouraged citizens and communities to become more deeply involved in the forest management process, the new law led to much the same practical outcome. The net result was a significant reduction of cutting in our national forests, from eleven billion board feet a year in the early 1970s to three billion board feet a year in 2008.

———

At NRDC, we had long been concerned that the timber in our national forests was being harvested at an unsustainable rate. We had already won one lawsuit barring the Forest Service and its parent agency, the

U.S. Department of Agriculture, from expanding timber sales without doing an environmental impact statement. Now we moved on to the economics of the sales that the Forest Service was making.

Tom Barlow and Tom Stoel researched timber sales in every national forest over a five-year period from 1973 to 1978. The conventional wisdom had always been that the sales were profitable, and the district offices of the Forest Service liked them because they brought in revenue that paid for salaries and other costs. What Barlow and Stoel found was shocking: in half of all cases, the Forest Service was selling federally owned timber to private companies for less than the cost it incurred in building logging roads, mapping, managing sales, and reseeding areas that had been cut. The losses were biggest in the Appalachians and the semiarid areas of the Rocky Mountain West, where the relative maintenance costs were higher and the productivity was lower. The big forest products companies that were buying this subsidized federal timber were making out like bandits. Since below-cost sales drove down the market price, smaller competitors that grew their own trees were unable to compete; they saw the value of their stock decline and ended up as prime candidates for takeovers by corporations and speculators. The biggest losers were the taxpayers; in the five years that Barlow and Stoel had studied, the below-cost sales had cost taxpayers $150 million.

Our final report on the sales, published in 1980, was called "Giving Away the National Forests." It caused an uproar. One of the most satisfying results for us was that the report encouraged stockholders and tree farmers from the smaller, private timber companies to make their voices heard during the administrative process of writing the regulations by which the National Forest Management Act would be enforced.

Writing those rules took several years—it was an even more protracted process than we'd seen with the Clean Air Act and Clean Water Act, in part because the Reagan administration, which took office in January 1981, was distinctly unhelpful. Once the rules were finally written, the Forest Service developed individual fifty-year management plans for each national forest. In almost all cases, the new administration proposed a huge increase in logging—even after we had beaten back many of the worst proposals.

A young lawyer named Kaid Benfield, who came to NRDC from the U.S. Department of Justice in late 1981, took over the running of our forestry project. One of his early decisions was to retain the help of veteran litigator Ron Wilson, who had left a large law firm to work for us and the Sierra Club Legal Defense Fund on a range of issues, including forestry. Kaid and Ron decided to target a select group of national forests and take a microscope to their draft management plans. We would then file critical comments on the plans, and if the final versions failed to meet the NFMA requirements, we would jump in with an administrative appeal. The overall goal was to eliminate below-cost timber sales and reduce clear-cutting. We carried out this strategy in partnership with the Wilderness Society, and it was extremely successful.

The biggest landmark case involved the San Juan National Forest and the jointly managed Grand Mesa, Uncompahgre, and Gunnison National Forests, all in Colorado. Together, these forests occupied more than five million acres of public land, making our case the greatest administrative challenge to logging in the history of the Forest Service. We won both appeals in a joint decision, forcing the agency to redo its proposals to include a more complete and balanced analysis of the economic implications of the planned logging programs. To the credit of the Reagan administration, it honored its free-market principles and sided with us. It was a huge victory.

Since it was important to establish a similar precedent in the eastern part of the country, we went through the same process with the management plan for the George Washington National Forest in Virginia. No forest in the entire national system is as heavily used for recreation. Yet the Forest Service proposed to triple the volume of logging, almost all of it through clear-cutting—with no alternatives proposed, as the law required. The case unfolded much as the two cases had in Colorado: critical comments, a massive administrative appeal, another major victory.

One case after another followed—the Rio Grande National Forest in Colorado, the Gallatin National Forest in Montana, the Payette National Forest in Idaho. We didn't win them all, but we saved a lot of land, and in most cases the Forest Service was forced to scale back its plans and allow a much greater degree of public involvement.

———————

As these cases suggest, the bulk of the forestry work shifted to the West Coast, which became our command center for the great pitched battles of the 1980s and 1990s over the old-growth forests of the Pacific Northwest and Alaska.

The idea for a California office had come from Mike McIntosh. One evening in 1971, as we sat over dinner with Mr. Duggan in the Oak Room at the Plaza Hotel in New York, Mike raised his glass and threw out a challenge: "You have to open an office on the West Coast. You have to go and compete with the Sierra Club!" Always the strategist, he recognized that NRDC needed to expand its vision and that California was the obvious place to do so. The state was big, it was growing, and it had an abundance of natural resources. It was a hell of a good decision, one of the defining factors in NRDC's success and the springboard to our becoming a major national organization.

The new office was headed by John Bryson. He was definitely the right person for the job, having been the calm, reasoning voice during our struggles to work out an agreement with the Yale group in 1970. A native of Oregon, John was tall, outgoing, charming, confident, and ambitious in the best sense of the word. Meeting him, we immediately saw his potential for accomplishing great things, perhaps a career in politics. (He did become a luminary in the field of renewable energy and energy conservation, serving eventually as CEO of Edison International, the parent company of Southern California Edison.)

John and I scouted the West to find the best place for our office. We looked at Seattle, Portland, and Denver before settling on Palo Alto.

California had always been John's preference. He saw the Bay Area as a natural seedbed for environmental work. Having graduated from Stanford, he knew influential members of the community there, such as Charlie Myers, the dean of Stanford Law School, who was extremely helpful to us as the office got up and running. Still, it wasn't long before we decided to make the move to San Francisco. That was where the other major organizations like the Sierra Club and the Sierra Club Legal Defense Fund had their offices, and that was where the important local environmental organizations, such as Save the Bay, were located. And, to be honest, that was also where the West Coast funders were. Within a short time, our small staff had moved to the city, with one exception—Johanna Wald.

This Land Is Our Land

Johanna was new to the West. She had grown up in Croton-on-Hudson, New York, and in 1967, after graduating from Yale Law School, where John Bryson had been her classmate, she had moved to Palo Alto. Her husband, Michael, was a law professor at Stanford. Johanna had two small children and was practicing what she called "living room law," giving legal advice to students at home after dinner. This lost its appeal very quickly, and when the NRDC office opened in 1972, she called John and asked if he could offer her a part-time position. He said no, and Johanna, in frustration, accidentally left the wrong phone number for him to call her if the situation changed. Nonetheless, he managed to track her down six months later and said he would take her on.

As a child, Johanna had hiked and camped and spent much of her free time playing in the woods behind her home with her brother and sister, but when she arrived at NRDC she didn't think of herself as an environmentalist or an advocate for the outdoors. That passion developed on the job.

What she remembers best about those early days at NRDC, in addition to the excitement of practicing an entirely new field of law, was her sense of the fragility of the organization. There were only half a dozen staff in California, and they were stretched thin. Every few months I would fly out there, and the staff and I would go hiking together. John Bryson would travel to New York periodically for meetings of NRDC's senior staff, and Johanna says that when he was gone the rest of the office would hunker down and wait anxiously for his return, worried that he would announce that the funding had dried up and the great experiment was over. It never occurred to Johanna that the organization would still be around forty years later.

John offered her a choice: she could work on coastal issues or on the problem of grazing on public lands. She chose grazing, even though she knew nothing about the subject. When she started meeting people in the field, she says, they must have known perfectly well that though she might have eaten beef, she had never stood next to a cow.

Our public lands—especially the mountains, mesas, forests, deserts, and semiarid plains of the West—are the crown jewels of the American landscape, the wide-open spaces of our national myths and legends. As our children grew up, the beauty of these places touched us personally and inspired our belief in the importance of supporting Johanna's work. I vividly recall one occasion when Patricia and our son John Hamilton hiked Coyote Gulch in Utah, land controlled by the Bureau of Land Management (BLM). They slept under a night sky more brilliant than any they had ever seen and clambered down the two-hundred-foot walls of red rock canyons to the Escalante River. It was May, and they did not see another soul for five days. Tamper with these public lands, and you tamper with the country's very identity. To me, NRDC's work in this area raised a fundamental question about our values as a nation: what were we prepared to sacrifice in order to extract the earth's natural resources?

In the lower forty-eight states, the United States government owns hundreds of millions of acres, which belong to all of us. Most of that land is not wilderness. It is designated for "multiple use"— managed by the U.S. Forest Service and the BLM for forestry, grazing, drilling, and mining, as well as for recreation. All these interests were supposed to receive equal consideration from federal agencies charged with planning how the land should be used. In practice, as a result of the pressures from private interests, some uses were more equal than others. An old joke said that "BLM" stood for Bureau of Livestock and Mining.

John Leshy, a lawyer in our new San Francisco office (and later solicitor general in President Bill Clinton's Interior Department), began to work on mining issues in the 1970s, especially in trying to limit the extent and environmental impact of strip-mining in areas such as the Powder River Basin of Montana and Wyoming, which accounted for 80 percent of the country's coal production. John laid the foundation for the work we continue to do today, both in that region and in the Appalachians. Working on coal was an important adjunct to our big lawsuit against the Tennessee Valley Authority, which was considering the purchase of cheap coal from the West. But it was hard for us to accomplish much. In fairness to the BLM (which, unlike the Forest Service, is an agency of the Department of the Interior), it was—and still is—hobbled by the obsolete General Mining Law of 1872, passed in the days of the lone prospector with his burro and pickax. Producers of "soft minerals," such as oil, gas, and coal, had to pay only modest royalties on their income. For "hard rock" mining, anyone could file a claim as long as $100 a year in "assessment work" had been invested, and no one else could use it. No matter what quantity of minerals were extracted from the claim, they never had to pay royalties. Mines on federal lands were subject to very few environmental restrictions.

―――――

These extractive industries would become a much larger part of NRDC's work in later years, especially as we became more focused on climate change and the nation's energy policies, but for now John Bryson believed that we could get greater traction on the neglected issue of grazing.

Johanna discovered that livestock grazing was the largest single use of federal lands. It was authorized on more than 150 million acres of BLM land in the eleven western states, 90 percent of the total under the agency's control, as well as on 100 million acres of national forests, national grasslands, national wildlife refuges, and national parks. The BLM was doing little or nothing to implement the few regulations that were in place, didn't revisit allocations to ranchers once they had been made, and didn't record violations. The BLM's inertia showed complete disdain for NEPA.

Not surprisingly, much of the land was severely overgrazed. In arid and semiarid areas of the West especially, cattle can have a hugely destructive impact. Grazing can destroy native vegetation and wildlife habitat; compact and erode topsoil, trample riverbanks, and degrade water quality; and introduce and spread invasive species. Livestock allotments often contain important wetlands, roadless areas, or archaeological sites, and grazing has often been implicated in the decline of animals and plants listed under the Endangered Species Act. And cattle do little for the scenic or recreational values of the landscape.

Because of these effects, it seemed obvious to us that the BLM should file an environmental impact assessment whenever it allocated land for grazing, as NEPA intended. Instead, the agency had chosen to issue only one assessment—enough, it claimed, to cover all 150 million acres. The BLM also paid little attention to the insistence of the new law on public input into the decision-making process. It was a secretive agency; when Johanna started our grazing project, almost nothing was known about the BLM, other than the total acreage it managed and the location of its offices. Maps of the West did not identify BLM lands, and nearby communities often didn't know where they were. Agency officials met privately with mining companies and livestock owners to determine what was in their best interests. "It was a completely closed door," Johanna says, "the curtains were down, and the keyhole was blocked."

She needed allies who could help her figure out how to force the door open, and she found her most important one by pure chance. Reading an article on the public lands in *Reader's Digest* one day, she realized that the author was the same man who had recently bought her parents' house in Croton-on-Hudson, the house in which Johanna had grown up. On an impulse, she called him. It turned out that he was able to put her in touch with one of the people quoted in the story, a retired BLM official from Idaho named Bill Meiners, who had strong environmentalist sympathies and had publicly criticized the management of the agency. Meiners became Johanna's mentor.

Their first visit to a BLM field office, in Idaho, spoke volumes. When the head of the office heard that the two had come to see him, he hastily left the building. Meiners saw him scurrying across the parking lot to his car. The BLM had had some dealings with the older-style conservation groups and their members, but never had to deal with anything like NRDC.

The relationship with Bill Meiners, as well as with a former Forest Service official named Earl Sandvig, who had worked to reduce the amount of cattle grazing on federal forest lands in the Southwest, was a revelation to Johanna. When she started out, she imagined that the best approach to learning about public lands and grazing would be to contact academic experts around the West. She soon realized that all the "experts" were at land grant colleges and that their scholarship was anything but objective. She learned a lot more by accompanying Meiners, Sandvig, and others to the places they knew intimately, meeting the hunters, anglers, and outdoor recreationists—people like the members of the Ada County Fish and Game Club in Challis, Idaho—whose interests were being directly affected by grazing.

This was a somewhat different style of work for NRDC. On the East Coast, most of our activities necessarily had a top-down character. We were *insiders*; much of our time was spent arguing before judges or sitting in hearings and administrative proceedings with federal agencies in Washington. In the program that Johanna was developing, everything revolved around a particular place and the people who lived there. She found Challis fascinating. Located in southeastern Idaho, on the Salmon River, it was an area of great natural beauty, with rich and diverse natural resources. Bighorn sheep roamed the mountains, and the rivers were alive with fish. People who lived in places like this had a deep attachment to the land—and that included the ranchers.

———

I picked up on some of this in a case I took in 1972 with Hamilton Kean, an attorney who was working for us pro bono and later became an NRDC trustee. Even though most of my time was taken up with building our new organization, I still enjoyed the challenge of handling the occasional case myself.

The issue in this instance was a poison called sodium monofluoroacetate, marketed as Compound 1080, which was widely used by ranchers to control coyotes and other predators. The problem was that it also killed countless thousands of bears, bobcats, mountain lions, bald eagles, and other "nontarget" animals, which suffered "secondary poisoning" when they fed on the carcasses. We petitioned the EPA to cancel the registration of Compound 1080 and three other predator-control poisons.

It was a significant case for a number of reasons. For a start, it was one of our earliest, successful attempts to build a coalition of like-minded organizations. The National Audubon Society, Sierra Club, Defenders of Wildlife, and half a dozen other groups agreed to join our petition, even though we were the new kids on the block. Ham Kean recalls being asked over and over again, "*National* Resource Defense? What was that name again?" (It still happens—a lot.)

Nathaniel Reed, who was the assistant secretary for fish and wildlife at the Department of the Interior under Nixon, and later became an NRDC board member, believed that the fastest way to get rid of Compound 1080 was by executive order. He had formed a committee to document the number of nontarget animals being killed.

"This lawsuit by Sierra Club and NRDC caught my attention," Nathaniel remembers. "I said to Secretary of the Interior [Rogers]

Morton, 'You know, before we assume that we're right and they are wrong, it would be a great idea to invite their attorneys to sit down and go over their complaint.' But two guys from the Department of Justice stood up and said, 'Mr. Secretary, that's not the way we do business in DC!'"

"Why not?"

"Our job is to protect our government from these eco-freaks."

Part of our problem was that the ranchers had powerful friends in Washington. But at the same time, we had to see the situation from the ranchers' point of view. They were losing their sheep—meaning their livelihood—to coyotes. Rather than simply opposing the poisons they were using to protect their livestock, we had to show that there were alternatives that would not have the same terrible impact on other species. For help, we turned to the National Zoological Society, whose experts demonstrated various ways that coyotes and other predators could be controlled without using Compound 1080. This was the key to our victory in the case. The EPA accepted our argument, canceling the registration of strychnine, cyanide, and Compound 1080 for predator control and banning thallium sulphate for all purposes.

Seeing matters from the ranchers' point of view, and understanding the long tradition they represented in American life, made a real impression on many of us. Roger Beers, a brilliant Harvard Law School graduate from Texas who had joined Johanna on the grazing project in 1973, recalls a trip he made to meet some ranchers on the New Mexico–Texas border. "When we passed a house after fifty miles of open country, one rancher said that things were getting crowded. We ate dinner on the Chisholm Trail, which went right through his property. As we talked about the importance of a dialogue between environmentalists and ranchers, I saw that we really wanted the same things. But I also realized that these ranchers, who represented a way of life that had gone on for generations, were also an endangered species. Their way of life was ending."

Johanna came to see things in much the same way. The relationship was never easy, and there was often a huge cultural gap to bridge, but she came to admire many of the ranchers she met and the way of life they had chosen. "What they do is really hard," she says, "and doing it badly may be even harder. What brought us together was the shared sense of place, an affection for the land. They do what they do because they want to get up in the morning and see the mountains, walk down to a free-flowing creek, and ride their horse."

———

Roger Beers was not everybody's idea of a perfect fit when he first came to NRDC. During his interview with Dick Ayres, he made the mistake of saying how much he liked Dallas, because there were so many parking lots and it was always easy to find a place to leave your car. Dick, scowling at him, said, "We're trying to get rid of parking lots." Nevertheless, Roger passed the test. He was a terrific born litigator with a sophisticated grasp of strategy, and he handled the lead argument in our biggest lawsuit against the BLM—*NRDC v. Morton*.

The essence of our case, which we brought in 1974, was straightforward: grazing had a substantial environmental impact on federally owned lands, and according to NEPA, every permit or group of permits granted by the BLM should be accompanied by its own environmental impact assessment. It was impossible for the agency to generalize about the impact of grazing on 150 million acres of every kind of public land, from the forested slopes of Oregon to the sagebrush flats of Wyoming to the red rock desert of Utah. A single global assessment would not give a particular range manager useful guidance; everything depended on the specific local situation. Should this specific area be grazed at all? If so, at what time of year, how much, by how many animals, how often, and for how long? The devil was in the details, and these had historically been a matter of private negotiations between the BLM and the ranchers.

The government's lawyers responded that individual assessments were not what Congress had intended; they would be a waste of time, money, and resources. Things worked just fine the way they were, thank you very much, and if local problems arose, they were probably due to a drought.

Obviously we could not provide chapter and verse on every one of the 150 million acres of BLM grazing land, but that was where Johanna's contacts were crucial. What we were able to do, with the assistance of local groups like the Ada County Fish and Game Club in Idaho, Earl Sandvig's friends in Oregon, and the Nevada Outdoor Recreation Association, was to paint a detailed and authoritative picture of the impact of grazing in a small number of specific areas. With no case law to draw on, we had to show a federal judge in the East that these local conditions were representative of a larger national problem, and the professional reputation and expertise of former agency officials like Sandvig and Bill Meiners were such that the judge found our argument persuasive. The case was heard on appeal by Judge Thomas J. Flannery of the U.S. Court of Appeals for the District of Columbia, the same judge who presided over our case against the EPA for its failure to regulate toxic substances in our water. Once again he ruled in our favor. It was another landmark victory for NRDC.

For the first time, the government would be forced to consider the value of federal lands from an environmental point of view and in an open, public process. Site-specific environmental impact statements "which satisfy the National Environmental Policy Act in all respects" were required for all local grazing allotments. That included outlining alternative management plans for the land that did not emphasize grazing as the major use. Roger Beers often joked that we held the record for the largest number of such statements ever obtained in a single lawsuit—150 for 150 million acres, though the number was subsequently whittled down to 112. One of the first individual environmental impact assessments—whose defects we challenged in court—was for Challis, Idaho, where Bill Meiners and Johanna had begun their work together.

In the wake of *NRDC v. Morton*, Congress passed the Federal Land Policy and Management Act of 1976, which ordered the BLM to manage our public lands in the future for "sustained yield" and multiple use. The law also ended the monopoly that ranchers had exercised for decades over the BLM's advisory boards; from now on, a variety of interested parties had to be represented on these bodies.

We had changed the law, changed the way our public lands were exploited, and changed the culture of the Bureau of Land Management. To deal with our lawsuit, the BLM had brought in a lot of new staff, and these people stayed on, bringing with them a much more open and accepting attitude to critics from outside the agency. Johanna Wald learned later that they called themselves the "Morton Babies."

———————

By the end of the decade, we had accomplished great things. We had written important parts of the nation's Clean Air and Clean Water Acts. We had challenged and defeated previously all-powerful government bureaucracies like the BLM, the TVA, and the Atomic Energy Commission. Judges and senators had heaped praise on the quality of our work. We had helped the new EPA do its job against often crippling odds and helped bring some of the country's biggest corporate polluters to book. Along the way, we had brought scores of other, less publicized lawsuits on everything from nuclear safety, offshore oil drilling, and energy conservation to subway noise, disposable packaging, and carcinogenic food additives. In the process, we had given a cadre of brilliant young litigators an unparalleled opportunity to fight and win landmark cases before the highest courts in the land. As an article in *Science* magazine said, "The young public interest lawyer may have the heady experience of handling big cases almost before he has had time to learn where the restroom is at the courthouse."

With our model of "responsible militancy," we had also shown a knack for principled compromise. We had gone to the negotiating table to find common ground with our adversaries, and while we kept up the pressure on the EPA to meet its new obligations, we also knew how to back off when the new agency was overwhelmed by the demands on its staff.

We had begun life in an era of bipartisan support for the environment, with a new generation of laws enacted under a Republican administration. For the last part of the decade, we had been able to count, for the most part, on the support of a Democratic administration with strong environmental sympathies. But even under President Jimmy Carter, the mood had begun to shift. This had a lot to do with the energy crisis and with the nation's supposed "malaise" (a word Carter never actually used during his infamous "cardigan speech"). There was a growing scarcity of the natural resources that Americans had always taken for granted, and the environmental movement made a convenient whipping boy. Our critics began to say that we were against everything—coal, pipelines, nuclear plants, dams, offshore drilling—and for nothing. All we wanted to do was regulate. We were accused of being self-righteous zealots, puritanical elitists, litigious opponents of industry and profit, determined to tie the legal system up in knots. That charge seemed particularly ridiculous to us: after all, it was the large corporations that could afford to deploy the batteries of expensive lawyers who could tie things up in the courts. Not only had we won the great majority of our cases—we never had a single suit dismissed by a judge for being frivolous or capricious.

Yet it was impossible to deny that the times had changed, and that while NRDC would never abandon litigation as a core strategy, we would also need to add a variety of new tools to meet the next round of threats to the environment. If we had any doubts about this, they were laid to rest in November 1980, when a radical new administration was elected with an unapologetic promise to undo all that we had accomplished.

Second Decade

1980–1990

The Dark Ages (and How We Survived Them)

I'd have a hard time choosing which was worse for the environment—Ronald Reagan or George W. Bush. I'd probably have to say the Reagan administration, because it was the first time we had to deal with such a determined assault on our core values. By 2001, we had had lots of practice.

From the very beginning, we knew what lay in store. The backlash against the nation's new environmental laws had already started under the Carter administration. The incoming president had made his views on the environment quite clear when he was governor of California. "A tree is a tree," he once famously said. "How many more do you need to look at?"

The new administration was intensely opposed to all forms of government regulation. On the campaign trail, Reagan liked to say that government was not the solution to our problems—it *was* the problem. His new budget director, David Stockman, and the chairman of the Council of Economic Advisers, Murray Weidenbaum, were passionate advocates of deregulation. A particular object of their hostility was the EPA, which they wrongly held responsible for stifling economic growth and energy production during the Carter years.

Over the previous decade, the EPA had grown to become a sizeable enterprise with 14,500 employees, ten regional offices, and an annual operating budget well over a billion dollars. In addition to its responsibility for enforcing keystone laws like the Clean Air Act and Clean Water Act, it was in charge of the $1.6 billion Superfund program, which Congress had established in 1980 to clean up the nation's hazardous waste sites. Stockman declared that he intended to slash the EPA budget in half.

Reagan set the new tone on his first day in office by rescinding executive orders banning the export of hazardous materials, revoking temporary regulations designed to strengthen energy conservation, and removing the solar panels that Carter had installed on the White House roof. Stockman's Office of Management and Budget followed up by compiling a target list of 242 actual or proposed federal regulations to be repealed, including rules on airborne pollutants such as sulfur dioxide and nitrogen oxides (SO_x and NO_x) and carbon monoxide, food labeling, PCBs, energy efficiency in buildings, the labeling of hazardous chemicals, and the allocation of wilderness areas in Alaska for energy development.

Then came the appointments to Reagan's "environmental" team.

The new EPA administrator was a young Colorado legislator named Anne Gorsuch, a hard-charging, ideologically rigid member of a Colorado group that proudly referred to itself as "the crazies" and was energetically supported by big oil companies that had made huge profits from their leases on public lands along the Rocky Mountain Front. The fossil fuel industry had become so powerful in Gorsuch's home state that Denver was sometimes referred to as "Houston North."

The post of secretary of the interior, in charge of forests, public lands, and national parks, went to James Watt, a born-again Christian from Wyoming who believed that the end of the world was approaching, saw human dominion over nature as a biblical mandate, and likened environmentalists to Nazis. He had been the first head of the Mountain States Legal Foundation, set up by wealthy Colorado brewer Joseph Coors in 1977 and backed by the likes of Exxon, Conoco, and Amoco to "fight in the courts those bureaucrats and no-growth advocates who create a challenge to individual liberty and economic freedoms." Watt was also a luminary in the Sagebrush Rebellion, a western campaign against efforts to limit the environmental abuse of our public lands. One of the main things triggering this rebellion had been our landmark suit on grazing, *NRDC v. Morton*. Those who saw their traditional prerogatives threatened by the new climate of environmental regulation now proposed that these federal lands should be privatized or turned over to the states.

Watt, who made no secret of his intentions, had what the eighteenth-century Irish philosopher George Berkeley called "an outward contempt of what the public esteemeth sacred." His first step would be a purge of the Interior Department, and he warned the president that his take-no-prisoners approach was bound to be controversial. According to Watt himself, who liked to tell the story, Reagan looked him right in the eye and said, "Sic 'em." In a way, I suppose, Watt's appointment was a bizarre stroke of luck for us. He was so extreme, so downright weird, that he made a great rallying point for our efforts to oppose the rollback of environmental protections.

Reagan's other appointments were in much the same vein. The new head of the U.S. Forest Service was James B. Crowell, who had been the general counsel of Georgia-Pacific, the largest buyer of timber from federal lands and a major cutter of redwoods. Crowell advocated massive logging of what he called "highly decadent old-growth stands" in the Tongass National Forest—for export to Japan. Perhaps the biggest new challenge we faced was at the Department of Energy, which slashed its budget for conservation by almost 80 percent and dedicated $762 million for the development of fast breeder nuclear reactors. Reagan was a militant proponent of nuclear power, which he called "the cleanest, most economical electric power we can have." His secretary of energy, James Edwards, a former governor of South Carolina, bragged that his home state, which housed several nuclear plants as well as the Savannah River nuclear weapons facility, was "the world's nuclear energy capital." Opponents of nuclear power, Edwards declared, were being used by "subversive elements" to do the bidding of the Soviet Union. Questioning the new administration's energy policies, in other words, would take us into the realm of national security—hitherto unknown territory for environmentalists.

———————

With this new climate of hostility in Washington, we had to do some retooling of NRDC. After ten years, we were a robust organization, with three busy offices and a staff approaching a hundred, but we were still heavily dominated by lawyers. We had pioneered the field of environmental public interest litigation, but we no longer had the field to ourselves. Other fine organizations, such as the Sierra Club Legal Defense Fund, were doing similar work, and sometimes we partnered with them on cases. What set us apart, I think, was that we constantly added new tools and experimented with new tactics. Winning lawsuits was not an end in itself; our goal was to change public policy, and the courtroom was not the only venue for doing that.

We would continue to litigate, to defend the laws and regulations we had worked so hard to create and uphold. But with a new administration in Washington, we also recognized that having the facts and the law on our side—something we had never doubted—was not going to be enough. We could no longer count on a cooperative relationship with the EPA or other federal agencies. Our opponents would always have more, and more highly paid, lawyers. If the other side had the dollars and the levers of power, what we needed was the numbers—in the form of voters, communities affected by environmental abuses, and NRDC members. If we hoped to persuade the public of our arguments, we would have to learn how to communicate with them more effectively. We had taken some modest steps in this direction in the two years before Reagan came to office; now we needed to do a lot more.

The most obvious way to get the word out was by using the media. However, we did not have anything resembling a professional media operation or an official spokesperson. We had structured NRDC so that each specialist took care of his or her own media exposure. Some people argued that we should have a single identified leader, a "face" for the organization, but I said no. I believed then, as I do now, that NRDC is not about the individual; it's about the team. We may have leaders, but they don't wear generals' hats. That still left us with a problem. No matter how brilliant they may be, lawyers and scientists are not always very good at communicating with lay audiences.

There are exceptions, of course. One was our staff attorney Jonathan Lash, a former federal prosecutor, who led our campaign against Gorsuch and Watt. Jonathan was the scion of a famous family of liberal Democrats (his mother, Trudy, had been a close friend of Eleanor Roosevelt's). He subsequently wrote a hard-hitting book, *A Season of Spoils*, which gave a detailed account of the Reagan administration's attempt to reverse the environmental gains of the 1970s. Jonathan would later become secretary of the environment for the state of Vermont and president of the nonprofit World Resources Institute.

We had also been blessed with another fine writer, Marc Reisner. Marc, whose parents had fled Nazi Germany, shared a house in Garrison, New York, with Frances Beinecke and others. He had come to NRDC in 1971 straight out of college and was the first person we hired to work on fundraising and membership. This included producing a modest newsletter. Marc's "office," which he shared with two others, was the library, where he also kept his bicycle and his duffel bag. In these cramped quarters, puffing away on his pipe and often sleeping there overnight, he worked feverishly to get each issue of our one-man newsletter to the printer on time. Eventually Marc left NRDC to work on a brilliant book, *Cadillac Desert: The American West and Its Disappearing Water*, published in 1986 and still considered the classic work on the subject.

When Marc moved on in 1979, I was anxious to find the right person to build on the work he had done. I approached former *Time* magazine journalist Peter Borrelli, who was the director of the Catskill Center for Conservation and Development (where I was on the board) and had also worked for the Sierra Club, and asked him to review what we should do to raise our public profile. NRDC needed to establish a specific identity, he said. Being an environmental law firm wasn't enough. We were still small compared to older organizations such as the Sierra Club and the National Audubon Society, and unlike them we didn't have a "founding father" like John Muir or John James Audubon.

Our nascent membership department felt the same way. When staff lawyers were asked to describe NRDC, the usual answer was: "We're the shadow EPA; we make the EPA do its job." That was accurate enough and effective in Washington political circles. Although we might have the respect of every elite lawyer and scientist in the country, most people didn't even know what the EPA was. As far as the general public was concerned, NRDC wasn't even a shadow; we were the shadow of a shadow.

Peter suggested upgrading the newsletter to a quarterly magazine, a journal of thought and opinion. He even suggested a name: *Man and Nature*, after the book of the same name by George Perkins Marsh, the nineteenth-century author, diplomat, and conservationist. When he presented this idea to the staff, Sarah Chasis gave him one of her inimitable looks and asked, "What is this, *Man* and Nature?"

Jonathan Larsen, the former editor of *New Times* and the *Village Voice*, came up with the alternative that stuck. The new magazine would be called the *Amicus Journal*, and Jonathan became the chair of its editorial board. Joan Davidson, one of our earliest trustees and the president of the J. M. Kaplan Fund, gave us the support we needed to start up the publication. Despite the name, which alluded to the amicus or friend of the court briefs we often filed in lawsuits, it would not be a narrowly focused legal journal. Nor would it be limited to the issues on which NRDC was working. The journal would take a broader critical look at the great environmental issues of the day. At the insistence of board member John Oakes, who had just retired from editing the op-ed page of the *New York Times*, it would not be "an organ of NRDC." The organization would not exercise editorial control over its content, and under Jonathan's expert guidance, the *Amicus Journal* and its successor, *OnEarth* (the name was changed in 2001), would aspire to the highest standards of journalistic excellence.

I thought this was exactly the right approach, and the publication has been vindicated over the years by a slew of awards and a stable of writers and photographers equal to any in the country. In recent years, thanks to editor Doug Barasch and his superb team, *OnEarth* has set a standard that no other environmental magazine in the country can match.

During the Reagan years—and for all the years that followed—one person did more than any other to raise NRDC's public profile. This was Robert Redford. He had already taken on the misdeeds of one president on the movie screen, and he was ready to do the same thing with another president—this time for real.

I first met Redford in 1973, when he came to lunch with Mike McIntosh and me. He had grown up in a working-class neighborhood in Southern California, where his father worked as a midlevel official for the Chevron oil company. As a kid, he had fallen in love with the ocean and the high Sierras, and he'd worked a summer job in Yosemite. By about 1969, when his movie career was taking off in earnest, he had decided that the environment was his great passion. "There was not a big population of environmental activists," he recalled at an NRDC event many years later. "So you were up against tremendous odds. When you went out to speak, you got hammered pretty hard."

He started small, with a successful fight to block the widening of a two-lane highway through Provo Canyon in Utah. In 1975, he took on a much bigger opponent: Southern California Edison and its plan to build a huge coal-fired power plant near Zion and Bryce Canyon national parks. By now he was a big movie star, and Dan Rather covered the story on CBS's *60 Minutes*. The giant utility ended up canceling its plans for the plant, but only after a bitter public struggle. In Kanab, Utah, Bob was burned in effigy by people who blamed him for the loss of jobs and cheap energy. They called him an extremist and a "backpacking kook." His family received threatening letters. He had been in the lion's den.

From this he drew a couple of important conclusions. One was that the bitterness that had marked the fight against Southern California Edison was something to be avoided if possible; perhaps there was a way to bring all parties in a dispute to the table and see what common ground existed. To pursue this idea, he created the Institute for Resource Management and invited me to join the board. It was an amazing group that included not only local communities, Native Americans, renowned scientists, and prominent environmentalists such as former Secretary of the Interior Stewart Udall, but also corporate executives like George Keller of Chevron, Charles Kittrell of Phillips Petroleum— and even Howard Allen, chair of Southern California Edison. I learned a lot from Bob's determination to reach out to traditional adversaries and engage them at the highest levels. He reasoned that you were much more likely to win lasting, meaningful victories if you could find common ground with others who had a real stake in the issue. In this he was way ahead of his time, and his philosophy had a significant influence on how we subsequently worked at NRDC.

His second conclusion was that his own work would be strengthened if he joined forces with an existing environmental organization. He supported all of them, he told me, and had talked to many, but in the end he was nervous about spreading himself too thin. He wanted a partnership with just one group, and he chose NRDC. The reason, he explained, was the effectiveness of our litigation. We took people to court, and we won. He said that he would like to kick off the relationship by having the premiere of his next movie, *All the President's Men*, be a joint benefit for NRDC and the Consumer Action Network, which had been started by his then wife, Lola.

The evening was a tremendous success, with a dinner attended by Carl Bernstein and Bob Woodward, Lillian Hellman and Nora Ephron, and Liza Minnelli and her entourage. The great draw, of course, was Bob himself. Pattie Sullivan jokes, "Everyone was far too 'waspy' to approach him, so I took him around to the tables and he spoke to people. He was always a good sport about this." The benefit started a tradition that continued with other Redford movies such as *The Electric Horseman* (1979), *Out of Africa* (1985), *The Milagro Beanfield War* (1988), and *A River Runs Through It* (1992), each bringing in money and new supporters for NRDC.

Public interest organizations are always eager to find high-profile supporters from the world of arts and entertainment, and in our celebrity-driven culture that can sometimes be a mixed blessing. From the time of our first meeting, it was obvious to me that Redford had a very sophisticated view of the pitfalls of celebrity. He made it apparent that he had no time for the glitz of Hollywood and hated spending time there, yet he also had a clear understanding of the power of movies and the arts to advance social causes—witness his later creation of the Sundance Institute and Festival. The key to our relationship over the past thirty-five years has been Bob's professionalism and his discretion. He is not afraid to use his name, but at the same time that imposes the obligation on us not to overuse it or to ask him to do anything inappropriate. He has always been willing to use his celebrity to help us, the condition being that he would only support those issues he knew and cared deeply about. And on those, he proved to be as knowledgeable as NRDC's own lawyers and scientists. This became clear when Secretary of the Interior James Watt announced plans to open up a billion acres of the Outer Continental Shelf to oil and gas drilling.

Leases for drilling on the Outer Continental Shelf did not begin with the Reagan administration. With memories of the traumatic 1969 Santa Barbara oil spill fresh in everyone's minds, we had already gone to court several times in the 1970s to demand adequate environmental impact statements before drilling leases were issued in coastal waters off Louisiana and several northeastern and mid-Atlantic states. When the Department of the Interior expanded its leasing program in 1974, we grew more and more concerned about the potential impact on major fisheries. What worried us was not only the risk of major one-time events like Santa Barbara but the more insidious effects of chronic, low-level spills and discharges from drill rigs and platforms, as well as from tankers bringing the oil ashore.

However, no one was prepared for the magnitude of what Watt proposed. Immediately after his confirmation, he wrote to the governors of California and Oregon announcing that his first priority was to increase domestic oil and gas production. Accordingly, he proposed to auction off drilling leases on the continental shelf off the beautiful Northern California coast, in areas that had been withdrawn from the leasing program after the Santa Barbara blowout. That disaster had been the impetus for California's coastal protection law (passed over then Governor Reagan's objections) and then for the federal Coastal Zone Management Act of 1972. Watt was known as a vindictive man, and it seemed as if he had singled out the state of California, and its association with one of the main symbols of the modern environmental movement, for special treatment.

Although a federal appeals court ruled against Watt's plans, he announced an even more sweeping plan in June 1982 that would open up a billion acres of the continental shelf—an area equal to half of the entire continental United States—to drilling over the next five years. The total extent of all drilling leases approved since 1953 was ninety-five million acres, and that was mainly limited to the Gulf of Mexico. Under the new plan, no section of our coastal waters would be spared. Some of the world's most important fisheries, such as the Georges Bank in the North Atlantic and the southeastern Bering Sea, would be imperiled. The leasing area off Alaska would be larger than the state itself. Off the coast of Maryland and Delaware, oil rigs would sprout as little as eight miles from shore.

Writing in the new *Amicus Journal*, Sarah Chasis and Frances Beinecke denounced Watt's plan as "one of the most callous and irresponsible public lands decisions ever made." Joined by six other environmental organizations, as well as the states of Alaska and California, we took the secretary of the interior to court, citing the Outer Continental Shelf Lands Act of 1978, which called for a balance "between the potential for environmental damage, the potential for the discovery of oil and gas, and the potential for adverse impact on the coastal zone."

Watt's drilling plan also alarmed Robert Redford, and he decided it should be the focus of a conference at his Institute for Resource Management. Sarah Chasis and I flew out to the meeting, which was held in Morro Bay, California. Bob had also invited the oil companies to

THE INSTITUTE OF RESOURCE MANAGEMENT MEETING CONCERNING OUTER CONTINENTAL SHELF DRILLING, MORRO BAY, CALIFORNIA, 1982
Left: John Adams, Founding Director and Trustee, NRDC;
Right: Robert Redford, NRDC Trustee

join in, and although I was deeply skeptical about what that was likely to accomplish, Sarah and I were astounded by what ensued.

"The differences were pretty apparent," Sarah remembers. "The oil executives were a generation older than we were and dressed in suits, while we were in khakis and down vests. The first evening we took a boat ride out in Morro Bay. We had some wine, and then the water got quite rough, so we were all swaying back and forth together. Redford joked that it was his way to make sure we 'got closer.'"

Bob laid down a challenge for the group: was there any room to negotiate on offshore drilling? He suggested we take a particular area that we all cared about and see if we could reach some agreement. We chose the Bering Sea, bordering Alaska. These are some of the roughest waters in the world, and we thought it was crazy to drill there. The risks were high, and the oil reserves were marginal. Although we didn't have detailed scientific data in those days about ocean ecosystems, we did know—because local fishermen and native Alaskan people told us when we met with them—that these fisheries were among the most productive in the world.

At our first meeting to discuss the Bering Sea, Doug Foy, the director of the Conservation Law Foundation of New England, held up a map and said to the industry folks, "If our priority areas overlap all of yours, then we have a problem. But at least we will know where our problems are. We can throw out the other 90 percent and stop fighting over the stuff nobody cares about."

Each side agreed to draw circles around the areas of the Bering Sea it would fight for. If we wanted an area but the oil companies didn't, we would jointly recommend to the Department of the Interior *not* to include it in the five-year leasing program. If an area was of lower environmental concern, it could be considered for leasing and included in the five-year planning schedule (although it would still be subject to further environmental review before a final decision was made). In areas where the interests of the environmentalists and the companies came into conflict, we either negotiated or agreed to disagree.

As we looked at the map, one oil executive pointed to an area we had circled and said, "Are you saying that if we give up drilling in this area, you will give up trying to stop us over here?"

I leaned forward and said, "Yes."

"When I saw this," Redford told us years later, "I realized that we were breaking through. It was a defining moment." Shortly after, we reached an agreement about which areas could go into the five-year leasing program and which would be protected.

I could see even then that the work we were doing would have major implications for NRDC's future. Our coastal project, run by Sarah and Frances, was still quite modest in scale. We had begun by opposing James Watt's plans for offshore oil drilling, and we were on the verge of becoming major players in determining the health of the nation's fisheries. If we continued down this road—and I was convinced that we should—it would mean more money, more staff, capacity to work simultaneously on the East Coast, on the West Coast, off Alaska. Over time, it would mean transforming our modest effort into a much more sweeping program to protect the world's oceans.

After we'd reached agreement with the oil companies over the Bering Sea, Sarah and I flew with Redford to Washington to make the announcement at a press conference. When we met with the secretary of interior, his attitude was, "Who are you to tell us how to manage the Bering Sea? That's our job!"

But in a sense, that was no longer true. The recommendations that we were presenting had been accepted by the oil companies, and eventually most would be accepted by the government.

It was 1985, and James Watt was gone by now. The interior secretary with whom we met was his replacement, Donald Hodel. Watt had fallen victim to his own excesses. In 1983, when he banned the Beach Boys from playing at a July 4 concert on the National Mall, he became a figure of public ridicule. Later that year, he sealed his fate by boasting that the members of his coal advisory board included "a black, a woman, two Jews, and a cripple." He had become an embarrassment to the administration he served.

Anne Gorsuch was gone, too. In her case, it was the result of a series of scandals at the EPA involving corruption, misconduct, and conflicts of interest. The official she had appointed to oversee the Superfund program was in jail for lying to Congress under oath. Gorsuch herself was held in contempt of Congress for failing to release documents relating to Superfund and the chemical industry. Eventually she was forced to resign in disgrace.

Yet the president heaped praise on both of them. He said Gorsuch's tenure at the EPA had been "splendid" and declared that Watt had "done an outstanding job . . . in his stewardship of the natural resources of the nation."

The personalities might change, but we saw that Reagan's policies would continue—and that we would continue fighting them. One of our first, and biggest, battles took on the administration's obsession with nuclear power.

A Terrible Power

Plutonium is one of the most hazardous substances on earth. The scientist who discovered it, Glenn Seaborg, once described it as "fiendishly toxic." One-millionth of a gram lodged in a lung carries a very high risk of causing cancer. Less than fifteen pounds are needed to manufacture a nuclear weapon the size of the one that obliterated Nagasaki.

Plutonium can also be used to fuel nuclear power plants, once it has been separated from nuclear waste by "reprocessing," and in the early 1970s, the Atomic Energy Commission saw plutonium as the magic bullet that would solve all our energy problems. In particular, the AEC was infatuated with so-called Liquid Metal Fast Breeder Reactors (a "breeder" reactor being one that produces more plutonium than it consumes), and in 1970 President Nixon designated this as the nation's highest priority technology research and development program. Thanks to fast breeder technology, the AEC saw a radiant future in which as many as fourteen hundred nuclear power plants would be in operation by the year 2000.

Although his main focus was on clean water, Gus Speth immediately saw the tremendous risks of the fast breeder reactor program—not only the danger it posed to human health and the environment, but the risk of weapons proliferation and terrorism, not to mention the huge economic cost. Then there was the problem of what to do with the waste, most of which would be shipped to the Hanford Reservation, on the Columbia River in Washington state. Originally established as part of the Manhattan Project, Hanford had grown to a sprawling complex of nine nuclear reactors and five plutonium reprocessing facilities. It was responsible for producing most of the country's nuclear weapons arsenal during the Cold War, and already it was storing millions of gallons of highly radioactive waste in underground tanks—with no coherent plan for moving it to safe storage in the kind of deep, secure geological formations where it could remain safely sequestered for several hundred thousand years. That's how long it would take until the waste radioactively decayed to the point where it no longer posed a significant health risk.

We thought the "plutonium economy" was madness and decided to fight it with all the resources at our disposal—precedent-setting litigation, administrative actions, testimony before Congress, scientific reports, and citizen education.

Before taking the AEC to court over the fast breeder reactor program, Gus wanted to find the right science-based partner organization (NRDC was just beginning to develop its own scientific capability). He found this in the Scientists' Institute for Public Information, a recently established advocacy group. His counterpart at SIPI was Dean Abrahamson, a nuclear physicist from Minnesota who also had degrees in biology and medicine. Of Swedish origin, Dean had close ties to Sweden's active nuclear disarmament community. He later joined the NRDC board.

In 1971, acting on behalf of SIPI, we filed suit in the U.S. Court of Appeals for the Fourth Circuit. No specific statute addressed the dangers of plutonium. Therefore, as in so many other cases, we turned to the National Environmental Protection Act, which required an environmental impact statement for any federal agency action that "significantly affected the quality of the human environment." The Atomic Energy Commission insisted that it *had* filed individual assessments for each of the first plants it proposed under the Liquid Metal Fast Breeder Reactor Program, but Gus argued that this was not enough: the agency also needed to file an impact statement that covered the entire program, including the shipping and storage of highly toxic material. What would be the cumulative effect of *all* these new nuclear plants on the environment?

After two years of litigation, the court upheld our position. The AEC was furious, but there was nothing it could do. The court's decision was cut-and-dried, and the agency declined to file an appeal. We celebrated with a big victory party that night in our Washington brownstone.

Although we felt that we had stopped the fast breeder reactor program in its tracks, we knew our work was far from over. The environmental impact statements would open the program to public scrutiny. There would be congressional hearings and administrative proceedings, hundreds of technical documents to review, thousands of written questions to prepare, and briefs and memoranda and testimonies to draft. We needed the best scientific experts we could find to guide us through the review process.

Gus and Dean hired Arthur Tamplin, a biophysicist on leave from the Atomic Energy Commission, and Thomas Cochran, a nuclear physicist on the staff of Resources for the Future, a nonprofit organization in Washington, where he had been writing an economic and environmental critique of the breeder program. Tom's passion for nuclear issues is legendary: his idea of a honeymoon was to drive across the country with his wife, stopping off on the way to look at nuclear plants.

A plainspoken man from Tennessee with a dry wit, Tom originally wasn't sure if he wanted to join what he called "this wild ass group." In the end he said, "I agreed to work at NRDC, but only if I was treated as an equal, not just a research scientist for a bunch of lawyers. Maybe because of that Art Tamplin and I were given the living room of the old house for our office. We even had our own private bathroom!"

Tom went on to become one of the most important people in building NRDC.

One lawsuit followed another, and we expanded the fight beyond the fast breeder reactor program to nuclear power in general. When Congress shut down the Atomic Energy Commission in 1974, we took on its successor, the Nuclear Regulatory Commission. We opposed the use of plutonium recovered in reprocessing in existing light water reactors; sued the NRC to force it to conduct an environmental review before licensing any new plutonium reprocessing facilities; demanded tighter radiation protection standards for plutonium to reduce the risk of cancer; challenged proposals for new nuclear facilities such as the Vermont Yankee plant and eight floating nuclear plants, the first of their kind, off the coast of Florida; forced federal weapons plants to obey the same safety rules as privately owned facilities; and challenged proposals to license the export of nuclear fuel to other countries, demonstrating the ease with which sensitive nuclear technologies could be converted from civilian to military uses. This effort resulted eventually in the 1978 Nuclear Non-Proliferation Act.

We also became the most important citizen watchdog organization monitoring the federal nuclear waste program—work that was run out of our Palo Alto office, with the litigation being handled by John Bryson and Roger Beers. We succeeded in forcing the government to begin dealing for the first time with the hundreds of thousands of gallons of radioactive waste leaking from underground storage tanks at Hanford and the Savannah River plant in South Carolina.

The government's gung ho attitude toward nuclear power changed radically when Jimmy Carter was elected president in 1977. Gus Speth left NRDC to join the new administration; still only in his early thirties, he was appointed chair of the president's Council on Environmental Quality. Carter was no fan of nuclear power, which he described as a "last resort" in addressing the nation's energy needs, and in April 1977 he called for an indefinite suspension of all work on the fast breeder reactor program. The linchpin of the program, authorized by the Atomic Energy Commission in 1970, had been the Clinch River Breeder Reactor in Tennessee, a 350-megawatt plant where the highly enriched uranium for the Hiroshima bomb, "Little Boy," had been produced. Carter denounced the Clinch River project as "a technological dinosaur," "an assault on our attempts to control the spread of dangerous nuclear materials," and "a waste of one and a half billion dollars of taxpayers' money."

Two years later, Americans watched in horror as the reactor core at the Three Mile Island nuclear plant near Harrisburg, Pennsylvania, overheated. It was subsequently found that 70 percent of the fuel was damaged and that 35 to 45 percent of the core had melted. Although catastrophe was narrowly averted (as much by good luck as by good engineering), the incident seemed to be the final nail in the coffin of the nuclear power program in the United States.

But then came the Iranian revolution, the "second oil shock," and the election of Ronald Reagan, and once again we found ourselves up against an administration that saw nuclear power as the panacea for all our troubles. Despite congressional opposition and a soaring price tag (an original estimate of $400 million had risen to over $4 billion, including $1 billion for an adjoining reprocessing facility), the new administration broke ground on the Clinch River plant early in 1981.

Oil shock or no oil shock, we opposed Clinch River for the same reasons as before. We had to show that environmental laws were not something that could be picked up or dropped in response to passing economic and political circumstances; these laws expressed bedrock principles about the responsible use of our natural resources. But in opposing the Reagan administration's plans to press ahead with Clinch River, we were also aware that we were involving ourselves for the first time in issues of national security. Reagan's attachment to nuclear power was inseparable from his renewal of the arms race. The plutonium from a civilian reactor's spent fuel could easily be used to make bombs, and the Department of Energy was considering transferring its entire eighteen-ton stockpile of plutonium to the weapons program, where it could be used to manufacture as many as four thousand warheads. Weapons production as well as more traditional environmental oversight was on our minds as we pressed on with our renewed litigation against Clinch River.

Gus Speth and Tom Cochran had been organizing a broad coalition to oppose the program, including not only environmental groups and the Union of Concerned Scientists but fiscal conservatives appalled by the cost. After Gus left NRDC to join the Carter administration, we sought the assistance of two public interest lawyers in Washington and then brought on board a young lawyer, Barbara Finamore, who came to NRDC from the Department of Interior. Barbara had been hired by the department right out of Harvard Law School and had worked briefly on issues that included surface mining and offshore oil drilling. She lasted just six months before falling to James Watt's ax. Technically she wasn't fired; it was called a reduction in force but amounted to the same thing.

For Barbara, the Clinch River fight was a baptism by fire. In 1982, shortly after her arrival, she was to accompany Tom and one of the outside lawyers to Oak Ridge for a construction permit hearing before an NRC licensing board. At the last minute, however, the other lawyer said he could not attend. He coached Barbara on what she would have to do. It was easy, he said: just propose that Tom be certified by the judge as our representative in this particular hearing.

The hearing room was packed, with ten lawyers for the other side at one table and Barbara and Tom at another. The judge banged his gavel and said, "Begin your case."

"I would like to nominate Tom Cochran to be the NRDC representative," Barbara answered.

"Denied. Call your first witness."

Tom whispered something in Barbara's ear, but she was so flustered she couldn't hear him.

"No whispering in the courtroom," the judge bellowed.

Tom started writing Barbara a note.

"No passing notes."

Tom nervously tapped his finger on the table, trying to figure out what to do.

"Let the record show," growled the judge, "that Mr. Cochran is tapping his fingers in a cantankerous manner."

They asked for a recess, with Barbara ready to explode in frustration, but Tom told her not to worry: "We're going to get those SOBs." Barbara went on to perform brilliantly under the circumstances. She even caught one of the lawyers representing the Clinch River project secretly colluding with an NRC staff attorney in an attempt to avoid Barbara's withering cross-examination of the government's witnesses.

The construction licensing battle would drag on for another two years. Before it was concluded, Tom got a call from someone at Oak Ridge, who told him that the Y-12 plant had been dumping mercury into a nearby creek for years, without notifying the communities downstream. The informant said that a total of seven tons of mercury had been disposed of in this way.

Barbara took the Department of Energy to court, this time under the Clean Water Act and the Resource Conservation and Recovery Act (RCRA) of 1976, both of which require "cradle to grave" handling and cleanup of such hazardous substances. The Energy Department admitted that it had been dumping mercury from the Y-12 plant, going all the way back to 1950—but argued that under the Atomic Energy Act it had sole authority to regulate activities at nuclear weapons facilities and that the EPA and state regulations did not apply. The EPA thought otherwise. Anne Gorsuch's disastrous tenure had ended, and the man brought in to clean up the mess was William Ruckelshaus, who had already served one term as the agency's first administrator, from 1970 to 1973. Ruckelshaus said that RCRA did indeed apply to the Y-12 plant, and the judge agreed. The ruling applied only to a single facility, but two weeks later the Department of Energy wrote to every one of the country's thirty or so nuclear weapons plants saying that they too had to comply. This landmark case opened the entire nuclear weapons

FAST BREEDER REACTOR VICTORY PARTY, FALL 1983
Left to right: Tom Cochran, Director, Nuclear Program, NRDC; James Gustave
Speth, Founding Staff and Trustee, NRDC; Barbara Finamore, Senior Attorney,
China Program, NRDC; John Adams, Founding Director and Trustee, NRDC;
Jacob Scherr, Director, International Program, NRDC

complex to EPA and state oversight and led to the largest environmental
cleanup program in the nation's history.

As for the Clinch River reactor construction project, we did not
prevail in the licensing hearings; the NRC was simply determined to
press ahead. It didn't matter, because the issue had shifted to Congress,
and though we had lost the licensing battle, we won the war. On
October 26, 1983, over the objections of Republican Majority Leader
Howard Baker of Tennessee, the Senate voted fifty-six to forty to deny
further financing for the project. The Clinch River Breeder Reactor—and
for all practical purposes the entire Liquid Metal Fast Breeder Reactor
Program—was dead. On purely economic grounds, it had been folly.
The original estimate of the cost of the Clinch River reactor had been

$400 million. In 1977, Carter said $1.5 billion. By 1981, it was $4 billion. By the time the project was finally canceled, the cost estimate had risen to $8 billion. Senator Dale Bumpers, Democrat from Arkansas, who led the effort to kill the fast breeder reactor program, said, "We put some money down a rathole and decided not to spend any more."

Going Underground

Our work on the nuclear issue also gave NRDC a more international focus, starting with our opposition to licenses for the export of nuclear fuel to India. This followed India's 1974 test of a nuclear device built with plutonium produced in a reactor supplied for peaceful research. We had always taken a holistic view of our work, recognizing that big issues like air, water, and wilderness were intertwined. By the same token, we knew that environmental threats could not be contained within national boundaries.

With our limited resources, we had done a modest amount of work outside the United States in the 1970s. In 1972, a group of us—myself, board member Jim Marshall, and some students from the clinic that I was running at New York University Law School, together with Patricia and two of our kids, Kate and John Hamilton—had flown to Stockholm for the first United Nations Conference on the Human Environment. Beatrice Abbott Duggan, who had been present at the creation of NRDC and whose husband was still our chairman, was our representative at the UN in New York. In those days, environmental advocacy was still largely limited to the developed world, but we had created a fellowship program in honor of the Duggans that allowed us to bring outstanding young activists from developing countries to the United States. One was Wangari Maathai, who later became internationally famous for her work to protect the environment in her native Kenya and was awarded the Nobel Peace Prize. The Duggan Fellows program was overseen by Jacob Scherr, a graduate of Georgetown University Law School, who later took charge of all our international work.

We briefly considered opening one or more foreign offices but decided that we could have a greater impact by working in Washington with the big international aid and financial agencies, whose programs had never before been held up to scrutiny on environmental grounds. Many of these programs were designed to support agricultural development, and they often encouraged the heavy use of toxic pesticides—exported from the United States. With a lot of help and advice from our new board member, former Ambassador Robert Blake, an expert on the World Bank, the Inter-American Development Bank, and the U.S. Agency for International Development (AID), I think we accomplished a great deal. In 1977 Congress ordered AID to incorporate environmental considerations into its assistance programs, which affected everything from fish farming in Ecuador to floodplain development in West Africa.

In 1980 Mr. Duggan decided it was time for him to retire, and I needed to look for a successor. Ross Sandler introduced me to the perfect candidate at a meeting of the New York City Bar Association. The topic was nuclear weapons. Adrian DeWind—universally known as Bill—was from a Northern Ireland family, and for that reason alone I felt an immediate kinship. He was the outgoing president of the bar association and a senior partner at Paul, Weiss, Rifkind, Wharton, and Garrison, a law firm with a distinguished history of support for pro bono work. He was also one of the country's leading tax experts and had served on presidential tax commissions under both Kennedy and Johnson.

Bill was articulate and outspoken, with an incredible reputation for integrity. His manner was low-key, and he had a great sense of humor. He was fun. I had always looked on Mr. Duggan as a mentor, but Bill was my pal, my traveling buddy. Whenever a trip came up, I could rely on Bill being on the airplane, and he refused to travel first class. On one occasion, years later, when we were in Brazil for the UN's 1992 Rio

NRDC BOARD MEETING, DECEMBER 1991
Left to right: Adam Albright, NRDC Trustee; John Adams, NRDC Founding
Director and Trustee; Adrian (Bill) W. DeWind, NRDC Chairman 1981–1992;
Stephen P. Duggan, NRDC Founding Chairman 1970–1980

Conference on the Environment, we slept in bunks in a crummy apartment building where there were gunshots and bloodstains in the hallways. None of it bothered Bill, who had already spent several years
traveling to dangerous and unsavory places as one of the founders of
Human Rights Watch. He didn't have any specific background in environmental issues. What he brought to us was caring, common sense,
great connections in the foundation world, and an instinct for how to
build institutions. Over the next decade, under Bill's guidance, NRDC
grew exponentially.

At this time, Bill cared most about the threat of nuclear annihila-
tion. The Cold War was raging, and in his farewell address President
Carter had warned, "In an all-out nuclear war, more destructive power
than in all of World War II would be unleashed every second during
the long afternoon it would take for all of the missiles and bombs
to fall." For many, President Reagan's foreign policy, denouncing the

Soviet Union as the "Evil Empire" and later launching the Strategic Defense Initiative, commonly known as Star Wars, made this danger more imminent. Even the accidental launch of a nuclear weapon, which many people thought had become more likely in the new hair-trigger atmosphere, would be a catastrophe.

Bill immediately saw the possibilities for NRDC to play a big part in reducing the risk of nuclear war, and he championed the issue with our board. Some members were skeptical: how could a nuclear test ban be considered an environmental issue? No other environmental groups were working in this area. Bill's response was simple: "If there is a nuclear holocaust, there *will be no* environment!"

Tom Cochran realized that if we were going to work on arms control issues, we first had to establish our credentials. The Senate Armed Services Committee was not exactly known for its high opinion of environmental groups. In those days, most of the information about nuclear weapons—how and where they were made, their characteristics, and where they were deployed—was shrouded in secrecy, which severely limited public participation in decision making. Tom decided that we should start by writing a series of reference books on nuclear weapons.

He teamed up with William Arkin, a former U.S. Army intelligence analyst, and the two of them recruited consultants, including Stan Norris, who subsequently joined our nuclear program and is still one of our senior research associates. The first volume of the series was the *Nuclear Weapons Databook: U.S. Nuclear Forces and Capabilities*, written in 1984 by Tom, William Arkin, and Milton Hoenig. The book received a glowing review in the *New York Times* from McGeorge Bundy, former national security advisor to both Presidents John F. Kennedy and Lyndon B. Johnson, who described it as "a powerful antidote to the simplistic deceptions peddled with such zeal from high places." Over the succeeding years, Tom, Stan, and other coauthors produced additional comprehensive studies of the Soviet, British, Chinese, and French nuclear arsenals. Similar in style to the classic *Jane's Fighting Ships*, the series provided the most complete collection of nonclassified data on nuclear weapons production, stockpiles, and deployments. The NRDC board followed up by adopting a resolution calling on the United States and the Soviet Union to negotiate a mutual and verifiable freeze on the testing, production, and future deployment of nuclear warheads, missiles, and other delivery systems.

––––––––

In 1985, when Mikhail Gorbachev declared a unilateral moratorium on all nuclear tests on the fortieth anniversary of the Hiroshima bombing and invited the United States to join in, Reagan insisted that this was just propaganda. He maintained that even if the United States agreed to stop testing, there was no way to accurately monitor underground Soviet tests—and therefore there could be no verification—since Moscow had never allowed American scientists to establish seismic stations within the Soviet Union.

However, while collecting material for the *Databook*, Tom realized that we could challenge Gorbachev and Reagan to permit American and Soviet scientists to establish and jointly operate seismic stations within the Soviet Union and the United States. These stations would demonstrate that in-country verification was not an obstacle to a comprehensive test ban and that scientists from both countries could work together toward the common goal of a ban. Such a project would also show whether Gorbachev was sincere, or whether Reagan was right in assuming that the Soviet moratorium was just propaganda. American scientists didn't have to work for the government to operate the seismic stations, and the stations didn't have to be located on the government-controlled test sites.

In early 1986, John Fialka, a reporter for the *Wall Street Journal*, arranged for Tom to present his proposal to Vitaly Churkin, a defense expert who was stationed at the Soviet Embassy in Washington and is now the Russian ambassador to the UN. The meeting proved unproductive. A few months later, Tom presented his proposal at a meeting organized by the Federation of American Scientists (FAS). The initial response of the Soviet delegation, led by Soviet defense expert Andrei Kokoshin, was encouraging. Shortly thereafter, Frank von Hippel, a professor of nuclear physics at Princeton's Woodrow Wilson School and an FAS council member, met with his fellow physicist Evgeny P. Velikhov, a vice president of the Soviet Academy of Sciences. Velikhov agreed to host a workshop on nuclear test verification in Moscow.

I remember warning Tom, "This could well be through the KGB, so be careful. Call up the FBI and let them know you were contacted, and keep a record of all meetings you have with the Soviets."

Tom and Frank von Hippel organized a group of Americans for the trip to Moscow in May 1986, just a month after the disaster at Chernobyl. The group included Frank; Tom; Bill DeWind; Charles Archambeau, an expert theoretical seismologist at the University of Colorado; and Christopher Paine, a legislative aide to Congressman Edward Markey. At the time, Chris worked with the House Subcommittee on Energy, Conservation, and Power, where he drafted the amendment that initiated the ultimately successful series of legislative efforts to end U.S. nuclear test explosions. Chris went on to become assistant for nuclear weapons issues to Senator Edward M. Kennedy, and in 1991 he joined the staff of NRDC. He is now the director of NRDC's nuclear program, having taken over from Tom.

To gauge the administration's receptivity to our initiative, Bill DeWind, through his friendship with John Whitehead, Reagan's deputy secretary of state, arranged for Bill and Tom to meet with Whitehead and Paul Nitze, the president's special advisor and secretary of state on arms control and one of the principal architects of U.S. policy toward the Soviet Union during the Cold War. The result was that while the State Department did not support our plan, it did not *disapprove* of it. We took this as a green light to go to Moscow.

At the workshop at the Soviet Academy of Sciences, Tom proposed installing seismic stations around the Soviet nuclear proving grounds near Semipalatinsk, in the Central Asian republic of Kazakhstan, and around the Nevada Test Site in the United States. All the stations would be operated by a joint team of American and Soviet scientists. Although two other proposals were also presented, Velikhov favored the NRDC plan, which did not require U.S. government approval. He sent the American delegation to St. Petersburg for three days while he sought Soviet government permission for the NRDC plan. We later learned that no permission was granted, and although Velikhov knew he was taking a chance, he decided to go ahead anyway. When we got back to Moscow, he told the American delegation that he agreed to Cochran's proposal. "Whom am I agreeing with?" he asked. "The Natural Resources Defense Council," Cochran answered, "and this is our chairman, Mr. Bill DeWind."

Velikhov asked the American delegation and his Soviet colleagues to stay and draft an agreement, which both sides could sign that evening. Bill sat in Velikhov's office and drafted the text in longhand on a legal pad. It was typed up and translated into Russian. That evening, May 28, 1986, DeWind and Velikhov signed the agreement, without even wanting to send it back to correct the typos. Everyone shook hands, and that was it. Bill and Tom immediately went to the Moscow bureau of the *New York Times*. Philip Taubman, the bureau chief, picked up the story under the headline "New Yorkers Sign Soviet Test Pact."

Hoping to pressure Gorbachev to extend the Soviet test moratorium beyond the summer of 1986, Velikhov insisted that NRDC return to the Soviet Union with our team and equipment in one month. Starting practically from scratch, we went into high gear. Tom enlisted Charles Archambeau to be our scientific advisor for seismic monitoring. Archambeau in turn recruited Jon Berger of the Scripps Institution of Oceanography to field the American team of seismologists and supply top-of-the-line scientific instruments. Berger recruited seismologists from his own program at Scripps, the University of Nevada, and the state of California. Bill DeWind and I had thirty days to come up with the first million dollars to fund the initiative. We managed to raise it with the help of Sally Lilienthal, who had founded the Ploughshares Fund to prevent the spread and use of nuclear, biological, and chemical weapons. The Rockefeller and Ford foundations also contributed, and we received a generous gift from Joan Kroc, the wife of the founder of McDonald's.

Jacob Scherr, acting as our quarterback, managed the day-to-day logistics for the NRDC project. John Whitehead's behind-the-scenes support helped Jacob obtain—in record time—the necessary licenses from the U.S. Department of Commerce to take monitoring equipment to the Soviet Union. Jacob was already familiar with nuclear issues, having led our litigation over nuclear fuel exports to India. He had also taken the lead in our work to highlight the dangers of "nuclear winter"—the theory that the smoke and dust from even a limited nuclear exchange could trigger weeks or months of darkness and cold that might extinguish much life on earth.

To meet Velikhov's tight schedule, Tom and the team of seismologists arrived in Moscow on July 5 with twenty tons of seismic equipment. There was one hitch. Velikhov still did not have permission for the Americans to go to Semipalatinsk. The Soviet military and several members of the politburo were opposed. After an inconclusive meeting with the politburo, Velikhov appealed directly to Gorbachev. The details of that conversation have been revealed in David Hoffman's book *The Dead Hand: The Untold Story of the Cold War Arms Race and Its Dangerous Legacy*:

> Gorbachev replied, in his maddeningly vague way: "Follow the line of the discussion at the meeting."
> "As I understood it?" Velikhov asked.
> "Yes," said Gorbachev.
> Velikhov took this to mean "yes." He gave the green light to Cochran's team.

On July 9, the American and Soviet seismologists began setting up their first joint seismic station at Karkaralinsk, in Kazakhstan, about a hundred miles west of the Semipalatinsk Test Site. Cochran had accomplished what every administration since Eisenhower had attempted without success—seismic monitoring on Soviet soil. Seismic data from Karkaralinsk were presented to an international test ban conference in Moscow a few days later, and on July 14 Cochran, von Hippel, Velikhov, and others met with Gorbachev in his office at the Central Committee headquarters. On August 18, Gorbachev extended the test moratorium.

The Soviet Army dug underground vaults at the three sites around Semipalatinsk, lined them with concrete, and put a pad in the middle for the measuring instruments. Archambeau and Berger had insisted on fielding top-of-the-line scientific instruments in the vaults. This nearly broke the bank at NRDC, but the generosity of numerous foundations and our members kept us afloat.

After setting up the stations, the American and Soviet teams wanted to demonstrate the sensitivity of Berger's seismic equipment for monitoring underground nuclear tests. The Soviet side prepared three underground chemical explosions—two ten-ton explosions and one of twenty tons, adjacent to the test site at Semipalatinsk. Tom and Jacob recruited three members of Congress—Thomas J. Downey of New York, Jim Moody of Wisconsin, and Bob Carr of Michigan, all Democrats—to go to Kazakhstan in September 1987 to observe the monitoring experiments. The group included Tom, Charles Archambeau, Chris Paine, several other congressional staff members, and reporters from a number of news organizations.

Cochran went back to Moscow after observing the tests and almost immediately got a call from Velikhov to assemble the delegation to go to Siberia to inspect the giant, top-secret Krasnoyarsk radar, which was under construction. The Reagan administration maintained that its location was in violation of the 1972 Anti-Ballistic Missile Treaty. This was the first of a series of glasnost-inspired visits to secret military installations that Velikhov arranged for NRDC delegations.

In 1987 the American seismologists decided they wanted to establish additional seismic stations in the Soviet Union to collect data from other regions of the country. One of the new locations selected was the Soviet Academy of Sciences seismographic station in Garm, Tajikistan, nine hundred miles from Semipalatinsk. If a 125-kiloton blast at Semipalatinsk (smaller than the yield of the warhead on the Minuteman, the mainstay of the United States' nuclear arsenal) showed up on the monitoring equipment in Garm, it would prove that there was no technological impediment to a verifiable nuclear test ban.

Patricia and I were part of an NRDC team that visited the Garm site in September 1988. The team included Jacob and Tom and board member Henry Breck, who had once served with the CIA. The final member of our group was Frances Beinecke. Frances was living in Washington at the time with her husband, Paul Elston, who was working at the EPA. She had been away from NRDC for several years to be with her three young daughters, but had come back to stay. Dr. Mikhail Gokhberg, the deputy director of the Soviet Institute for Physics of the Earth, and Dr. Ilona Lapushonok of the Soviet Academy of Sciences accompanied us to Garm.

We were on an important mission to show the feasibility of a nuclear test ban, but at the same time we were in one of the most exotic and interesting places we had ever visited. We were north of the Hindu Kush and east of the River Oxus in the Pamir Mountains, which are the westernmost range of the Himalayas. It was the land of Kubla Khan and Tamerlane. The people and communities in these mountains had changed little since "Alexandrovich" (the Russian name for Alexander the Great) came over the mountains two thousand years ago.

In the capital, Dushanbe, we boarded a plane that knocked and shook as we lifted off from the runway and followed the Surkob River up a narrow valley. There were no air controllers, no second engines, no confident smiling attendants—just the NRDC nuclear verification team and a group of Tajik men dressed in beaded hats, high boots, and long black coats tied loosely at the waist.

The Soviet research center in Garm was surrounded by mud walls and an iron gate. Inside, the facility had the appearance of a model socialist commune, organized around the common pursuit of scientific research. There were fruit trees, vegetable gardens, farmyard animals, and an abundance of flowering shrubs. The children were rosy cheeked; the girls wore wide hair bows, and the boys short pants. A Russian cook prepared delicious meals in the cafeteria, with large roasts and fresh vegetables and mounds of caviar for breakfast. It was a very different atmosphere than we had experienced in our few days in stark Moscow and could have been a propaganda movie for the good life in the Soviet Union.

In the evenings, we watched Mikhail Gorbachev on the communal television. He was talking about perestroika as he traveled through Siberia, listening to angry workers as they complained vociferously about the lack of everything from hand soap to fresh fruit. In spite of the comfortable environment at Garm, the Russians watching this on television also muttered about the "bad system" and how things simply "do not work!"

The other surprising thing was that this little community was in very hostile country. When we went out with the Russians, even schoolchildren gave us the finger, and merchants scowled at us. As soon as they heard us speak English, however, everything was different. Mikhail and Ilona said that the people of the Central Asian Republics were "wild peoples" who had some poetry, colorful art, and music, but did not contribute to the progress of the Soviet people. It was clear to us they did not *want* to contribute to the Soviet Union. The Soviet Socialist Republics were that in name only.

On September 14, 1988, just before eleven a.m., we gathered in front of the seismometers with the Soviet scientists to await the explosion. We had no way of knowing if the explosion would take place on time since there were no phone lines between Semipalatinsk and Garm. The only evidence we would see would be on the computer screens and seismographs, which at 11:02 were stable and quiet.

"How can you tell the difference between an earthquake and a nuclear blast?" Frances asked. This was a critical point.

"A nuclear blast applies uniform pressure to the walls of the cavity it creates, making what we call compressional waves," Dr. Gokhberg explained, "while an earthquake generates shear waves from all parts of the fault that rupture. The seismic signals from these earth movements are different."

At 11:03 we saw the initial tremors on the computer. At the same time, the thirty-year-old Russian seismograph recorded the blast with a series of short horizontal tracings. There was great excitement in the room as the blast was monitored. Standing beneath an incongruous-seeming poster of Kurt Vonnegut, we toasted with vodka and congratulated one another.

As part of the agreement with Velikhov, we then hosted a group of Soviet scientists in Nevada, where we set up a ten-ton chemical explosion similar to those monitored in Kazkahstan the previous year. The experiment took place at an underground test site in the desert two hours from Reno. Compared to the logistics of setting up the tests in the Soviet Union, Nevada was relatively simple. This experiment was also successful, and the scientists were able to compare two different methods of monitoring the size of nuclear tests. Again, the Nevada tests showed that the yield of a weapons test could be accurately calculated using distant instruments.

We knew that we had accomplished something very important and that the two countries, if they chose to, could move forward on verification. After the test was over, we drove the two hours to Reno to take our Soviet friends for a night in a casino. They had brought along a film crew, with an old eight-millimeter camera, and I gave them a demonstration of how the slot machines worked. As it happened, I hit the jackpot. I couldn't help but see the irony of Russians watching a film of money pouring out of machines in the United States.

We made another trip to the Soviet Union in July 1989, and looking back at this one, it's clear to me that we were probably much more deeply involved than I realized at the time in the political endgame of the Cold War. Congressman Bob Carr came with us again, accompanied by two other Democratic congressmen, John Spratt of South Carolina and Jim Olin of Virginia.

This time we were invited first to Yalta, the home port of the Soviet Black Sea Fleet, where we were allowed to see if handheld radiation detectors could detect the presence of nuclear weapons on ships. Velikhov had arranged for us to have access for a day to the *Slava*, a Soviet cruiser and flagship of the Black Sea Fleet, with one nuclear-armed missile in its launch tube. On the third day, we flew to the

CELEBRATING IN RENO AFTER WITNESSING A DEMONSTRATION OF THE
SENSITIVITY OF THE SEISMIC STATIONS SET UP AROUND THE NEVADA
TEST SITES, RENO, NEVADA, APRIL 1988
Left to right: Dr. Nikolai F. Yukhnin, Geophysicist, Institute of Physics of the Earth;
Academician Evgeny P. Velikhov, Vice President, Soviet Academy of Sciences;
Dr. Mikhail Gokhberg, Geophysicist, Institute of Physics of the Earth

Chelyabinsk-65/Mayak Chemical Combine in the Ural Mountains. This was a closed city—a city of "no name" that Stalin had established to build the Soviet Union's first nuclear power plant. It was the equivalent of our Hanford Reservation, and to the best of our knowledge, we were the first westerners to go there. Soviet physicists gave us a guided tour down into two reactors that they had just shut down. Although we wore protective clothing, I'm sure I received more exposure to radiation that day than in the rest of my days put together.

In the evening we were taken to the chief physicist's dacha by a lake, where we feasted on suckling pig and toasted each other with vodka. Before dinner, the eighty-six-year-old physicist invited us to join him as he stripped off his clothes and jumped into the icy water. Several of us followed him, but not the congressmen, surely because we were accompanied by American and Soviet reporters with cameras.

Back in Moscow, Tom got a call from Velikhov, who told us that the defense minister's jet was ready to take us on another trip to Kazakhstan, this time to look at the controversial Sary Shagan missile test center near Lake Balkhash. The United States claimed that Sary Shagan housed an air-defense and antiballistic missile system, as well as a facility that researched capabilities for attacking satellites. We saw a very different picture: just a large concrete building with a beat-up, nonworking computer from the 1950s that took up an entire room. The place had been abandoned. There were no lightbulbs. Rain came in through the roof. We saw little potential here for shooting down our missiles.

In a congressional hearing after our return, the CIA insisted that we had not been taken to Sary Shagan, but to some other site. However, Congressman Spratt, angry at being called a liar, managed to get hold of American satellite photographs of our trip, which Tom now produced. They clearly showed us standing in front of Sary Shagan. As our hosts had often told us, the Soviet Union in the late 1980s was a country where the system "did not work." The military threat it posed had been grossly exaggerated, and our three visits had lifted the curtain on that reality.

Henry Breck, with his CIA background, had been convinced back in Garm that Mikhail Gokhberg and Ilona Lapushonok must be with the KGB. Tom's answer was "So what?" They had their agenda; we had ours. But Henry, in true James Bond fashion, marked his briefcase to see if anyone went through it. Someone did. After the fall of the Soviet Union, Misha and Ellie (as we now knew them) told us that, yes, of course they had worked for the KGB—anyone high up in the Soviet government did.

Henry maintains that Gorbachev wanted to use NRDC as a back channel to get his message out: that the "Evil Empire" did not have the technology or the ability to continue the Cold War. "The fact that we were closely watched by the KGB did not affect the value of the project," Henry says. "We proved you couldn't cheat on underground nuclear testing, and that was very important." Tom never let the KGB slow him down. I still recall on one of our trips together the sight of Tom striding into the Kremlin past guards yelling "Stop! Stop!"

NRDC had organized the largest privately funded scientific exchange with the Soviet Union, and our work was a vital part of the larger effort to implement a lasting test ban. The Soviet Union no longer exists, and the United States has not conducted a nuclear test since 1992.

As far as I'm concerned, the person who deserves most of the credit is Tom. It was because of him that the Soviets were persuaded to let us in and show us as much as they did. If it were up to me, Evgeny Velikhov and Tom Cochran would have been awarded the Nobel Peace Prize.

The Poisoned Chalice

Even as we fought threats to humanity's survival from the Cold War and the nuclear arms race, we were fighting the less visible legacy of another conflict. Before World War II, very few synthetic chemicals existed—laboratory-made compounds not found in nature. But the war effort brought a surge of creativity from the nation's chemists. A new generation of plastics, solvents, insulators, and other compounds produced better weapons. Synthetic insecticides, herbicides, and fungicides brought increased crop yields to feed the troops and their families on the home front. With the future of the world in the balance, the focus was understandably more on success than on safety.

When the conflict ended, the new chemical industry was one of the driving forces in the unprecedented economic boom that followed. Chemicals seemed to make our life easier, safer, and more fun, giving us abundant cheap food, TVs and household appliances, greener lawns, new drugs to keep us healthy. In the process, however, they created an invisible, ticking time bomb that would threaten our health, our intelligence, even our ability to reproduce. These newly invented chemicals entered our bodies through every conceivable pathway. They were sprayed on our food, so we ate them; they leached from landfills into our water supply, so we drank them; they floated on the air, so we breathed them. They crept in through the barrier of our skin via cosmetics and household products. Pregnant women passed them on to their unborn fetuses, and nursing mothers fed them to their babies in breast milk. In effect, all of us were the subjects of a gigantic, unplanned, and almost totally unregulated science experiment.

There were occasional public alarms over a particular chemical, such as the 1959 "Thanksgiving cranberry scare" involving the carcinogenic pesticide, aminotriazole. But in general, our faith in better living through chemistry (an ironic catchphrase that began life with an advertising slogan of the DuPont chemical company) went largely unquestioned for the better part of two decades.

That began to change in 1962 with the publication of Rachel Carson's book *Silent Spring*. Carson, a marine biologist who had worked for the U.S. Fish and Wildlife Service, showed how DDT, which had been sprayed on millions of acres of farmland and forest, thinned eggshells and killed birds, including the iconic bald eagle. One of Carson's most important messages was the failure of federal and state authorities to exercise any meaningful oversight of the chemical industry. In response, the industry attacked her furiously. They said she was mentally unstable; they called her an amateur, a Communist, a lesbian.

After DDT, the next toxic chemicals to arouse widespread public concern were polychlorinated biphenyls (PCBs), highly effective coolants, insulators, and lubricators that were used in a variety of industrial applications: electrical capacitors and transformers; hydraulic fluids and plasticizers; inks, waxes and adhesives. PCBs were a proven human carcinogen, and like DDT they had devastating effects on wildlife. In 1971 the Monsanto Company, the main manufacturer of these chemicals, voluntarily suspended their production, and in 1979 the EPA banned them totally. But by that time 150 million pounds of PCBs had been dispersed in the air and water, and a further 290 million pounds had been dumped in landfills. The biggest single user, General Electric, had dumped enormous quantities of PCBs into the Hudson River in New York and the Housatonic River in Connecticut, sites that are still the object of multimillion dollar cleanup operations.

This focus on disasters that had already happened could only take us so far. How were the public—and wildlife—to be protected in a more systematic way from future harm?

Over and above the provisions of the Clean Air Act and Clean Water Act, the manufacture, use, and disposal of synthetic chemicals and other toxics are covered by two laws. The Toxic Substances Control Act (TSCA) of 1976 was born out of increased concern in Congress about the production and marketing of chemicals whose potential toxicity had not been assessed. It required manufacturers to notify the EPA of new chemical substances, and the EPA would then maintain an inventory of all chemicals, which currently number about a hundred thousand, with thousands more added every year. TSCA requires testing where there is evidence that a particular chemical poses a risk. Any "significant new use" of an existing chemical must be reported, as must imports and exports.

Pesticides are not covered by the act. These fall under a different law, the Federal Insecticide, Fungicide, and Rodenticide Act (FIFRA). It's an old statute, passed in 1947 and sometimes referred to as the orphan stepchild of environmental legislation. Enforcement was originally the responsibility of the U.S. Department of Agriculture (USDA), but the pesticides act was revised in 1972 and oversight passed to the new EPA. The law required that pesticides must be registered with that agency, once their effectiveness and potential hazards have been assessed, and then they must be labeled for proper use. Some may be approved for general use; others for use only by a "certified applicator" licensed by the EPA or by a state or other appropriate authority. As with the toxic substances act, any significant new use must be reported, so a chemical already being applied to cotton, for example, can't be sprayed on tomatoes without additional notification and approval.

The problem is that virtually all the research into the effectiveness and potential risk of these compounds is done by the manufacturers themselves, with little effort made by the EPA to check its accuracy. And very little could be done about all the grandfathered pesticides whose use had been approved before 1972. Oversight by the USDA, oversight by the EPA: it made little difference. The basic rule remained the same—give the companies what they want. This continued even after a scandal in the late 1970s, when a private lab called Industrial Bio-Test was found to have engaged in wholesale falsification of pesticide safety test results.

The essential goal of both TSCA and FIFRA was to protect the public from "unreasonable risks." But who was to define what was "reasonable"? And on what basis? The EPA was given the power to ban the manufacture and import of chemicals that posed such a risk, but it was extraordinarily difficult for the agency to amass the data that would allow it to make a determination. Manufacturers were rarely required to test. If the government attempted to do so, how much testing needed to be done in order to prove a specific risk? How could regulations be designed that would effectively protect public health? Companies asked how proprietary information would remain confidential once it was in the hands of the government. Then there was the sheer volume of new chemicals coming out of industry labs each year, which made it impossible for the EPA, with its limited resources, to test more than a handful.

As a result, the EPA's standard practice was to wait until a particular chemical was shown to cause a problem, rather than to prevent toxic chemicals from getting into the environment in the first place. It was the opposite of the precautionary principle; chemicals were "innocent until proven guilty."

During the 1970s, we had weighed in on the toxics and pesticides acts in much the same way as we did with the other key environmental laws, seeking to ensure that they were properly enforced by taking part in EPA working groups and submitting extensive comments on the agency's evolving regulations and procedures.

We had also done a modest amount of work during our first decade on specific products. This foreshadowed an approach that we would later use much more widely: targeting particular toxic substances in everyday use and in the process creating market incentives for the development of safe alternatives. We worked hard for a ban on asbestos, for example, which is known to cause lung and other cancers. This led eventually to a 1989 EPA decision to phase out 90 percent of all asbestos uses, and a petition from NRDC was instrumental in ending the largest single unregulated use—in the manufacture of brake linings and other friction products.

At about the same time, NRDC scientists conducted a study of the toxicity of art materials used by children, whose developing bodies are particularly vulnerable to harm. Using paints and crayons in the classroom exposed children to chemicals in a variety of ways, through frequent skin contact, inhalation, and ingestion each time they put a finger in their mouths. Teachers and school boards had no way of knowing which materials were toxic. We identified possible hazards, proposed nontoxic alternatives, and suggested precautions.

A brilliant young lawyer, Jackie Warren, joined us at the end of 1980 and took charge of our work on toxics and public health. Like Jacob Scherr, the head of our international program, Jackie was a graduate of Georgetown University Law School. Before coming to NRDC, she had been the first female lawyer at the Environmental Defense Fund. Her husband had been chief of staff for Senator Jacob Javits, Republican from New York, and had been very involved in writing New York's state law on toxics.

Jackie, whose team included two scientists, Karim Ahmed and Ricky Perera, had an unusually sophisticated grasp of the complexity of the problem posed by chemicals. In developing a plan to protect public health, based on the principle of prevention, we would need a multifaceted approach that combined law, science, and—as events would show—a more effective way of communicating with the public.

"My goal was to cover everything—air, water, land," Jackie says. "To go through every single act, permit, and regulation and make a list of the toxics. Then we would present our findings to the EPA so it would list these chemicals and establish a set of rules for testing them."

One big problem was that we were no longer dealing with the same EPA we had grown used to over the past decade. As the "shadow EPA," NRDC had generally taken a collegial approach by setting out to work together, although the agency knew we would not hesitate to take it to court if we had to. But within a few months of Jackie Warren's arrival at NRDC, President Reagan named Anne Gorsuch as the head of the agency. At the staff level, the spirit of cooperation continued, but the attitude at the top changed, and many of the senior people with whom we'd worked were replaced.

Part of our difficulty was that the agency had grown so big that its leaders felt they no longer needed us. The relationship also became openly adversarial. When Reagan appointed Vice President George H. W. Bush to head a task force on "regulatory relief," one of its main targets was pesticides. The White House directed the EPA to streamline "burdensome, unnecessary" regulation and to speed up the review and approval of new pesticides being introduced into the marketplace. The agency's assistant administrator under Gorsuch suggested that the substances should no longer be described as "pesticides" but as "crop protection chemicals."

Under Gorsuch, the EPA became dysfunctional, mired in procedural squabbles. Looking back, Jackie Warren compares it to the intelligence community before 9/11: "Just as the CIA made a list of potential terrorists but customs officials didn't have that list, the EPA department studying toxics in the air didn't talk to the department studying toxics in the water. There was no coordination."

Jackie's team used all the tools at their disposal: they would go to Congress to introduce changes to the law on hazardous waste, demand that a governmental agency release specific information, use the media to get public sentiment to support a ban on a particular substance, or as a last resort turn to litigation. Knowing that we would eventually call the agency in front of a judge, EPA officials would drag their feet for months on an issue.

In 1982 we launched a special project on pesticides. Although the general public didn't yet see pesticides as an urgent environmental issue, alarm was growing in the public health community.

In a sense, pesticides were our single most pervasive environmental problem, since all of us were exposed to them on a daily basis. In fact, most of us were walking around with pesticides in our bodies that had been banned years earlier, including DDT, chlordane, heptachlor, aldrin, and dieldrin. By the 1980s, more than two and a half billion pounds of pesticides were being used in the United States each year, not only on our crops but also on our lawns, parks, forests, lakes, and playing fields. And we were using more and more of the stuff as insects, weeds, and fungi developed resistance. Ironically, the more pesticides we sprayed on the fields, the more bugs there were.

Over the course of the decade, a growing body of scientific evidence linked pesticides with a variety of cancers, birth defects, genetic mutations, neurological damage, and reproductive disorders. The neurotoxicity of insecticides was hardly surprising, since organophosphates, which include such common pest-control chemicals as malathion and parathion, were designed to disrupt the functioning of an insect's central nervous system and worked on the same principle as nerve gases developed during World War II. As for cancer, a 1987 report by the National Academy of Sciences concluded that pesticides might be responsible for one million cases over our lifetimes. This figure did not take into account the pesticides in drinking water. Farmers and farmworkers exposed to pesticides had a greatly increased incidence of certain cancers; children who grew up in homes that used household and garden pesticides had a seven times greater risk of getting leukemia.

For many of us at NRDC, cancer had struck close to home. Frances Beinecke fought it—and won. So did our son, John Hamilton. My wonderful assistant, Mary Donnellon, who ran my life with an iron fist and a great sense of humor, battled it—and lost. Inevitably, we wondered about the cause. Why were young people like this stricken? Was it something in the water?

Proving the direct cause-and-effect link between a particular chemical and a particular disease was difficult, especially because it might take years of exposure to make someone sick. For obvious reasons, clinical tests could not be conducted on humans, so scientists had to build their case slowly on the basis of animal studies, not all of which could easily be extrapolated to humans, and a growing body of epidemiological evidence. In trying to establish liability, lawyers and judges demanded cut-and-dried answers, but scientists had to be cautious about drawing categorical conclusions. The chemical industry, which had always taken full advantage of this problem of the burden of proof, could easily cite mountains of data of its own to show the public benefit of its products. People needed to look no farther than the overflowing shelves at their local supermarket, for which synthetic agricultural chemicals were largely responsible.

NRDC's San Francisco office, which now had about two dozen staff, took the lead in our work on pesticides. California had become a hotbed of public interest law in the 1970s, with many former members of Robert F. Kennedy's Justice Department heading out to the West Coast after Nixon's election. Many of these lawyers were motivated by their concern for the plight of migrant farmworkers, whose unsafe working conditions included massive exposure to pesticides.

Al Meyerhoff, who came to NRDC in January 1982, had graduated from Cornell Law School ten years earlier and had promptly taken a sixty-dollar-a-week job with California Rural Legal Assistance, representing migrant workers and other poor people in rural areas against abuses by large agribusiness. Al was joined a year later at NRDC by Lawrie Mott, who had just received her master's in molecular biology from Yale, where her particular field of study included mechanisms of DNA repair after environmental damage. Al and Lawrie were known to all of us as "the Dynamic Duo."

I always thought Lawrie was one of the nicest people who ever worked at NRDC. She was smart and practical, with a warm and caring personality; everyone liked her. With Marc Reisner, the former editor of our newsletter, it was more than a matter of liking. Marc had moved out West to write his book on western water, *Cadillac Desert*, and the two met, fell in love, and were soon married.

Al, who died tragically young in 2008, was a larger-than-life character. We called him "the big man"—big frame, big hair, big voice, and, above all, big ideas. "He always had about twenty ideas, nineteen of which didn't work, but one of which would be brilliant," Lawrie remembers. Al was full of life; his presence filled up a room. He was going to correct the ills of the world, and with his enormous charisma you instinctively wanted to help him do so.

Al added a crucial new dimension to NRDC's work. His interest in the environment was rooted in his commitment to social reform, and he wanted to introduce the voice of ordinary people into mainstream environmentalism. More than anyone, he made us see that it was essential for us to connect to a grassroots constituency. Al was also a born campaigner, and while he spent seventeen years working for us on national issues, his biggest single victory may have been Proposition 65, the 1986 California law that required businesses to notify the public of any exposure to substances that caused cancer and birth defects and prohibited the discharge of those chemicals in or near any source of drinking water. Al helped bring the force of Hollywood behind Prop 65, enlisting celebrities like Jane Fonda (whose then husband, the former antiwar activist Tom Hayden, was a state assemblyman), Whoopi Goldberg, Michael J. Fox, Morgan Fairchild, and Chevy Chase as he built public support for the campaign.

Over time, Al and Lawrie would develop a sweeping agenda: strengthening legal standards, raising risk awareness among the public, requiring health and safety testing and labeling for all pesticides on the market, seeking special protections for children, and encouraging safe alternatives to agricultural chemicals. But they started with a more modest goal: gaining public access to the facts, which was supposedly guaranteed by 1978 amendments to the pesticides act. Despite those legislative changes, Americans still had no idea which pesticides were in their food or what levels of pesticide residue were safe.

In 1982 Al decided it was time to sue the EPA, which we did together with the AFL-CIO. The court ruled in our favor, and Lawrie headed to Washington to ask the EPA for the data we were after. But she ran into a stone wall. The reality was that the agency didn't *have* any data to show the public that pesticides were safe. It became clear to us that regulatory decisions were being made on the basis of closed-door meetings between the EPA and pesticide manufacturers, with none of the relevant data being made public.

It was time for another lawsuit, and in the usual NRDC fashion, Al looked around creatively for the right statute to use. He found it not in any environmental law, but in the 1972 Federal Advisory Committee Act, which stipulates that information from the hundreds of committees that advise government agencies must be "objective and accessible to the public."

Al subpoenaed a host of chemical company documents and files that showed the extent of the ties between the industry and Anne Gorsuch's EPA. "These were hot documents," Al remembered later. "We found enough smoking guns to start a gun store." Chemical industry lobbyists and lawyers, he said, had become "the science advisory committee for the EPA."

Coming in the midst of the unfolding EPA scandal, which centered on the concealment of documents related to the chemical industry and the Superfund program and eventually led to Gorsuch's downfall, our litigation had an enormous impact. Congressman Mike Synar, Democrat from Oklahoma, worked closely with us on the case, and we were called to testify at hearings before the House Subcommittee on Oversight and Investigations. The media were all over the story. With the White House under enormous pressure, we entered into a settlement in 1983, a few months after Gorsuch's resignation. The settlement was designed to put an end to closed-door decision making and would give the public access for the first time to EPA health and safety data on pesticides.

Changing the law itself, which Lawrie and Al proposed to do next, was a much tougher challenge. To do so, we helped build a coalition of more than forty environmental and consumer organizations, the Farm Bureau, and the National Agricultural Chemicals Association. It turned out that there were some enlightened people among the chemical manufacturers, and I've found that to be true of most industries if you are prepared to be patient and open-minded.

NRDC has always believed strongly in the value of coalitions, and an essential part of the exercise, as Robert Redford had shown in the fight over oil drilling in the Bering Sea, is to define the common interest that exists among unconventional or nontraditional allies. Even so, this one broke new ground. Never before had citizen groups hashed out an agreement with a regulated industry on a major piece of environmental legislation. After months of intense, good faith negotiations, we reached an agreement in early 1986. It proposed a review of health and safety studies for pesticides that were currently on the market; additional testing by companies where studies were found to be inadequate or outdated, followed by reregistration of the chemical in question; suspending the registration of chemicals where past industry data was shown to have been falsified; and release of health and safety information to the public *before* a product was registered. Also part of the agreement was a "right to know" provision ensuring that local communities and authorities would be notified of the location of agricultural chemical plants and told what was being produced there.

Next, we had to get the statutory language through Congress. Reform bills were defeated twice, even after we made compromises on pesticides in groundwater to satisfy the farm lobby, but in Al's words, "it kept coming back, like Lazarus from the dead." Al became a one-man frequent flyer program, shuttling back and forth between San Francisco and Washington on the now-defunct TWA. (During his seventeen years at NRDC, he testified before Congress more than fifty times.) As the bill came up for a vote, every single member was important. "We were trying to get one congressman to help us," Lawrie remembers, "but couldn't figure out how to convince him of the danger of these pesticides. Someone said that he had gone to Catholic schools and would believe a nun. So we found a nun who had formed an organization for labor rights, and she convinced him that pesticides had serious long-term effects on farmworkers."

Eventually, in 1988, the reform bill passed. Though pesticides continue to be a serious environmental and public health problem, we had the first meaningful controls over their manufacture and distribution.

Our work on toxics and public health shed light on some profound changes that had taken place in the environmental movement during the 1980s. We had grown and matured, and the larger and more established organizations based in Washington and New York were looking for ways to work together more effectively. With the help of Bob Allen and the Henry P. Kendall Foundation, NRDC joined with the Environmental Defense Fund, the Environmental Policy Institute, Friends of the Earth, the Izaak Walton League of America, the National Audubon Society, the National Parks and Conservation Association, the National Wildlife Federation, the Sierra Club, and the Wilderness Society to form the Group of Ten, and in 1985 we hammered out a consensus document that we called "An Environmental Agenda for the Future."

We knew that beneath the surface the movement was confronting some serious problems. Several members of the Group of Ten were facing financial difficulties after the costly all-out fight against James

Watt, Anne Gorsuch, and the rest of the Reagan agenda. Some groups were dealing with turnover in their leadership. For NRDC, the law had always been at the core of our identity. However, the daily grind of snapping at the heels of the federal bureaucracy had taken its toll, and our litigators were concerned that landmark cases that could significantly alter public policy on the environment were getting harder to find. But as Al Meyerhoff reminded us forcefully, drawing on his experience with migrant farmworkers, perhaps our most important challenge was to connect the work we had been doing in the courtroom and the halls of Congress to the real people and communities who were on the receiving end of environmental abuse.

The dynamic of the environmental movement had begun to change as a result of the events in a small community on the eastern edge of Niagara Falls, where an old abandoned canal—Love Canal—had been used in the 1940s and 1950s by the Hooker Chemical Company as a toxic waste dump. Hooker had closed the dump in 1953 and covered it with earth, and a school and a modest residential development had been built on the site. In 1978 a heavy rainstorm produced scenes from a horror movie: rotting barrels of carcinogenic chemicals protruding from the soil, dying trees, foul-smelling pools of liquid oozing from basements and backyards. Doctors began to report a wave of miscarriages and birth defects. Love Canal was one of those events that galvanized public awareness of the environment, like the Cuyahoga River fire and the Santa Barbara oil spill a decade earlier. It dramatized the fact that the worst impact of toxic chemicals fell on poor and underrepresented communities, and it also raised a question that would occupy a great deal of NRDC's time in succeeding years: who would be held responsible for cleaning up the toxic legacy of the past?

Opponents of environmental regulation had always attacked us for being out of touch with the interests of "ordinary Americans," who only wanted jobs and progress. Yet Love Canal made it apparent that these were precisely the people who were most at risk. At the same time, the burgeoning grassroots movement that had grown up in the wake of

Love Canal, and included thousands of small, local organizations, saw our work as remote, elitist, and bureaucratic. The issues on which they concentrated were those that struck closest to home: the toxic dumps on their doorstep, the safety of the food they ate and the household products they used, the health of their children. Ironically, those were the same things we had worked to address through law and science. Yet we saw that there was a huge cultural gulf to be bridged. This challenged us to find better ways of communicating with the public, to build new relationships of trust with local communities, and to focus directly on the things that affected people in their daily lives.

By going rule by rule through the regulatory system, we were never going to climb the mountain. We also needed to publicize the specific threats that people faced in their everyday lives and get those threats off the market, one chemical or family of chemicals at a time. We started where the chemical industry boasted of one of its greatest success stories—the produce aisle of the local supermarket.

An Apple a Day

When we ate the carrots and celery that we bought in the supermarket, what specific pesticides were we being exposed to? Al Meyerhoff and Lawrie Mott had begun to ask that question as early as 1983, initially because they were looking to illustrate the laxness of pesticide regulation as part of our effort to reform FIFRA, the national pesticides law. As a first step, Lawrie went to the supermarket, filled a basket with vegetables, drove from San Francisco to a laboratory in Santa Clara, and returned later to pick up the test results. They were shocking. Every vegetable in her basket contained chemical residues, and half showed traces of DDT, which had been banned fifteen years earlier.

A year later, NRDC's New York office carried out a similar survey. The East Coast market basket contained a somewhat different assortment, produced under different environmental conditions, and we thought it might reflect the use of different agricultural chemicals. By doing a bicoastal study, we hoped to broaden the evidence we could present to the EPA, as well as increasing the public impact of our findings.

The East Coast study was directed by Robin Whyatt. Robin had a master's in environmental health sciences from Columbia and had worked for Scenic Hudson with the legendary folk singer Pete Seeger and the beautiful Hudson River sloop *Clearwater*, a floating environmental science study center. In 1982 the EPA offered her a consultancy to put together a toxics hotline. She remembers going outside on a moonlit night soon after starting work with the agency and having something she describes as "close to a vision." She had just given birth to her first child, and it struck her that all the risk assessments that had been done on the effects of pesticides had been based on the exposure to toxics of an average 160-pound male adult. But what about an infant or a 30-pound toddler? No one had thought of the problem that way, and Robin decided that this would be her mission.

Everyone who worked on our nascent public health program in the early 1980s shared this kind of entrepreneurial instinct—those were the kind of people we always looked to hire—and for many Robin's personal motivations as a new parent resonated strongly. Ricky Perera had four young children. Lawrie Mott and Marc Reisner were married and had a baby. Wendy Gordon, who worked with Robin on the East Coast study, had just given birth to her first child. (She had recently married Larry Rockefeller, another romance that started life in the NRDC offices when Wendy, having just gotten her master's in public health from Columbia, was working as an intern.) For all of them, the fact that children were more susceptible to pesticides was as plain as the nose on your face, but as scientists they knew they had to prove it.

To measure pesticide residues in children, we needed to collect data on what children ate. We didn't have the resources to do this ourselves, but the U.S. Department of Agriculture had done a survey on the diets of mothers and their young children in 1985, so we started with that. Although the USDA's focus had been on nutrition, not pesticides, it told us what children ate and how much. For instance, how many apples did a two-year-old eat daily? How much apple pie or apple juice did a preschooler consume? We compared that to the amount of apples, juice, and pie eaten by the mother. Children consumed much greater amounts of fruit than adults, particularly in the form of apple sauce and apple juice. When we calculated how much apple juice a child drank *per pound of body weight*, we found that it was thirty times as much as an adult. We also knew that if those apples contained pesticides, the risk of exposure in early childhood, when the body is developing quickly, was much greater than it was for adults.

This early work evolved into a full-fledged study of twenty-three different pesticides and other agricultural chemicals. The study showed the prevalence of both carcinogens and neurotoxins in fruit and vegetables and the failure of the EPA to regulate them. We knew that we were on to something important, but we had no way of foreseeing how big the consequences would be. Our final report, which we called "Intolerable Risk," was ready for publication in February 1989. At that point all hell broke loose.

Although the study looked at twenty-three different compounds found in children's food, eight of which were suspected or known carcinogens, we used our new "one chemical at a time" approach to draw attention to a single product that had been the subject of an ongoing controversy at the EPA for years. First registered for use in 1968 and produced by a single company, Uniroyal, the chemical was called daminozide, better known by its trade name, Alar.

Alar was covered by the provisions of the pesticides law, although it was not strictly a pesticide but a growth regulator and color enhancer. Alar, sprayed on apple trees, not on the apples themselves, caused the fruit cells to grow more densely and all the apples in an orchard to ripen at the same time. For growers, that was a great convenience: use of Alar reduced the waste of fruit that dropped early and greatly reduced labor costs since the entire crop could be harvested at the same time.

The most serious problem with Alar was its breakdown product, or metabolite, a chemical with the unwieldy name of unsymmetrical dimethyl hydrazine, or UDMH, one of the principal ingredients in rocket fuel. UDMH was released during heating, for instance when the fruit was turned into apple sauce or when apple juice was pasteurized. These were the forms in which children mainly consumed apples, and UDMH was what mainly accounted for the carcinogenic risk posed by Alar.

The problem had been known for years. Tests done on mice in the 1970s had shown that elevated levels of Alar produced rare cancers of the lung, brain, and blood vessels. The EPA conducted a formal review of these studies in the early 1980s, but Uniroyal scientists presented data of their own to try and discredit each of the studies in turn. In the end, the EPA decided not to ban Alar, despite an outcry from the American Pediatric Association, NRDC, and others, although it did order Uniroyal to carry out additional tests. By 1989 Alar was a bomb waiting to go off.

"Intolerable Risk" brought about a major shift in the institutional culture of NRDC. Until now, almost all our resources had gone into program activity—the legal work, the scientific research, and the administrative infrastructure necessary to keep the organization running. But this report and our "one chemical at a time" strategy in general were aimed squarely at the general public. Alar was about children and motherhood and apple pie, and the public impact of our findings was potentially enormous. We realized that we needed to beef up our skeletal communications department and learn how to do smarter public advocacy. To design our first major media campaign, we turned to Fenton Communications, a firm that had built a reputation for its work on public health, human rights, and other public interest campaigns.

The result was a trial by fire for NRDC, beginning with a special segment on CBS's 60 *Minutes*, with Ed Bradley reporting. It aired on February 26, the eve of the publication of "Intolerable Risk." Our team now included Janet Hathaway, an attorney in the Washington office, and she had the kind of natural media skills that made her the obvious choice to represent us on the program. Although our campaign was being managed by professionals, Robin Whyatt recalls that there was no such thing as "risk communication" training in those days, "where people who appear in the media get coached on how to look directly into the camera, how to frame their words and use sound bites."

Essentially Janet was winging it, as was the EPA representative on the show, Jack Moore, who was head of the toxic substances and pesticides division and the agency's acting administrator. Fortunately for us, she was very good.

Janet insisted that our report, despite its title, actually *underplayed* the risk of pesticides, since we had examined only eight that were carcinogens, and the EPA had acknowledged that sixty-six such pesticides were legally in use. The EPA's Moore told Ed Bradley that though the agency had the power to review potentially harmful chemicals like Alar in advance of their introduction, once they were on the market the EPA could do little to remove them. In saying this, Moore was simply being honest and accurate—indeed it was exactly the same thing Al Meyerhoff and Lawrie Mott had been saying throughout their long campaign to reform the pesticides act. But the message that the public heard was, "Yes, Alar is the most dangerous chemical, and we can't do anything about it."

Moore's comments on *60 Minutes* created a firestorm. The morning after the show aired, we unveiled our report at press conferences in a dozen cities. We put out a short booklet about Alar that sold twenty-five thousand copies in a matter of days. We were swamped by requests for interviews and TV appearances. Lawrie, Wendy, and Robin appeared on *The Phil Donahue Show* and *Good Morning America*. Pesticides made the cover of *Time* magazine and *Newsweek*. The *New York Times* and the *Washington Post* ran major stories.

A week after the *60 Minutes* report, when the first flurry of news coverage had run its course, we rolled out the second phase of our campaign. Wendy Gordon, who had just returned from maternity leave after the birth of her second child, announced the formation of a new group called Mothers and Others for a Livable Planet. Actress Meryl Streep, a person of enormous warmth and integrity and a great friend to NRDC over the years, agreed to join the board of Mothers and Others and filmed a series of public service announcements for TV in which she stood at the kitchen sink with her own children scrubbing fruit and vegetables with soap to remove the toxic residues. Together, the *60 Minutes* story and Meryl's appearances had an incredible impact. School lunchrooms removed apples from their menus, and mothers staged public protests in which they poured bottles of apple juice down the drain. In June 1989, still protesting that Alar was harmless and insisting that it would continue to export it, Uniroyal voluntarily withdrew the product from the U.S. market to quell the alarm among consumers.

The saga was far from over. In retrospect, I have to admit that we were rather naive, particularly in failing to anticipate the ferocity of the backlash from industry. The counterattack began with a second *60 Minutes* segment, aired six weeks after the first. This time Bradley switched the focus to Uniroyal and the criticism from apple producers and the chemical industry that CBS's first piece had been biased. We came away from the program unscathed, because it had done nothing to undermine the validity of our research. Then the apple growers hit us with a lawsuit—*Auvil v. CBS, Fenton Communications, and NRDC*—charging that the "scare" had cost the industry $100 million and driven thousands of apple growers into bankruptcy proceedings. We had liability insurance, but realized that the stakes here were too high to depend on the insurance company lawyers and hired an excellent Seattle law firm, Davis, Wright, and Tremaine, to represent us.

Things turned ugly. Bushels of rotten apples were sent to me at our San Francisco office; the same thing happened to Meryl Streep, and her family was threatened by an apple grower who lived near her home in Connecticut. Meryl was unbelievably brave and steadfast, but with the safety of her children uppermost in her mind she understandably decided to lower her profile for a time.

It was a scary time for NRDC. Once, when I was particularly worried about the whirlwind of publicity, accusations, and threats, I said to our chairman, Bill DeWind, "Bill, this is a hell of a fight. How did we get into this mess?" He looked at me and replied, "Because NRDC takes a stand on what we believe; there's no middle ground for us. There are only two things in the middle of the road—a yellow line and a dead skunk." I did my best to show that same unwavering support to the staff whose work was under attack.

There was no denying that the lawsuit put us in a precarious position. If any single fact in our report could be refuted, or if any error, no matter how small, were found in our methodology, we risked losing not only our credibility but perhaps the lawsuit.

Shortly after the release of "Intolerable Risk," Ricky Perera happened to be attending a conference in Finland, where she saw Dr. Chris Portier, an internationally recognized expert in toxicology data and risk assessment who had been asked to review the report. Portier took her aside and told her that he'd found a mistake. It looked as if a factor in our assessment had been double-counted in the write-up in the appendix. Even this small discrepancy—essentially just a typo—could have been disastrous. Ricky remembers that she literally grabbed Portier and took him up to her hotel room, where they called her NRDC colleagues and got the information cleared up to his satisfaction. Our credibility remained intact.

In 1993 the National Academy of Sciences (NAS) confirmed the validity of our study, and both the World Health Organization's International Agency for Research on Cancer and the federal government's National Toxicology Program concurred that Alar and its metabolite, UDMH, were carcinogenic. Dr. Philip Landrigan, who chaired the NAS committee, said, "NRDC was absolutely on the right track when it excoriated the regulatory agencies for having allowed a toxic material to stay on the market for twenty-five years." In 1994 the apple growers' suit was thrown out of court, and the charges against NRDC were dismissed.

Yet industry scientists ("biostitutes," as Bobby Kennedy calls them) continued to challenge our data and our research methods. Again we underestimated the virulence of the attack and how much of the mud would stick. I find it deeply ironic that despite the vindication of our findings and the removal of Alar from the market, the episode is still taught in college communications and advertising courses as "the Alar scare"—supposedly a case study of how environmentalists alarmed the public unnecessarily by exaggerating the health risks of a chemical.

But those are things you learn to live with. Much more important was that we had forced the government, the chemical industry, and above all the general public to take a hard look at the presence of pesticides in our food supply. The Alar case also gave a huge boost to the embryonic organic food movement. It's interesting to look back at an article that Lawrie Mott and Karen Snyder wrote about pesticides in the *Amicus Journal* in 1988. In the article, they looked to offer practical advice to readers struggling to find alternatives. The best they could come up with was, "Organic produce is available in certain Boston food stores." Lawrie recalls an organic baby food company that was about to go out of business because there seemed to be no market for its product. A month after the publication of "Intolerable Risk," the company couldn't keep up with demand. Within eighteen months, we had a national organic food law, and organic farming was on the road to becoming a multi-billion dollar industry. The Organic Foods Production Act, part of the 1990 farm bill, was a new and different kind of statute: previous laws had made lists of toxic chemicals we wanted to take *out* of the environment; this one stopped us from putting them *in* in the first place.

Under Wendy Gordon's expert direction, Mothers and Others continued to work on changing consumer behavior through its newsletter, *The Green Guide*, which steadily expanded its focus beyond food to such things as household cleaning products and the plastics and chemicals used in home furnishing. Mothers and Others also published a series of books with titles like *For Our Kids' Sake* and *The Way We Grow*, and its membership grew to over fifty thousand. In 1998 the group became independent from NRDC, and in 2006 the *Green Guide*, still edited by Wendy, was acquired by *National Geographic*. Wendy is now back at NRDC as a consultant to our communications team, where she is re-creating her early successes through one of our Web sites, simplesteps.org.

Simplesteps in turn is part of our Green Living project, which has been expanded by senior project analyst Jonathan Kaplan in our San Francisco office. Most recently, Jonathan has established the Growing Green Awards, which recognize leaders in sustainable food production who are committed to alternatives to pesticides.

This award made us realize that a visionary leader in this field already existed, Patrick Dollard, who runs the Center for Discovery in Harris, New York. The Center treats almost 1,500 people, mostly children, for multiple disabilities, primarily autism and cerebral palsy. Their buildings are green, their cleaning products non-toxic and, most important, their food is grown at the Center and is totally pesticide and chemical free.

Tom Burnham, our nephew who is the Center's Vice President of Environmental Policy, explains: "Someone with autism has a very nervous stomach. Food that's hard to digest causes them to become more agitated and aggressive because their stomach is churning. With our food, simple, organic and non- processed, they are more comfortable and healthier. We see results in one meal."

Leadership like Kaplan's with Growing Green and Dollard's at the Center, has taken these issues to another level at a time when all of America is looking for safe food.

For me, the Alar episode remains one of the epochal moments in NRDC's history. It forced us to develop totally new ways of communicating with the public. It catapulted us to a level of public recognition and credibility we had never dreamed of. It showed that we could take on a huge public fight against powerful opponents—and win. Our membership numbers soared.

The most lasting influence of the Alar case was the lesson it taught us about how we could best protect the public and influence the behavior of industry. NRDC would no longer focus only on government, law, and regulation. From now on, we would also look to the marketplace and the powerful force of consumer choice.

Third Decade

1990—2000

Uptown, Downtown, All Around the Town

At the time of the Alar case, NRDC was in the midst of a huge organizational transition. The case itself and the public exposure it gave us were a big part of this. Even more important was the decision we made to redefine our relationship to our hometown, New York. In the late 1980s, the New York office was by far our biggest (it still is), and the city was home to the majority of our members. It was a place that constantly reinvented itself, and most of us who worked at NRDC loved it.

"Cities are good for the environment," says Eric Goldstein, a former student of mine at the New York University law clinic, who arrived at NRDC in 1976 and became the director of our New York City urban program in 1986. At the time, this was a challenging notion for many people; surely cities were the antithesis of "the environment," which meant fields and forests and oceans. But Eric, one of the nation's leading experts on urban environmental issues, understood that "city residents use less energy, produce less air pollution with their compact living patterns, need less water (no lawns to water), and use mass transit. City dwellers live within the existing infrastructure. If we want to protect forests, wetlands, and wilderness, cities must be places where people want to live."

In line with Eric's vision, our New York program came to embrace all the key elements in the life of the city—clean drinking water, air quality, mass transportation systems, disposal of garbage and waste, conservation of the rural hinterland, preservation of historic buildings and monuments, and quality of life in the poorest neighborhoods. Starting with our own offices, we also saw New York as a place where we could create environmental models that could be replicated elsewhere, not only in other cities but around the world.

Our decision to engage with the built environment of New York had begun in 1982, when the city was in deep trouble. Crime was rampant, the streets and subways were filthy, and the air quality was atrocious. Homeless people were a daily reminder of the need for social reform, and AIDS was becoming a part of our lives as friends and relatives were stricken with the disease. More and more people were fleeing the city.

Times Square was the symbolic heart of New York, the center of the theater district, and a magnet for visitors. By the early 1980s, it had become an emblem of urban decay, best known for prostitution and street crime. Its fate was a matter of deep personal concern for one of our first and most important trustees, Joan Davidson.

Joan was president of the J. M. Kaplan Fund, set up by her father with the fortune he had acquired from the sale of the Welch Grape Company. Her special passion was historic preservation. She deplored what developers like Donald Trump were doing to the city and had been one of the leaders of the unsuccessful fight to prevent the historic Penn Station from being torn down. She was also devoted to NRDC, and it was her support that had enabled us to launch the *Amicus Journal* in 1979.

As part of the effort to renovate Times Square, developers were tearing down the classic old theaters, in spite of bitter opposition from preservationists. The historic Helen Hayes and Morosco theaters were destroyed to make way for the Marriott Marquis Hotel, designed by John C. Portman (and nicknamed the Toaster Hotel because of its shape). Because of the uproar from New Yorkers, the city designated every surviving Broadway theater built prior to 1930 as a landmark. The theater owners responded by suing the city.

Joan started a group called Save Our Theaters, composed of actors, directors, choreographers, set designers, and others working in the field. She brought them to NRDC looking for help, and Mitch Bernard, our star litigator, agreed to represent them. For Mitch, this was personal as well as professional; he had written musicals and had taken time off from NRDC to compose music while sharing childcare with his wife, Adrienne, also a lawyer."

The theater owners' lawsuit failed. The New York State Court of Appeals upheld the landmark decision, and the historic theaters still stand.

Not everyone at NRDC was happy about our involvement in the issue, questioning what it had to do with the natural environment. One board member, who came from a prominent family of real estate developers, resigned (one of only three to do so in our forty-year history), saying that real estate was too important to the city's economy for us to interfere. Nevertheless, after this first taste of urban warfare, we were ready to take on other powerful developers, even if we were David to real estate Goliaths—such as the Rose family.

Rose is one of the most famous names in New York City real estate, and the family is rightly lauded for its notable gifts to the public, such as the Rose Room at the New York Public Library and the Rose Center for Earth and Space (more commonly known as the Hayden Planetarium) at the American Museum of Natural History. In 1984 Rose Associates was planning to build the Atlantic Center, a twenty-seven-acre development in Brooklyn on the site of the old Atlantic terminal train station. The brainchild of Jonathan Rose, a third-generation member of the family firm, the Atlantic Center would be the city's first transit-centered development, embodying a set of principles later known as "smart growth." The mixed community would have town houses, some afford-able housing, courtyards with gardens that provided cross breezes for residents, a recycling center, a public square, and offices. Rose had obtained a zoning variance that would discourage car use by cutting down on the number of parking spaces.

Despite Rose's good intentions, South Brooklyn Legal Services represented residents who were concerned about an environmental issue: Did the project's EIS adequately address the secondary displace-ment of lower income residents and small businesses? They contacted Mitch. NRDC had an institutional interest in consideration of this issue; it was a matter of enforcement of the law. Mitch filed an amicus brief in the appellate division of the state court, which did not oppose the devel-opment as such but demanded full analysis of relevant environmental impacts. Mitch soon began to feel pressure from the real estate commu-nity, which insisted that Jonathan Rose had made a conscientious effort to build a well-planned, environmentally sensitive development. Several members of the NRDC board also called me to express their concern. I called Rose and invited him to meet with me and Mitch in my office.

It was not an easy meeting. Neither of us had met Rose before, but I learned that Rose's NRDC membership renewal had been returned with a handwritten note at the bottom: "I don't give to people who sue me."

Rose was frustrated that we should stand in the way of this sus-tainable development, especially since he had gone far beyond what city rules required. Mitch and I responded that an EIS is a matter of legal principle, and this one did not meet the standard because it did not include secondary displacement.

"Mr. Bernard, I like to do things," Rose said. "You like to stop things."

The Appellate Court deliberated for around 11 months, and although it ruled in favor of the Atlantic Project, due to the delays, Rose Associates sold the project. But it was not the last we had seen of Jonathan Rose.

Although I had pigeonholed Rose as a typical real estate developer, the dispute was never about the principles behind his project. On the contrary, NRDC's thoughts were moving in a similar direction as we examined our relationship to the city. With a hundred staff members, we had outgrown our offices in the Chanin Building, and besides, I wondered, did we really want to be stuck away out of sight on the forty-fifth floor of a Midtown Manhattan skyscraper? It was time to move.

I wanted to find somewhere that would establish a physical presence in the heart of the community and at the same time embody the idea of NRDC as a family. Since 1971, we'd had an annual summer picnic, when people came to our home with their families for a day of (very competitive) softball and volleyball and long hikes. Since we had no swimming pool, the children happily ran around under sprinklers, and I gave them rides on our tractor. Everyone contributed something to the picnic table. Back in the city, meanwhile, we had a softball team that we called the Environmental Extremists, which still makes it to the finals in New York's "green league" every year. It's managed by our facilities coordinator, Matt Cohen, who even makes player cards for the team with pictures, schedules, and personal stats.

We needed a real home in the city, and Pattie Sullivan, typically, found exactly what we needed. On Friday, October 16, 1987, with the help of the real estate developer and philanthropist Marshall Rose (no relation to Jonathan), we signed the contract to buy an empty hat and tuxedo factory, an art deco building on West Twentieth Street, and made a down payment of a million dollars, thanks to the generosity of trustee and friend John Robinson. The following Monday, the stock market crashed. Rising to the challenge, Marshall Rose found another buyer to join us, the Library for the Blind, and Bill DeWind's law firm, Paul, Weiss, brought in Cambridge University Press as a third. We would occupy the upper three floors of the twelve-story building. Board members and other supporters helped with emergency infusions of cash.

We decided that 40 West Twentieth Street would be a model energy-efficient building, the first green retrofit attempted in New

York—and still to this day the most ambitious—visited over the years by thousands of architects. Doubters on the board and among the staff worried that we were digging ourselves into a deep financial hole, but we were confident that we were making the right long-term decision and plunged ahead.

Over the decades we have had a string of creative geniuses on staff at NRDC, and near the top of any list would be Rob Watson, our green buildings expert, who worked with Kirsten Childs of Croxton Collaborative Architects to oversee the design of the building. I've always believed that when you hire people with Rob's level of talent, you let them operate on a very long leash, without a lot of close supervision. Rob was the classic Lone Ranger type. We never quite knew where he was or what he was doing. We might look for him to get advice on some detail about the windows on the new building and finally track him down in Russia or some other faraway place where he was advising someone on how to install solar panels. Later he would become famous as the father of the U.S. Green Building Council's LEED (Leadership in Energy and Environmental Design) certification system. (Another NRDC staffer, Kaid Benfield, who had initially worked on our forestry program, was subsequently instrumental in developing the LEED-ND system, which expanded the idea of green building into smart growth at the neighborhood level.)

There are very few skyscrapers in our Chelsea neighborhood, and Rob and Kirsten took full advantage of the natural light on the upper floors of our new home. The motion-sensor lighting, air-conditioning, and heating systems were all based on the principle of energy efficiency. As a result, we cut our energy consumption by 70 percent compared to a conventional office.

Pattie chose the artwork and furnishings, using only carpets and fabrics made from recycled materials. A friend of mine, the artist Don Nice, offered one of his signature murals, *The Peaceable Kingdom*, a beautiful nine-by-thirty-six-foot depiction of dozens of animals, birds, fishes, and plants that had been shown in four museums and had to be brought out of storage in sections. The workers took a break from putting in the air-conditioning to install the mural, which rises two stories above our reception area.

It was a beautiful, welcoming place, but the skeptics who worried about the cost definitely had a point. Buying the building had left us with a $700,000 deficit. There was a cash reserve of less than $1 million, and every year it was used to pay end-of-year bills and then replenished. In 1989, realizing that the organization was seriously overstretched, we brought in a team of management consultants— the Management Assistance Group—who advised us to revamp our leadership on all fronts.

We needed a capital campaign to take care of the deficit, give us the reserves we required to launch new programs, and cushion us against fluctuating fundraising cycles as well as the ups and downs in the economy. To accomplish this, we made two of the most important hires in NRDC's history. Judy Keefer, who had worked in the mayor's office in New York, became our first director of finance and operations. Jack Murray, who had extensive fundraising experience in universities and hospitals, was hired as our director of development. Under his direction, the capital campaign was a huge success. We paid down the debt on the building and amassed working capital of close to $10 million.

These weren't the only major changes. In the wake of the Alar campaign, we hired a new communications director, Charles Fulwood, who had been the media director for Amnesty International's 1988 World Tour to celebrate the Universal Declaration of Human Rights. Frances Beinecke, who had recently returned to NRDC, became our program director. She had been living in Washington, where, in addition to raising her three young daughters, she had gained valuable experience chairing the Wilderness Society. Most important, though, everyone in the organization liked and respected Frances for her honesty, openness, and thoughtfulness.

Finally, Bill DeWind came to the end of his ten-year tenure as board chair and was replaced by F.A.O. (Fritz) Schwarz Jr., a senior partner at the law firm of Cravath, Swain, and Moore. Brilliant and idealistic, Fritz was one of the most respected public servants in the city. As corporation counsel from 1982 to 1986, he had overhauled the city's ethics and lobbying laws. At a time when we were devoting so much attention to New York City, we couldn't have made a better choice.

It was 1990, and heading into the new decade with a new building, a new chairman, and money in the bank, it was the best of times. NRDC was alive with ideas and ambitions, and we were set to take on one of the biggest experiments we had ever attempted.

The twentieth anniversary of Earth Day in 1990 was dedicated to recycling. It was the most widely supported environmental cause in the country, and understandably so. Any vision of sustainability—a word that was just coming into vogue—depends on recycling the materials we use. Ninety-five percent of the environmental impact of any product happens before you open the package.

NRDC was part of a large coalition of environmental groups pressing for Congress to pass a National Recycling Act, and our efforts in Washington were headed by Allen Hershkowitz. Allen had studied resource economics and combustion engineering, and had written his PhD on the need to deregulate big utilities such as Consolidated Edison. He believed that Con Edison was taking advantage of its protected status to block efforts by Congress to develop new and more efficient energy technologies in the wake of the oil shocks of the 1970s.

In 1983 New York City Mayor Ed Koch came up with a plan to burn the city's garbage and sell it to Con Edison as a new source of energy. Allen was intrigued by the idea, but also saw it as a potential environmental disaster. Over the next several years, he made a study of garbage burning in the United States, Europe, and Japan, and by the time he was done he had turned himself into one of the nation's leading experts on waste management and recycling. Along the way he met NRDC's Eric

Goldstein, who chaired a city task force on resource recovery. Eric hired Allen as a consultant, and then, in 1989, Allen came directly onto our senior staff as the director of our national solid waste project.

He spent the next four years lobbying for the National Recycling Act, working closely with Senator Max Baucus of Montana, chairman of the Senate Environment Committee, and Congressman Al Swift of Washington, head of the House Subcommittee on Transportation and Hazardous Materials. It was a long war of attrition against lobbyists for the plastics industry, the incinerator industry, the paper industry, the mining industry, and the food packaging industry, all of whom resented being told what raw materials they could use. By the time the bill reached the markup stage, both incineration and the use of virgin timber by-products had been redefined as recycling, and the federal government was to be given the authority to overrule local zoning ordinances to decide where incinerators should be sited, as if they were a matter of national security. Rather than let the bill go to the floor, the environmental groups killed it.

Allen saw this as a watershed moment. He reasoned that we were never going to legislate or litigate our way to sustainability, as we lacked sufficient political muscle. The pace of change in Washington and the courts was out of sync with the intensity of pressures on the planet, and while ordinary Americans had become more aware of environmental issues, they were more and more pessimistic about finding solutions. Allen wondered if market forces, rather than the law, could provide the models of success that people craved. With Alar and pesticides, we had turned to the power of consumers to influence corporate behavior. Allen proposed to show industry that sustainability was compatible with the pursuit of profit.

A few months before the collapse of the recycling bill, Allen had traveled to Europe on a fact-finding trip with Senator Baucus and Congressman Swift. Wherever they went, they found that politicians and CEOs needed no convincing that industry had a responsibility to protect the environment. Allen was especially impressed by a paper mill they visited in a small town near Stuttgart, Germany, which produced high-quality recycled paper without the use of chlorine. NRDC had just created a model office building in New York, Allen thought, so why shouldn't it build a factory?

A paper mill was the obvious choice, since waste paper was New York's biggest export—Allen liked to call the city "the Saudi Arabia of Waste Paper"—with most being sent to China, India, and Canada.

Allen went to Eric Goldstein and told him about his idea. Eric looked at him in disbelief and said, "What? We don't build paper mills."

"Build it," Allen said, "and they will come."

He presented the idea at our annual retreat in 1992. According to *New Yorker* reporter Lis Harris, who wrote a profile of Allen that later turned into a book, *Tilting at Mills*, "from the expressions on many of his colleagues' faces Hershkowitz felt as if he had just told them they were all soon going to be assuming the roles of lead dancers in the Bolshoi Ballet."

But Allen, who is one of the most persuasive people you will ever meet, pressed ahead and took his proposal to the NRDC board, which gave it the green light.

By now Bill Clinton and Al Gore had moved into the White House, and in looking for a site that might provide hundreds of jobs for an impoverished inner-city neighborhood—helping to build a "sustainable community," in the jargon of the time—Allen's plans were perfectly in tune with the new administration's priorities. Clinton's favorite slogan, after all, was "It's the economy, stupid!" I'd known Vice President Al Gore since the late 1980s, when he was in the Senate, and when I met with him just after the inauguration, he told me that he hoped all our environmental initiatives would be geared to creating new jobs.

Thanks to his years of involvement in waste management, Allen was also acutely sensitive to the concerns of the environmental justice movement, whose ranks had been growing rapidly. Hazardous waste, incinerators, and landfills were the main threat faced by minority communities in the United States. In 1982 Congressman Walter

Fauntroy, the head of the Congressional Black Caucus, had demanded an investigation by the General Accounting Office into the siting of hazardous waste landfills in eight southern states. The GAO found that three-fourths of them were in black neighborhoods, even though African Americans made up only 20 percent of the population. A wave of lawsuits followed, charging discrimination under the Civil Rights Act. When the government mandated the closing of open dumps, landfills and incinerators emerged as alternatives. But these turned out to be a source of serious air pollution, and once again most were located in poor and minority neighborhoods.

In January 1990, I and the leaders of seven other environmental organizations received a scathing letter from a group of civil rights leaders charging that "racism and the 'whiteness' of the environmental movement is our Achilles heel." The following year, Michael Fisher, then president of the Sierra Club, and I were invited to a People of Color Leadership Conference at the National Cathedral in Washington. We were the only whites there. I could see that the "mainstream" environmental organizations had been living in a different world.

The environmental justice movement was asking for our trust and respect. To amplify their voices, they wanted us to share our legal and scientific skills and our access to those in positions of power. And they wanted us to hire people of color in senior professional positions. I had always thought of NRDC as being color-blind and gender-blind in our hiring, but as Patricia says, the proof is in the pudding. We couldn't just pay lip service to the concerns of the environmental justice movement. We had to provide concrete results, and that is exactly what Allen Hershkowitz was proposing to do with his paper mill.

The plant would be the largest private sector manufacturing enterprise in New York City since the end of World War II. It would take waste paper from the city's trash, remove the ink without using chlorine bleach or other toxics, and form the cleaned fibers into rolls of newsprint. The three million gallons of water used each day would be treated "gray water" from a sewage treatment facility close to the site, an abandoned railyard in the South Bronx recommended by Banana Kelly, a well-regarded community organization (named for a crescent-shaped street where it had done its earliest work rehabilitating derelict housing). The neighborhood was the poorest in New York City. It was 98 percent Latino and African American, and more than half the households were headed by single women. Male unemployment was close to 20 percent. Childhood asthma rates were the highest in the city. The neighborhood stood to benefit from the paper mill project not only through the six hundred jobs it would create but through financing for a learning and health center, a day-care center, and a dormitory for homeless, at-risk young people.

Much of Allen's time was taken up with obtaining permits for the project, which he found ironic. We had worked hard for years to create strict rules governing things like clean air and clean water, and now we had to jump through all the same regulatory hoops as someone who wanted to open a hazardous waste dump.

One day, as he was wrestling with a permitting problem, the switchboard called to say there was someone on the line asking about the environmental attributes of a certain stone she was using in a sculpture. Could he help her? The caller turned out to be Maya Lin, who had received worldwide acclaim for her design of the Vietnam Veterans Memorial in Washington, DC. Allen answered her question about the stone, then told her about the Bronx paper mill. He asked if she would be interested in designing the building, and she agreed. She produced a beautiful design, filled with energy-saving features, with gardens, fountains, and glass walls that would allow the public to see what was happening inside. The Bronx Museum of Art called it "the most important work of art ever created for the Bronx." Maya subsequently became an NRDC trustee.

So did one of Allen's potential investors, a developer who declined to put money into the project but said he'd be happy to contribute his expertise. This was none other than Jonathan Rose. He had left the family business to start Jonathan Rose Companies, which went on to become an important developer of green mixed-use, mixed-income communities. In the wake of Hurricane Katrina in 2005, for example, Jonathan's firm launched "Louisiana Speaks," an initiative to design a sustainable, long-term vision for the region devastated by the storm.

We looked back ruefully on our first encounter over the Atlantic Center project. I had to acknowledge that my first impressions of Jonathan had been wrong, and he regretted that he and Mitch Bernard had gotten off on the wrong foot. "When Mitch and I met in 1984," he said, "I was a jazz music producer and he was writing songs. If we had started out with that, perhaps things would have been different."

He told us, "I saw that NRDC could see the potential for development to improve a community. What we've learned is that we have to see beyond the labels to the reality behind them. The label says a developer is bad and an environmental organization can't sponsor a development. But what we must do is sit down and talk to one another." These days we do that all the time because Jonathan joined our board.

Everything seemed to be falling into place. Several big paper companies, starting with MoDo of Sweden, expressed interest in operating the mill. New York Governor George Pataki approved its construction, New York City came up with $75 million in tax-exempt financing, and the city and state together said they were willing to issue an additional $275 million in financing. About 150 people were working for the mill project in various capacities, along with four law firms and five engineering firms. We had all the permits we needed, and we felt close to breaking ground. When the Clinton administration issued an executive order requiring all federal agencies to use more recycled paper, Vice President Gore singled out the Bronx project for praise. The president himself sent a handwritten note saying that he and Gore would come to the groundbreaking ceremony.

But it didn't happen.

Perhaps we were naive. There were just too many moving parts to the puzzle, and the sheer amount of detail was overwhelming. The project involved everything that was toughest about doing business in New York: finding a site, raising money, obtaining permits, seeking community support, flattering local politicians. People had begun to refer to the paper mill as "the Beast."

In the end, Allen said, it was "death by a thousand cuts." Cost estimates for the project steadily escalated. Investors were made nervous by wild fluctuations in the price of newsprint. Some of the grassroots representatives whom we had seen as paragons of virtue turned out to be dysfunctional; others were corrupt. The innately conservative paper industry executives were hostile to Maya Lin's role in the project. At one point Allen remarked, "The only toxic chemical this project suffers from is testosterone."

NRDC had always prided itself on its nonpartisan approach. We saw this as a virtue, but in New York City politics it proved to be a liability. Democratic politicians condemned Allen for standing too close to Governor Pataki—a Republican and a staunch environmentalist and friend of NRDC—at a press conference. Our relationship with the city government was stressful. We were used to dealing with federal agencies like the EPA, which understood that you could cooperate with it and sue it at the same time. Not so in New York, where we had several lawsuits going against the city even as we asked for its support for the paper mill. After Clinton and Gore expressed their vigorous backing for the project, Mayor Rudy Giuliani decided the city should have nothing more to do with it.

The "final cut" came when the NAB Construction Company, which had submitted feasibility specs for the project but had not been hired, sued NRDC and other sponsors of the plant for $600 million, charging breach of contract, or "tortious interference." The amount it claimed from NRDC was $80 million.

Ruben Kraiem, then a partner at Paul, Weiss, who chaired the legal committee of our board, had long been a champion of the project, but he came to the conclusion that its moment had passed. He told *New Yorker* writer Lis Harris, "NRDC was perceived, rightly or wrongly, as having responsibility to develop the project, which exceeded the role that NRDC was qualified to perform. We were perceived as having the lead role in areas that exposed the organization to considerable risk. However important the project was, the overall health and solvency and reputation of NRDC are much, much, much more important."

The negotiations for winding up the project, supervised by Ruben, took a long time, but in 2000, after an eight-year roller-coaster ride, our relationship with the paper mill was officially terminated.

———

Was it all a wasted effort? I don't think so. Allen came very, very close to succeeding, and without Giuliani's hostility we might still have made it. As Frances Beinecke told Lis Harris, the Bronx mill was "as great a model not having been built as it would have been being built . . . for the people who are thinking about issues of sustainability, it had terrific resonance. They know all about it even though it's not sitting up on the Harlem River Railyard, it's alive."

The project had taught us many vital lessons that would shape our future partnerships with the private sector. The law alone was better at stopping bad things than at making good things happen, especially on a project as complicated as this. Market forces might have created most of our environmental problems in the first place, but they were also uniquely equipped to find the remedies. We also concluded that if corporations were interested in sustainability—which, we believed, many were, at least potentially—they would need the kind of expert advice that NRDC could offer.

Allen was understandably bereft at the abandonment of the project. Soon after it ended, he went out to lunch with Frances, who had a couple suggestions. First, take some time off and write a book. Second, since he had learned so much about the paper industry over the past eight years, why didn't he go to the source and look at where all that paper came from in the first place? But that's another story, which led NRDC to all sorts of unexpected successes, and I will come back to it later.

———

Meanwhile, the battle for recycling in New York City continued, led by attorney Mark Izeman. Mark had first come across NRDC in 1988, at Brown University's career counseling office. Eric Goldstein hired him, though the only salary he could offer was the $15,000 we had allocated to pay interns. That wasn't enough for Mark to live on, but he supplemented it with an evening job at Bloomingdale's. Then he took time off to attend New York University Law School, returning to NRDC in 1993.

During the 1990s, New York's recycling program had waxed and waned, and we brought a lawsuit against the city to get it back on track. Mark also pushed the city to recycling the twelve thousand tons of daily residential and institutional trash by lobbying, writing reports, and working with allies on the New York City Council to put pressure on successive mayors. His work helped push the city from less than 1 percent residential recycling in 1989 to roughly 20 percent by 2002.

But then, in February 2004, Mark got a call from a reporter telling him that Mayor Michael Bloomberg had decided to suspend the recycling of metal, glass, and plastics. Faced with huge budget deficits, Bloomberg had been advised by the Department of Sanitation that this step could save the city $40 million. After Bloomberg's decision went into effect in July, Mark decided to prove to the mayor that recycling not only was the right thing to do (the sanitation department, a notoriously unresponsive bureaucracy, regarded it as "too '60s"), but could actually save the city money.

Into the controversy stepped the Hugo Neu Corporation, which had recycled most of the steel from the World Trade Center after 9/11. The company had developed a way of making garbage profitable by finding lucrative markets for waste paper and using modern mechanized equipment to separate garbage. The city was paying $70 per ton to truck its garbage to distant landfills. Neu said that the company could do it for $48, and Bloomberg responded by fully restoring the recycling program in April 2004. In his biannual "report card" on his performance, the mayor gave himself an F in waste management. By striking the deal with Neu, Mark said, "he just turned in an A paper."

The company's chairman, John Neu, and his wife, Wendy, became a welcome addition to the NRDC family, and in 2006 Wendy joined our board.

Smoke Alarm

One of the great ironies in the Bronx paper mill saga was the hostility we encountered from a small number of clean air activists in the local community. The city's air quality had been a priority for us from the very earliest days of NRDC, and we had always understood that the impact of airborne pollutants fell disproportionately on poor neighborhoods. Our philosophy was summed up well by the veteran environmental journalist Mark Dowie: the air in a factory is just as important as the air in the Grand Canyon. It was especially painful for Allen Hershkowitz to listen to baseless charges that the Bronx mill would add to the pollution in the neighborhood's air.

Our first concern in the early 1970s had been airborne lead, which can cause serious neurobehavioral problems in children. Although New York City had passed a law banning lead in gasoline by the end of 1973, the Clean Air Act said that regulating lead was a matter for the federal government, not the states or localities. On its face, this was logical, but the effects could be perverse, because states such as New York and California have often passed much more stringent pollution controls—and can implement them much faster—than the federal government.

David Schoenbrod, a classmate of the original Yale group, intervened on behalf of the city in federal court in Manhattan, arguing that Washington could not preempt state and local authority to regulate gasoline and then do nothing itself. The court agreed, and in February 1972 the EPA announced that all gas stations would be required to carry unleaded gasoline. However, under presidents Nixon, Ford, and Carter, enforcement of the lead ban was repeatedly postponed. The Ethyl Corporation, a General Motors subsidiary that produced the lead used as a fuel additive, sued the EPA. Oil companies and car manufacturers insisted, quite incorrectly, that cars would not run properly without lead. In the end, it was not until 1986 that the ban on leaded gasoline took full effect.

For years, as this political battle played out, the children of New York went on breathing in lead. Poorer children playing in heavily trafficked streets were inhaling street dust as rich in lead as the ore in lead mines. There is little doubt that this generation suffered lasting effects from the exposure. In an article in the *New York Times Magazine* in 2007, Jessica Wolpaw Reyes argued that violent crime in the city peaked in the 1990s, just as children exposed to the highest levels of lead in the 1970s were reaching their late teens, and that the decline in juvenile crime after 1990 was directly related to the phaseout of lead in gasoline.

In 1975 David and Ross Sandler (who was also deeply involved at this time in the Storm King case) hit upon a brilliant strategy to come at the city's air pollution from a totally different direction. New York State was experiencing a fiscal crisis, and as a way of increasing revenues, Governor Hugh Carey raised the city's subway fare from thirty-five to fifty cents. Ross and David were convinced that this would decrease subway ridership and encourage people to use cars instead. They filed a lawsuit to stop the fare hike, arguing that the pollution from increased vehicle traffic would violate Clean Air Act standards.

The case went to the New York State Supreme Court in 1977, although, unfortunately, we weren't able to persuade the court of our point of view. However, our lawsuit got a lot of attention, including an article on the front page of the *New York Times*, which made the larger point that the city's subway system was falling apart. The stations were filthy, many of the cars had no working lights, trains were constantly out of service, graffiti was scrawled everywhere, and malfunctioning lubrication equipment created "Big Screechers" with noise levels up to 116 decibels, as loud as a rock concert. According to health professionals, anything above 85 decibels can cause permanent hearing damage. Whether or not there was fare increase, people were already deserting the subways.

The Metropolitan Transportation Authority (MTA) had no plan to address the crisis, so David and Ross decided to write one. NRDC had never taken on anything like this before, but we recognized that like many of the environmental challenges we faced, this one had no simple, linear solution. If we wanted to fix the problem, we would need to carry out a comprehensive policy analysis of all aspects of the system—economic, technical, and operational—and propose an equally comprehensive set of remedies.

"A New Direction in Transit," which took David and Ross almost two years to draft, was a detailed blueprint for rescuing the troubled subway system. It was released in December 1978 at a press conference presided over by Mayor Ed Koch and promptly adopted by the MTA. This led to a multibillion dollar transit rehabilitation project that brought new tracks, new air-conditioned cars, and clean, redecorated stations. It lifted the morale of the city and gave us a subway service that rivaled any in the world.

———

Eric Goldstein had worked with David and Ross on the transit study, and when Ross left NRDC in 1986 to become the city's transportation commissioner, Eric took over the New York urban program. After the success of the subway project, he brought the same tools of detailed policy analysis to bear on other critical threats to the city's air quality. Three years later, we started a West Coast urban program after opening a new NRDC office, our fourth, in Los Angeles. We were the first national environmental organization to establish a presence in the city. James Thornton and Lynne Edgerton moved from New York to start the operation. It was a small office with just a half-dozen staff, and its priority, under the direction of Mary Nichols was also air quality. (Mary would later become head of the California Air Resources Board.)

By the early 1980s, the Clean Air Act had brought dramatic improvements nationwide—40 percent lower particulate emissions, a 65 percent reduction in airborne sulfur dioxide, and a 35 percent decrease in carbon monoxide levels, despite the fact that driving miles had risen by 30 percent since 1970. Yet in our two biggest cities, New York and Los Angeles, which together accounted for 8 percent of the nation's population, air quality still failed to meet federal standards in two months out of three.

One of the biggest reasons was the rapid growth of the diesel fleet, especially trucks and buses. Diesel is a less refined fuel than conventional gasoline, and the black, oily clouds that belched from diesel tailpipes at that time contained as much as seventy times more particulate matter than the emissions from a gasoline engine. Almost all of this came in the form of "fine particles"—defined as those smaller than 2.5 microns in diameter, or one-fiftieth the thickness of a human hair—which get past the body's filtering defenses and burrow deep into the tissues of the lungs. Thousands of toxic chemicals hitch a ride on these particles, including as many as forty known carcinogens.

When Eric took over the urban program, roughly two hundred thousand trucks were registered in New York's five boroughs, with tens of thousands more coming in and out of the city each day through the tunnels and across the bridges. Most of these vehicles were diesel powered. New York was also the nation's diesel bus capital. According to one 1985 study, the city's trucks and buses were spewing almost three thousand tons of diesel particulates into the air each year. Some of the highest concentrations—the "hot spots"—were around bus depots and truck loading zones, which, like hazardous waste dumps, were usually located in the city's poorer neighborhoods. To make matters worse, the EPA had not yet used the tools of the Clean Air Act to force diesel engine makers to build cleaner engines, so the industry never had the same incentive to clean up its engines in the same way that car makers had during the 1980s.

By 1990, with tighter federal emissions limits for buses about to kick in, the city and the MTA were beginning to think about buses that would run on alternative fuels such as methanol and clean natural gas. The following year, Eric hired a young lawyer for the urban program, Rich Kassel, whose work would end up having as big an impact on urban transportation as David Schoenbrod and Ross Sandler had had on the New York City subway system.

————

Public transportation was not Rich's initial focus. His first project was a study of the pollution associated with airports, including the emissions from idling aircraft and the use of toxic deicing materials. I didn't need to be convinced of the importance of the issue; hanging in my office was a Friends of the Earth poster that pictured a trail of black smoke coming from an airplane's exhaust, accompanied by a quotation from Henry David Thoreau—"Thank God men cannot as yet fly and lay waste the sky as well as the earth."

Rich started out with a detailed case study of the Westchester County Airport, an hour north of New York City, which handles mainly short-haul flights by a number of major carriers and private corporate aircraft servicing local businesses. Soon after, he broadened his scope to 125 of the nation's busiest airports and gathered a team of researchers and interns who devised a seven-page questionnaire for the airports that requested information on noise, land use, deicing techniques, air pollution, and future expansion plans. Their final report, "Flying Off Course," established that airports were one of the worst generators of urban pollution.

Finding remedies was difficult. Airports were regulated by a variety of different entities, including the Federal Aviation Administration (whose primary concerns were safety and the promotion of the aviation industry), the EPA (whose regulatory mandate over aircraft was limited by international agreements and took no account of the aggregate impact of the airplanes idling on busy runways), and state and local governments (which were preempted from regulating aircraft pollution by federal law). The airlines and the FAA never had to deal with an environmental group like NRDC and had little desire to. Furthermore, both had strong legal protections that limited our ability to litigate. However, Rich was able to accomplish a lot by highlighting good practices by individual airlines. Delta, for example, found that it made sound economic sense to keep only a single engine running while an airplane was idling. With Delta's quiet cooperation, Rich publicized this in his report; once other airlines realized that this didn't compromise safety, they followed suit. Idling on one engine has since become standard industry practice.

Rich's involvement with buses grew initially out of his love of bikes. He lived on Manhattan's Upper West Side and rode his bike to work each day. The first part of the journey took him through Central Park, on a dedicated bike lane, but after that came forty blocks of often gridlocked buses, trucks, and yellow taxis on Fifth Avenue, which he called a "Diesel Canyon." Cursing as he weaved his way in and out of the black clouds of exhaust smoke, he muttered to himself, "Why doesn't someone *do* something about this?" One day, in the summer of 1993, the obvious answer came to him: *he* would be the one to do something about it. That was the beginning of our "Dump Dirty Diesels" campaign.

Rather than lessening the diesel problem, New York City Transit, the MTA's bus operator, seemed intent on making it worse. The MTA was in the midst of an $800 million capital program that included buying another eighteen hundred diesel buses and reinvesting in the diesel infrastructure at its citywide network of nineteen bus depots. Despite all the talk about methanol and clean natural gas, a grand total of four buses in the city were powered by alternative fuels.

More than twenty years after the Clean Air Act, New York City had never met federal air quality standards for particulate matter. On Madison Avenue, more than half the particulate pollution came from diesel engines, even though gasoline-powered cars outnumbered diesel vehicles by more than ten to one. When Rich pressed the EPA on this and threatened to take the matter to court, the agency reacted within twenty-four hours, redesignating the city as a clean air offender. The public health risks were well established. The EPA was on the case. But still the MTA did nothing.

After two years of this foot-dragging, Rich felt an urgent need to alter the political dynamic of the debate. Diesel buses were still being treated as a technical matter for insiders, and he decided that it was time to stir up the general public. "I don't need more research," he said, "I need ads on buses."

We had never done an ad campaign before, but Rich had worked with public interest research groups and two presidential campaigns before coming to NRDC and knew how to create a buzz. The problem was that we wanted to reach millions of people but didn't have the budget for a large-scale media campaign. Our solution was to go for "guerrilla advertising"—a small, targeted effort that would create a splash in the media and result in lots of free publicity.

A newly formed ad agency, Green Team Advertising, agreed to work with us on a pro bono basis and came up with a great tagline for the campaign: "Standing behind this bus could be more dangerous than standing in front of it." The agency designed a big yellow banner ad that included a toll-free number for more information on clean-fuel buses: 1-800-NICE RIDE.

Ideally, we would have liked to place the ad just above the polluting tailpipe of buses traveling in all the busiest parts of the city. But we had allocated only $35,000 to the campaign. "All we could afford," Rich recalls, "was ads on thirty buses traveling through Harlem at 3 a.m." We sent the MTA our check, and they cashed it. When other MTA staff saw the ad, they balked at running it.

This was the best thing that could possibly have happened, and we were ready for it. Mitch Bernard, our head of litigation, was more than happy to turn this into a First Amendment case and filed a lawsuit in federal court, knowing that the MTA, unlike a private corporation, could not legally reject an ad that was critical of it.

Our tactics worked like magic. The dispute was all over the *New York Times* and the evening news. Rich appeared on the morning TV chat shows, and each time he would whip out a poster-size reproduction of our ad, hold it up for the cameras, and declare, "This is the ad the MTA doesn't want you to see."

The MTA realized that it had a PR disaster on its hands. But we weren't done yet. In the course of our First Amendment case, we had learned that ours was not the only ad that had been turned down by the transit authority. It had also refused to carry posters from the Gay Men's Health Crisis and the Straphangers Campaign, which works to defend the interests of commuters on the New York City subways. Another firestorm erupted.

After two weeks of unrelenting media pressure, the agency finally cried uncle. Our ads could run for free and on more buses than we had originally planned. Even if the buses carrying our ads ran most often in the middle of the night, millions of New Yorkers had seen the ads over and over in the newspapers and on TV.

The following January, we hit the MTA with a second ad—this one timed to coincide with the opening of the 1996 session of the state legislature in Albany, Governor George Pataki's State of the State speech, and the debate over the new MTA budget. This one read "Meet New York's Heaviest Smoker." We had a thousand large color copies printed and mailed throughout the political and media worlds of New York, hoping that friendly staffers in the state Capitol would stick them up on the walls and add to the embarrassment of visiting MTA lobbyists.

It was at about this time that I got to know New York Governor Pataki, whose support would turn out to be hugely important as our fight for clean city buses progressed. Pataki lived near our home in Garrison, and I'd first met him ten years earlier when he was campaigning for the state senate, introducing himself and shaking hands with commuters at the train station. I'd asked him what his position was on the environment. He remembered that encounter, and shortly after he was elected governor in 1994, he and his chief counsel, Mike Finnegan, came to meet with me at our home. Sitting outside under an old apple tree, we talked about the steps he could take to protect the state's environment. (Patricia and the governor also compared notes on the best ways of keeping raccoons out of the vegetable garden.)

Among other things, Pataki and I discussed the need for incentives for energy efficiency and explored how we might work together on a major bond act for both land and water protection. I'd always had

173

CANOEING CONSTITUTION MARSH, COLD SPRING, NEW YORK, 1998
Governor George Pataki and John Adams

a particular interest in the New York City water supply, 90 percent of which comes from six reservoirs in the Catskills, where I'd grown up. Over a billion gallons of water flow by gravity through tunnels to the city every day, meeting the needs of almost ten million people. The system is a marvel of engineering and the envy of water providers throughout the world. I knew the system firsthand, having worked summer construction jobs on the tunnels as a high school kid and again as a law student. While in law school, I worked on the Cannonsville Dam, sweeping mud out of the entrance to the tunnel to earn enough money for a new suit and rent for my New York apartment before starting my first full-time job, at Cadwalader, Wickersham, and Taft.

In 1986, however, a major complication arose. Like the conflict over lead in gasoline, it was a case of a federal statute potentially overriding a perfectly good state law. The federal Safe Drinking Water Act Amendments of 1986 stipulated that all drinking water had to be filtered unless the watershed was adequately protected. Eric Goldstein argued to the city that filtration was unnecessary if the water remained pure at its source—as it did in the Catskills. The millions of dollars that would be spent on a filtration plant were funds that would be taken away from protecting the watersheds and reservoirs from pollution in the first place.

The city agreed with Eric's argument, and we managed to hold off the filtration plan with a temporary waiver. But the city had no coherent long-term strategy for guaranteeing a clean water supply. The solution it came up with was to protect the land around the reservoirs from development by asserting eminent domain. This opened up a long-festering dispute with upstate residents, many of whom still resented the high-handed way in which New York had seized farmland and submerged villages to build the Catskills reservoirs in the first place. The situation was potentially volatile, and Pataki was determined to heal the rift. He also saw the importance of having environmentalists at the negotiating table, and Mike Finnegan (who later became an NRDC board member) suggested that we should bring in both Eric and Bobby Kennedy. Bobby was working at NRDC at the time as a staff attorney. He also served as director of Riverkeeper, where he had been deeply involved in protecting the purity of the Croton reservoir system, which supplied the 10 percent of New York City's water that did not come from the Catskills.

In the spring of 1995, Pataki came to an informal meeting at the Riverkeeper's headquarters in Garrison. Sitting at the table in jeans, with his shirt sleeves rolled up, he told us that although he didn't favor invoking eminent domain, he was determined to find a way to protect the water supply from septic systems and highway and agricultural runoff, while not threatening the livelihood of people in the upstate counties around the reservoirs. He said he would try to mediate the dispute personally.

It wasn't easy. Finnegan scheduled twenty-eight meetings between politicians, community activists, state and city officials, and environmentalists, with Eric representing NRDC. Those first twenty-eight meetings turned into more than a hundred. There were four main issues on the table: compensation for upstate residents; city money to buy land to protect the watersheds; the necessary environmental infrastructure, such as storm drains, stream bank stabilization, and controls on agricultural runoff; and, most important from Eric and Bobby's point of view, a guaranteed way of monitoring the enforcement of whatever settlement was reached.

The breakthrough came in October 1995, when Bobby publicly stated his support of the economic demands of Delaware County—where per capita income was well below the state and national average. Coming from a recognized environmentalist, one with such a famous name, this changed the tone of the dispute. Within a short time, the city agreed to spend $1.5 billion to buy approximately 120,000 acres of land in the Catskills, build the infrastructure required to protect the water supply, and give the upstate counties money for economic development. Before they would sign on to the 1,500-page agreement, Bobby and Eric insisted not only on independent monitoring but on having a seat on the committee that would distribute the city funds. On

November 3, 1995, after an all-night session of talks led by Mike Finnegan, we had a deal that would protect the city's precious water.

Meanwhile, having won the fight over the ads on city buses, Rich Kassel proposed the formation of a task force that would hammer out a plan to replace diesel with cleaner fuels such as compressed natural gas (CNG). The proposal needed the approval of the MTA's Capital Program Review Board, comprised of leaders of both houses of the legislature in Albany, the mayor's office, and the governor. Pataki readily gave his blessing, and a broad-based task force was established that included key stakeholders from the environmental, environmental justice, transit, and utility sectors. It was cochaired by Rich and Charlie Monheim, at the time New York City Transit's senior vice president for buses.

The group studied each of the city's nineteen bus depots to determine whether it was feasible to convert them from diesel to CNG. With each conversion a complex and costly engineering challenge, the discussions dragged on for many months. Monheim turned out to be a trusted ally. "He and I worked endlessly through the blizzard-choked winter of 1996," Rich recalls. "In fact, the two of us once met at the NRDC office via cross-country skis during one blizzard, just to keep the talks going!"

In the end, the MTA agreed to a pilot CNG program at three bus depots, in the South Bronx, Brooklyn, and West Harlem. All were in poor minority neighborhoods, which made an important statement about the environmental justice dimension of the diesel problem. Over the next seven years, five hundred diesel buses would be converted to CNG, which emits almost no particulate matter, few toxic chemicals, and many fewer smog-forming nitrogen oxides.

The agreement was announced at a ceremony at the New York Coliseum, where Rich and I shared the podium with Governor Pataki and the chairman of the MTA, E. Virgil Conway. Even as we stood there, I knew Rich was thinking that this was far from the end of the story.

Three out of nineteen depots . . . little more than 10 percent of the city's buses . . . seven years. It would take decades and cost a fortune to convert the entire fleet. We would surely be back at the negotiating table before very long, looking for a bigger and better deal. Even then, could any plan for New York's buses be replicated elsewhere? Every city, every school district, every trucking company in the country was using fleets of dirty diesel vehicles. How could that change? Perhaps, Rich wondered, the work we had done in New York might be leveraged into new federal standards and a cleanup of the entire diesel industry.

———

Our Los Angeles office had also been hard at work on diesel pollution, though the approach it took was rather different, being more directly focused on local issues of environmental justice. Los Angeles was notorious as the smog capital of the United States, the result of the "thermal inversion" caused by the unique geography and climate, as well as the freeway system and car-centric culture. Although only 2 percent of the vehicles in the city were diesel, they accounted for 30 percent of the smog-causing nitrogen oxides. In 1988, as the NRDC office was about to open, James Lents, the head of L.A.'s Air Quality Management District, said, "If you took the air-pollution problems in Houston, Denver, Albuquerque, and New York, and added them together, they wouldn't equal the problem in L.A."

Gail Feuer, who took over the program in 1993 when Mary Nichols left to join the EPA, was just as concerned as Rich Kassel with the eventual cleanup of the city's bus fleet. She also wanted to take a crack at trucks, which were flooding poor, mainly Latino neighborhoods with diesel toxins. She faced the same catch-22 as Rich—namely the difficulty of demanding a phaseout of diesel while no viable alternative fuel was available and the EPA was not pushing hard for one to be developed. But Gail had one advantage that Rich did not, in the form of California state law.

Proposition 65, the Safe Drinking Water and Toxic Enforcement Act of 1986, was intended to protect the public from chemicals known to cause cancer, birth defects, and other reproductive damage, and to inform citizens when they risked exposure. For instance, if a ceramic bowl or plate contained lead, the manufacturers had to remove the lead or list it on a warning on the packaging. The law was enormously successful in getting lead out of consumer products.

By this logic, Gail reasoned, Prop 65 should also apply to diesel. After all, the state had listed diesel exhaust as a toxic pollutant, but no one using the fuel was warning the people living near the supply centers, fueling stations, or factories that they were being exposed to risk.

Her first task was to prove the risk, and that meant collecting precise on-site data. Working with the Coalition for Clean Air and the San Francisco–based Environmental Law Foundation, which specialized in Prop 65 cases, Gail decided to look at the low-income, Latino neighborhood around a huge trucking distribution center in South Los Angeles. They don't build these places in Beverly Hills, she noted dryly. Four of California's largest grocery store chains used the facility, and more than a thousand eighteen-wheeler diesel semitrucks came and went from it every day.

It was NRDC's first big undercover operation, and it was more than a year in the planning. In January 1998, Gail and her partners assembled their team of ten expert consultants and a group of student and NRDC volunteers and staked out the transfer center twenty-four hours a day for a week. They set up two monitoring stations, one to measure emissions upwind and one downwind, where the diesel fumes would be much more intense. Two rented vans with video equipment recorded every truck entering or leaving the facility, while the volunteers hunched over walkie-talkies whispering messages like "The bird is flying. Code Green!" and Gail sat in a nearby backyard among children's toys and tricycles radioing back instructions.

By the end of the week, they had all the evidence they needed. The levels of carcinogenic emissions from the truck exhausts were between ten and a hundred times the legal limit. The case that Gail and her colleagues had made was so persuasive that California Attorney General Bill Lockyer joined the lawsuit that they filed against the four supermarket chains—Lucky, Ralphs, Stater Bros., and Vons (and its parent company, Safeway). The companies filed motions to dismiss the case but lost. In 2000 we reached a settlement, and they agreed to issue warnings to the neighborhood. More important, they agreed to reduce the idling time for diesel trucks, convert the "yard goats"—the small, single-operator vehicles that move semitrailers—to natural gas or propane, and build alternative refueling centers.

While he remained in constant contact with Gail in Los Angeles, Rich Kassel was preparing for the second round of negotiations that he had long known would be necessary in New York. By now Governor Pataki had arrived at the same conclusion as we had: the 1997 MTA agreement had been only a limited stopgap measure. Like us, he wanted a permanent, fleetwide solution, and this time he took a decisive, hands-on role to make sure that we got results.

Made up of a dozen members representing a range of different constituencies, the task force that produced the first agreement had been a cumbersome body. This time the decisions would be made much more rapidly by a small group of very senior officials. The governor's representatives would be his chief counsel, Mike Finnegan, and John Cahill, who served initially as commissioner of the state Department of Environmental Conservation and later became Pataki's chief of staff.

The process took only nine months, and the solution that emerged was not centered on clean natural gas but used CNG emissions as a baseline for new, clean diesel-fueled technologies being developed with Rich Kassel's active and direct involvement. The governor announced the agreement in April 2000, just in time for the thirtieth anniversary of Earth Day. The MTA would build the world's cleanest mass transit fleet. It would take more than a thousand of the oldest, dirtiest diesel buses off the streets, in some cases six years ahead of schedule. The remainder of the fleet (more than three thousand vehicles) would switch to ultralow sulfur diesel fuel and be retrofitted with advanced emissions controls by the end of 2003, and 300 CNG and 250 hybrid-electric buses would be added to the fleet. All new buses purchased would have to meet the same emissions standards as a CNG bus, regardless of what fuel they used.

We had won great simultaneous victories in the two cities with the worst air pollution in the nation. But Rich had always intended to go further than that. As he had told the press at the time of the 1997 MTA settlement in New York, that deal sent "a clear message to the diesel industry that it needs to eliminate its toxic soot emissions or it will be out of the transit business in New York." And, by implication, everywhere else.

Since 1996, Rich had been meeting regularly with EPA officials in Washington. He was astonished that NRDC was the only environmental organization that had staff working full-time on the diesel issue at the federal level, since diesel was responsible for chronic air pollution and a multitude of serious public health problems.

Rich, together with a growing coalition of diesel advocates and like-minded scientists at the EPA, the California Air Resources Board, and other state agencies, examined the EPA data on diesel emissions. As they did so, they began to realize that there was a big discrepancy between the results of engine tests in the agency's labs and the emissions levels being measured on city streets. It turned out that in the search for greater fuel efficiency (a key concern for truck buyers), companies had designed engines that emitted up to three times more smog-forming nitrogen oxides at highway speed than they would have done if operating at EPA-certified emissions levels. We had stumbled on a major scandal. For years, the fiercely competitive diesel engine industry had been engaged in a kind of arms race to figure out which one could cheat the EPA emissions tests most successfully—clearly the wrong way to go about improving fuel economy.

We decided that this was a fight that should go all the way to the top. We fired off a letter to the president, and Rich and I brought up the issue with Vice President Gore personally. The administration responded almost immediately, and a special investigation by the Department of Justice led to a series of consent decrees that imposed on the engine manufacturers the largest penalties levied up to that time under the Clean Air Act.

After the consent decrees were signed, the diesel industry was in disgrace. This presented a unique opportunity for us to press hard for much tougher national diesel pollution standards than we had thought possible, standards that would clean up dirty diesel once and for all.

But was there such a thing as clean diesel? The idea was anathema to many environmentalists, who had always seen CNG as the fuel of the future. Thanks to his experiences in New York, Rich had already begun to think that CNG should be considered not as the *bottom line*, but as a *baseline*. "I don't care if the fuel is diesel, natural gas, or grapefruit juice, as long as it is clean," he often said.

There were two ways for the industry to go at this point. It could continue to fight the federal government, or it could recognize which way the regulatory wind was blowing and adapt. Most manufacturers decided to stick their heads in the sand, but one, the Cummins Engine Company of Columbus, Indiana, came to us and said that it would like to become the pioneer in developing the new diesel technology.

The top executives told us that Cummins had always prided itself on its sense of civic responsibility and that they shared our goals— even though I imagine they had never sat down before with a real-life professional environmentalist. After that, Rich began to spend a lot of time with the Cummins engineers and R&D people as they worked to develop diesel truck and bus engines that would be as clean as CNG. The key to cleaning up car engines had been to remove the lead; in the case of diesel, it was to remove the sulfur. There was no inherent technological reason why this couldn't be done; it hadn't been anyone's priority until now.

As Cummins developed its clean diesel technology, Rich continued to work closely with EPA and state air pollution officials and a coalition of environmental and public health groups to press for even more rigorous federal standards, In December 2000, despite massive opposition from the oil industry, President Clinton signed the Highway Diesel Rule. By 2006 all diesel fuel sold for highway use in the United States would be the same ultralow sulfur diesel that had been pioneered in New York City. By the following year, particulate emissions from all new diesel engines would be cut by 95 percent. It was the clean air equivalent of taking thirteen million trucks off the road.

The year 2000 had been a time of amazing victories, in New York, in Los Angeles, and finally in Washington. Once the principle of clean diesel was established, the idea became unstoppable. After 2000, Rich Kassel moved on from buses and trucks to help develop and enforce comparable standards for farm and construction equipment, marine engines, locomotives, and other off-road vehicles. When all of today's diesel engines have been replaced by engines that meet the new standards, more than twenty-one thousand premature deaths and $160 billion in health-care costs will be eliminated every year. That's why the White House Office of Management and Budget has called the EPA's diesel rules the most cost-effective regulatory program since the birth of the Clean Air Act forty years ago.

Today Rich has taken the idea that first came to him as he pedaled down Fifth Avenue in a cloud of black smoke not only to the rest of the United States but to dozens of countries around the world.

Looking back on these accomplishments, he says, "When we started, we didn't realize what a big fight was ahead of us. But it worked!

And the diesel campaign taught us some principles that continue to guide our work: focus on the most serious problems; focus on providing cost-effective solutions that are adaptable and can be replicated in other settings; and start small and think big, because sometimes a local project may lay the foundation for a national solution."

Our Toxic Legacy

Toxic chemicals. Whether it was taking Alar off grocery shelves, producing paper without chlorine, or finding cleaner fuels for trucks and buses, toxics continued to be one of the central focuses of our work throughout the 1990s.

The laws that govern toxics are a confusing alphabet soup— TSCA, FIFRA, RCRA, and so on. Now we turned our attention to another: the cumbersomely named Comprehensive Environmental Response, Compensation, and Liability Act (CERCLA), better known as Superfund.

The law creating Superfund was unlike any previous environmental legislation; it was not preventive but remedial. Unlike RCRA, which set stringent controls on the disposal or destruction of hazardous materials to prevent future contamination, Superfund took aim at the toxic legacy of the Industrial Revolution. The program was a response to the public fear and anger that swept the country after the events at Love Canal in 1978. Old, abandoned, unregulated dumpsites, landfills, and brownfields seemed to be everywhere. No existing law gave the government the authority, let alone the funds, to identify those responsible for the pollution or to recoup the cost of cleanups.

The central principle of Superfund was "polluter pays," and it established a system of what lawyers call strict, joint, and several liability. In other words, a company had *strict* liability if it caused the pollution, regardless of whether its conduct was negligent or illegal at the time. Banks, insurance companies, and previous owners were often involved, especially since some Superfund sites dated back a hundred years or more; so *joint and several* liability apportioned the cleanup costs to any parties who had contributed to any portion of the contamination. If those responsible refused to clean up their sites, the EPA could do so itself and assess the offender for three times the cost. If no responsible party could be found, the government would get the money from a trust fund created by taxes on the chemical and petroleum industries.

The law sounded great, and its promoters optimistically believed that all sites on a National Priority List could be cleaned up within a decade or so. But things turned out to be much more complicated, from both a scientific and a legal point of view. Every state had hundreds of potential Superfund sites. Some estimates placed the national total at thirty-two thousand, others as high as fifty-one thousand. Each site was different and had its own paper trail of ownership and liability. Hundreds of different chemicals were involved. Tracing the history and workings of a particular site was a bit like archaeology—the difference being that chemicals, unlike the physical relics of past civilizations, did not stay in one place. Instead they migrated through the soil, air, surface water, and groundwater along complicated and unpredictable pathways. Locating and containing the "plume" of contaminants were tough challenges for engineers. Once the problem was fully analyzed, a variety of remedial technologies existed. Some were effective, others were not, and many were unproven. The effective ones were often the most expensive.

The first few years of the program were a saga of incompetence and failure. The initial goal had been to remediate four hundred of the worst sites by 1985, but by 1982 only a handful had been completely cleaned up. The main culprits were Reagan's first EPA administrator, Anne Gorsuch, who was spending only 15 percent of the amount Congress had intended for the program, and the assistant administrator directly responsible for Superfund, Rita Lavelle, who was indicted for collusion with the chemical industry. Congress and the public concluded that, far from paying, the polluters were dictating government policy.

In 1986, with the EPA under new leadership, Congress reauthorized the Superfund program and tightened up its rules, over the president's opposition. The amendments explicitly required tough cleanup standards and expanded the cleanup fund to almost $9 billion. Congress wrote provisions that limited the EPA's discretion in applying the law and specifically discouraged the kind of cheap, short-term "solutions" that the agency had preferred, such as capped landfills and slurry walls, and instead demanded remedies that "permanently and significantly reduce the volume, toxicity, or mobility of the hazardous substances, pollutants, and contaminants."

The original law had called for "cost-effective" ways of protecting public health and the environment. The EPA had interpreted this to mean using the cheapest available methods, regardless of whether they met the primary goal. Congress sharply reminded the agency that protecting the public was the sole purpose of the law. The plain meaning of "cost-effectiveness" was that if there was more than one way of achieving this, the EPA should choose the more economical one.

The new, revised Superfund law was an excellent statute, and there seemed no reason it shouldn't have worked well if the political will had been there. Unfortunately, it wasn't. As I've seen many times during my career, it is impossible to legislate good intent.

By 1988, more than twelve hundred priority sites had been identified, and $9 billion were at the EPA's disposal. Yet still almost nothing had happened. Where was all the money going? What was wrong with this program? Frustration with the agency's performance became so acute that NRDC and several other major environmental groups joined forces with the Hazardous Waste Treatment Council (an industry group made up of companies involved in high-quality cleanups) to produce a detailed, case-by-case analysis of what had been accomplished in the first full year since the amendment of the Superfund law. Jackie Warren, the head of our toxics program, represented NRDC on the coalition, together with two colleagues, Jane Bloom and Doug Wolf. The principal investigator was a PhD in public health, Linda Greer, who had worked for several years with the Environmental Defense Fund and whose special expertise was pesticides and how they break down in soil.

The group found that while the law mandated the EPA to use permanent treatment technologies such as extraction, burning, and "bioremediation" "to the maximum extent practical," the agency had done so in only 8 percent of the sites it claimed to have remediated in 1987. In two-thirds of all cases, it had applied no treatment at all. Most of the actions it *had* taken had the same flaws that had plagued the program in its early years, with a continued preference for simply containing hazardous materials on-site in clay-capped landfills. This was a shell game; landfills were not a remedy, but a stopgap, a series of accidents waiting to happen. Standards were appallingly lax. Treatments were still being chosen because they were cheap, even in cases where the EPA knew they wouldn't work. Too many cleanup decisions were being based on site assessments carried out by contractors hired by the companies responsible for the pollution in the first place. Local communities had no voice in decisions affecting their health. At some sites, the "remedy" consisted of building a four-foot fence around the contaminated area and assuming that no one would climb over it. Clearly EPA officials didn't have adventurous children.

The nine EPA regions operated without any effective direction from Washington. Each site had its own documentation and its own suggested cleanup strategies, but this data was not even being collated into a single, centralized database. This case-by-case approach meant that the EPA was essentially reinventing the wheel each time, and not surprisingly there were egregious variations from region to region and site to site. For example, the "acceptable" level of benzene, a notorious carcinogen, was set thirty times higher at a site in Michigan than at a comparable site in New York. The coalition report concluded scathingly that "Superfund cannot operate like a restaurant franchise that lets each owner decide what he wants to serve."

This isn't to say that Superfund had no redeeming value. The fear of liability and the high costs of remediation, which averaged about $26 million per site, had given companies a powerful new incentive to avoid Superfund in the future by handling their hazardous waste much more carefully and preventing the spread of contamination. Many had cleaned up their act. At the same time, we recognized that not all the problems with Superfund could be attributed to the incompetence of the federal government. The program was uniquely complicated. By 1990, it was estimated that cleaning up all the Superfund, RCRA, and Defense Department toxic sites could take as long as thirty years and would cost in the neighborhood of $420 billion. Who was to bear that cost, and who was to decide if a particular cleanup was effective? How clean was clean? No one seemed able to answer those questions. Instead, as soon a site was placed on the Superfund list, it was dragged into a morass of litigation, which companies often found less costly than the prompt settlement of cleanup claims.

It was becoming clear that if we went on trying to untangle the Superfund mess through the conventional political process, we would never get anywhere. Two of my former colleagues at NRDC proposed an alternative source of pressure: an independent commission that would bring together as many of the interested parties as possible to propose a way forward. Congress was scheduled to reauthorize the Superfund program in 1995; this commission would give it specific recommendations for reform. The idea came from Gus Speth, who was now president of the World Resources Institute, and Jonathan Lash, whose book, *A Season of Spoils*, had chronicled the misdeeds of the Reagan administration, and who was director of the environmental law center at Vermont Law School.

Jonathan's argument was that while the disagreements were profound, all parties had a basic interest in simplifying the program and making it more predictable and consistent. That potential for common ground, he believed, had been obscured in the adversarial atmosphere created by so much litigation. He invited me to join the commission. "Never fear to negotiate," he wrote to me, quoting Churchill, and after some initial hesitation I agreed. With the prospect of a new administration in Washington (we met for the first time in December 1992, right after the election of President Clinton), I felt we might make real progress.

The Superfund Commission had twenty-five members. Among them were representatives from major green groups like NRDC, the Environmental Defense Fund, and the National Audubon Society; the CEOs of industry giants such as Amoco, the Olin Corporation, and Monsanto; the vice-chairman of Chase Manhattan; the dean of the school of public health at the University of California at Berkeley; and the president of the Oil, Chemical and Atomic Workers Union. Also included were environmental justice activists from the Navajo Nation and "Cancer Alley" in Baton Rouge, Louisiana, who wanted nothing less than 100 percent cleanups paid for by the corporations that had devastated their neighborhoods. I could never have imagined that a group like this would be sitting around the same table looking for common solutions.

We were each invited to nominate a staff expert to work with us, and I was fortunate to have Linda Greer in this role. Linda had been the lead investigator on the 1988 coalition report on Superfund and had been hired by Jackie Warren in 1990, since Jackie was based in New York and most of the Superfund action was in Washington. With her background in environmental toxicology, Linda was the perfect choice. She understood how toxics interacted with the environment (some are very persistent, while others disappear quickly, for example, breaking down in sunlight), and she knew what happened when they entered the human body. She recognized the importance of analyzing how chemicals were being manufactured and used by industry in the first place, which was especially relevant to the Superfund program. Linda also had a strong history as a lobbyist, having played a leading role in the reauthorization of the Resource Conservation and Recovery Act in the 1980s. NRDC went into this process with a strong grounding in both the science and the politics of hazardous waste issues.

Although huge arguments ignited along the way, and many irreconcilable differences remained at the end, the commission proved the skeptics wrong. Many people with long experience of Superfund politics said that CEOs would never talk to environmental leaders and community activists. When that happened, they said that while the corporations might lend their names to the process they would never sit down at the table with us. When that happened, they said that such a diverse group would never in the end reach agreement about anything. And when that happened, they said that the group would not stand together in support of the agreement once it faced scrutiny from the practitioners of politics as usual on Capitol Hill.

But we did all these things. After six meetings, we issued a sixty-seven-page report that offered detailed recommendations on everything from streamlining the cleanup process, setting consistent cleanup standards, using the best available remedial technologies, and simplifying the procedures for establishing liability, to strengthening community involvement, rectifying the clear biases in the program, and expanding research into the public health risks of the chemicals most commonly found at Superfund sites.

Were we successful? In part. With Clinton and Gore in office, and with an excellent new EPA administrator in Carol Browner, we were optimistic about the future prospects for Superfund. But we had not anticipated the hostility of the 104th Congress, which was elected just in time for the Superfund reauthorization debate and brought radical new Republican leadership to the House of Representatives in the persons of Newt Gingrich of Georgia and Dick Armey and Tom DeLay of Texas. The new Congress refused to reauthorize Superfund, rejecting out of hand the consensus view of the commission. It particularly opposed any proposal for new taxes on chemical and petroleum companies to replenish the so-called orphan fund that would be used to clean up sites where no one could be identified as responsible for the contamination.

Nevertheless, I don't think the Superfund Commission was a failure. Citizen groups and local residents were invited more into the discussions of site cleanups. With funding dwindling, the cleanups were not always perfect, but they did increase in number. The EPA stepped up its legal actions against individual corporations, and with the combined threat of RCRA and future Superfund designation, industry generally became more careful about the ways in which it used and disposed of chemicals.

Our daughter Kate Adams, who is senior vice president and general counsel of Honeywell, a Fortune 500 company that manufactures environmental controls, aerospace products, advanced fibers, refrigerants, and high-performance fuels, has spent years working with industry to clean up Superfund sites. Nowadays, she says, "The perspective of companies is to clean up the old mess and run our business in a way that protects us all from future Superfund sites. Cleaning up the 'legacy sites'—those sites where toxics were disposed of before Superfund existed—is a cost of doing business. It is in our company's interest to identify the right solution and move proactively with the administrators in government and get it done. Our goal is to manage these sites in a manner that is protective of human health and the environment, in consultation with the regulators and local communities, and we strive to be 100 percent compliant." I think Kate's attitude is typical of many of the younger generation of corporate officials in potentially hazardous industries.

After years of work with Superfund, Linda Greer had grown frustrated. "I began to compare the program to the pathology department of medicine. The mistakes had already been made, and there was only so much you could do. So I was motivated to look 'upstream' to see what companies were doing with chemicals in the beginning of the production process." This was unexplored territory; industry had historically wanted to keep environmental regulations as far away from their internal production processes as possible.

Thanks to Linda, NRDC had developed a great reputation for its work on the Superfund Commission. Therefore, it wasn't an issue we dropped lightly. But it was getting harder all the time to find funding for our Superfund work, and Linda persuaded me that it was time for our program on public health to "move upstream" and try a fresh, prevention-oriented strategy.

From our experience of dealing with big companies over the past several years, we knew that there were good guys in the corporate world, and there were bad guys. But there were also companies who had done bad things but could learn to do good ones—because they were nervous about liability issues or because they saw that being good corporate citizens was good for their brand, or simply because taking steps to reduce their environmental footprint might make them more efficient and profitable.

Linda wondered if we could work directly with individual corporations to help them minimize toxic wastes and emissions at the source while also looking for improvements in the efficiency of their production process that would save them money. She decided to start with Dow Chemical, one of the giants of the industry, which led to some criticism from other environmental groups. "How can you work with people like Dow?" Linda was asked. Her answer was simple: "It's like Willie Sutton said when they asked him why he robbed banks. It's where the money is."

In 1991, after an arduous day of negotiations with Dow about hazardous waste disposal, Linda fell into conversation over a drink with

Dow's environmental manager, Richard A. Olson. Both were frustrated. Linda saw federal regulations as an opportunity for Dow to clean up its act; Olson saw them as an impediment. The debate turned into a challenge: if Dow sincerely wanted to reduce pollution, Linda suggested, why didn't the two of them work together to figure out how? Olson was intrigued, and they agreed to go on-site at Dow's facility in LaPorte, Texas, and do a thorough analysis of the potential for changes in the production process that would work to everyone's advantage. "We never had the sense of being one big, happy family," Linda remembers, "but we were not screaming at each other across the room. The Dow CEO didn't refer to it as a collaboration; he called it 'a dynamic tension with informed activists.' We started from different places, but we all wanted results, so we rolled up our sleeves and got on with it."

We were lucky to find a pollution prevention expert in Texas, Bill Bilkovich, who was trusted by both sides. "These guys are not a dime a dozen," Linda stresses. While most engineers worked on pollution control devices—the so-called tailpipe approach, which emphasized technologies such as scrubbers on smokestacks—Bilkovich was a *process* engineer. What happens inside a chemical plant is that raw materials are mixed together under carefully controlled conditions; along the way, the process generates unwanted by-products and wastes, such as the solvents used to dissolve the chemical ingredients. Bilkovich understood how such processes could be improved to reduce waste and to use less water and energy.

With Bilkovich's expertise, we found multiple opportunities for cutting pollution at the source. Disappointingly, however, Dow regarded the LaPorte study as an "academic exercise" and did not implement our suggestions. There was nothing we could do about this, since we'd made the mistake of embarking on the experiment without an explicit prior agreement that Dow would follow our recommendations.

Faced with the prospect of bad press for its failure to act on the LaPorte study, Dow agreed to conduct a similar analysis of its giant plant in Midland, Michigan. This time Linda insisted on two conditions: the company would act on the recommendations, and the process should involve local environmental and public health activists who had a direct stake in the outcome.

Compared to Texas, Linda said, the Midland project—known as the Michigan Source Reduction Initiative (MSRI)—was "a deeper dive." Midland was one of the biggest chemical plants in the country, with more than four thousand employees, manufacturing more than five hundred different products, including Saran Wrap and a range of plastics, pesticides, pharmaceuticals, and industrial chemicals. It was the worst emitter in the state of Michigan of twelve especially dangerous toxics, including dioxin, a notorious carcinogen produced by the incineration of chlorinated wastes. Local communities had been fighting Dow for twenty years, especially over the health threat posed by the dioxin emissions.

Making the MSRI work required equal parts patience, persistence, and chemical engineering expertise. There was a huge cultural gap between the participants; many of the Dow executives had never met a real-life environmentalist before. Yet Linda was convinced that they were dealing with us in good faith and that this was not just a PR exercise. She understood that the trick was to stay focused on the areas of common interest that had brought us together and the practical solutions at hand, and to ignore the many areas of policy disagreement. The presence of five very strong and focused local activists was essential to the integrity of the project. So was Bilkovich's technical expertise. (The environmental health and safety officer at the Midland plant compared Bill's mastery of production processes to Michael Jordan's wizardry with a basketball.) Some of the money-saving solutions Bilkovich proposed were deceptively simple. For example, solvents that were being discarded after a single use could be reused several times with no loss of effectiveness. Certain chemical processes turned out to be just as efficient and to generate less waste when they were carried out at lower temperatures. And raw materials bought without impurities created much less dangerous waste streams.

The two-year project, which ended in 1999, was a huge success. Our initial goal had been a 35 percent cut in pollution from the Midland plant. In the end we achieved a 43 percent reduction in emissions and a 37 percent reduction in waste. Two-thirds of those wastes were of the more dangerous chlorinated variety. It might have taken years to achieve comparable results through regulation or litigation. For an initial investment of $3.2 million, Dow made $5.3 million a year in savings. The company got lots of good press as a result of the MSRI, which was given prominent coverage in the *New York Times*, *Fortune* magazine, and the chemical industry press. The whole exercise was an object lesson in the opportunities that were out there—provided someone looked for them. The specific conditions of the Midland plant were not transferable, of course, but we hoped the negotiating process would be, and we tried to publicize it as widely as we could as a model for a new kind of partnership between industry and environmentalists.

At the same time, we recognized the limitations. Our dealings with Dow Chemical taught us a lot about how corporate executives' minds worked. If a company could make $5 million a year from a one-time investment of $3 million and reduce pollution, we assumed it would do so. But we learned that this wasn't necessarily true. If other capital investments yielded a higher rate of return, those would be preferred. Not only did pollution prevention need to be profitable; it needed to be more profitable than any other investment being considered at the time. For the top decision makers at a company as large as Dow, which earned $1.3 billion in 1999, the sums we were dealing with were chicken feed. We were a long way from changing the corporate culture or greening Dow Chemical.

In the end, our experiment in appealing to the corporate bottom line to drive environmental initiatives proved limited. There was simply too much competition for capital investment at Dow Chemical. We also learned that despite the significant new opportunities, corporations were not necessarily going to seize them just because they liked us, or for the sake of good public relations. We still needed to hold in reserve the weapons of litigation and public pressure. If we showed companies like Dow that we understood the economic and technical details of their operations, and if we negotiated with them in good faith, we might win their respect. But they also needed to be afraid of what we would do if cooperation failed.

Contract on America

When Patricia and I went to Washington for the
Clinton-Gore inauguration in January 1993, the future
looked glorious. We watched George Bush board the helicopter and fly
away from the Capitol and then attended inauguration parties designed
especially for *environmentalists*. The Reagan/Bush era was over, the
Cold War was behind us, the economy looked promising, and with Al
Gore as vice president, we finally had the ear of people at the highest
levels in Washington. We looked forward enthusiastically to the next
four years. We were going to get a lot done.

Not so fast, our board warned us. "Don't forget," former
Ambassador Robert Blake reminded us, "the NRA has three million
members—and they will have an equally strong voice in Washington.
It doesn't matter if it's Democrats or Republicans, politicians will take
the middle road."

"If we're not pressing constantly and with a strong membership
behind us," Fritz Schwarz, our board chair at the time, insisted, "Even
the middle point will move away from us."

Fritz turned out to be absolutely right. Yet in those early days of
the new administration, it was hard to restrain our optimism. Although
Clinton didn't have a strong interest in the environment, it was Gore's
main passion. I had met the vice president in June 1992 at the big UN

Conference on the Environment and Development in Rio, and again in Moscow at an international inter-faith meeting of religious leaders. I found his manner somewhat aloof—very senatorial—but he was actively courting environmentalists, and many of us had actively supported him during the election campaign. His book *Earth in the Balance* had just been published and was on the best-seller list. Many Republicans derided him as "Ozone Man," which offered a foretaste of the bitter fights to come.

The first signals from the new administration could not have been more encouraging. The Democrats' campaign platform called for major cuts in pollution and waste; a new and improved Clean Water Act; the preservation of wildlands and forests; the use of market forces to punish polluters and create incentives for renewable energy and technological innovation; improved fuel efficiency standards; and a reassertion of the United States' global leadership on climate change and the environment in general. In his first major speech on the economy, in February 1993, Clinton called for an energy tax that would reflect the real "external" cost of fossil fuels—a step we had recommended in a major report, "America's Energy Choices," published two years earlier. The administration also showed real concern for the effects of pollution on poor and minority communities. The EPA's Office of Civil Rights began an investigation of environmental racism, and the U.S. Commission on Civil Right issued a report in 1993 on the disproportionate impact on African American communities from chemical plants and hazardous waste in Louisiana's infamous "Cancer Alley."

I began to spend a lot more time in Washington. The staff and I had open access to the new administration—from briefings in the White House Map Room to regular exchanges with senior officials. Environmentalists had worked hard to get good people appointed to top positions in the Clinton administration, and Secretary of the Interior Bruce Babbitt became a particularly close friend and ally. I even gave him a two-dollar bill that my mother had once given me as a good luck charm.

Our channels of communication expanded further as several of our top staff and NRDC alumni took high-level jobs with the new administration. David Doniger worked at the White House and subsequently became counsel to the head of the EPA's clean air program; Mary Nichols, one of the founders of our Los Angeles office, was now assistant administrator for air and radiation at the EPA; John Leshy of our forestry program became the Interior Department's solicitor; and Dan Reicher was appointed deputy chief of staff to the secretary of energy, later being promoted to chief of staff and then assistant secretary for energy efficiency and renewable energy. Gus Speth became administrator of the United Nations Development Programme, the highest-ranking American in the UN system.

This isn't to say that we always saw eye to eye with the new administration, especially when we thought it was dragging its feet on important matters. Perhaps the first sign of friction came when we urged the president to sign an executive order mandating that the federal government use only paper produced without the use of elemental chlorine bleach, a process that releases dioxins and furans, both powerful human carcinogens. Allen Hershkowitz and I went to the White House to present our case to a group that included Kathleen McGinty, head of the Council on Environmental Quality; Leon Panetta, director of the Office of Management and Budget and later Clinton's chief of staff; and Robert Rubin, assistant to the president for economic policy, who subsequently became secretary of the treasury.

Panetta told us that he would look into the matter only after we had prepared detailed scientific information and could present a compelling economic argument showing that the paper industry would not be hurt. Allen recalls that my response to this was to rise out of my seat, lean across the table to Panetta, and yell at him, "Come on! We can't wait for that—we've got to do something now!" Allen says he was sure that would be the end of the conversation—either that or they would call security. Instead, to our surprise, Panetta persuaded the president to sign the order. After that, he became one of our most reliable advocates in the administration. He and I became very good friends, and I felt I could always call him when I needed to be heard.

In June 1993 the administration created the President's Council on Sustainable Development, and I was invited to become a member. The term "sustainable development" was just coming into widespread use in those days; one oft-quoted definition is that such development "meets the needs of the present without compromising the ability of future generations to meet their own needs." Gore was the driving force behind the council, whose mandate was to bring together government officials, private sector leaders, and environmental advocates to help the country map out the path toward a self-sustaining future. Climate change was one of our main concerns, but that view wasn't shared by many of the industry representatives. This led to some of our more contentious discussions, especially after Clinton lost ground on the issue when he failed to get Congress to agree to an energy tax.

In addition to NRDC, the Environmental Defense Fund and the Sierra Club were represented on the Council on Sustainable Development, as were a number of Native American and environmental justice groups. The corporate leaders on the council included people like David Buzzelli of Dow Chemical, Harry Pearce of General Motors, Steve Percy of BP Amoco, Pete Correll of the paper giant Georgia-Pacific, and (perhaps surprisingly, given his later notoriety) Ken Lay of Enron. Jonathan Lash, who had taken Gus Speth's place as president of the World Resources Institute and had won a reputation as one of the country's most influential advocates of business-environmental cooperation, was invited to cochair the council.

The makeup of the group was somewhat reminiscent of the earlier Superfund Commission, but with one important difference: this time the full authority of the federal government was behind it, and a slew of cabinet officers sat on the council, including the secretaries of agriculture, commerce, education, energy, housing and urban development, interior, and transportation, as well as Carol Browner, the new administrator of the EPA.

The rules of the council meant that only I could speak for NRDC in meetings, but as far as I was concerned, the real leader of our effort was Frances Beinecke, our program director, who served as my staffer. It was Frances who did all the research, immersed herself in complex issues from fisheries to sustainable cities, met everyone, talked to everyone. As I observed her mastery of the facts, her diplomatic skills, and her sharp political instincts, I found myself thinking that if the time ever came for me to think about retirement, Frances would be my natural successor.

Our efforts on the council were an incredible education in the inner workings of Washington and the business community. Just as important was that we were on the road constantly. We went to workshops on the economics of organic food, on wind and solar power, on population stabilization. We attended public hearings with state governors, local officials, and political activists. Everywhere we went, we looked for projects that could be replicated elsewhere, trying to harvest the best ideas we heard so that they could be fed into deliberations at the federal level. Since a carbon tax or a carbon cap was not on the political agenda for the moment, we agreed with the EPA's Carol Browner that the best way we could attack the climate issue was to look at local initiatives involving energy efficiency, transportation policy, and land use planning.

Some of the cities we visited were obvious choices—we spent time with the Sustainable Seattle Coalition, for example, and with civic leaders in Portland, Oregon, which had built a model public transportation system and was widely regarded as the greenest city in the United States. We also found inspiring models in less likely places, such as Chattanooga, Tennessee, a derelict industrial city that had become a national leader in smart growth thanks to a visionary civic group, Vision 2000, and the leadership of city councilman Davy Crockett, a towering six-foot, six-inch giant of a man who was a direct descendant and namesake of the famous frontiersman.

When a delegation from the Council on Sustainable Development arrived in Chattanooga in January 1995, Crockett was highly amused by all the attention. "Many people still think of us as hillbillies down here in eastern Tennessee," he said, "and not as folks on the cutting edge of urban design and sustainable development."

Joking aside, Crockett was the first to recognize that Chattanooga had taken on a monumental task. It had a legacy of serious industrial pollution, blighted minority neighborhoods, and a devastated waterfront along the Tennessee River, which had been mutilated by the Army Corps of Engineers. In the early 1970s, the EPA called Chattanooga "the dirtiest city in America." When he brought in the renowned eco-architect William McDonough to revitalize the abandoned industrial area, Crockett warned him that greening the city might feel a bit "like teaching a mule to play the violin."

But steadily Chattanooga reinvented itself. In 1988 the EPA announced that it was "in attainment" of federal clean air standards. After that came a whole range of innovations—the downtown River Walk, free electric shuttle buses (and an electric bus manufacturing plant), the world's largest freshwater aquarium (with a child-centered environmental research center), urban farms, pocket parks, tree plantings, affordable housing, permeable paving to drain stormwater, oil-skimming devices in parking lots, and McDonough's zero-emissions eco-industrial park. At the time of our visit, Vice President Gore hailed Chattanooga for "[undergoing] the kind of transformation that needs to happen in our country as a whole."

Visits like these were an inspiration to me, expanding the range of NRDC's contacts nationwide and creating friendships that last to this day.

The great strength of the Council on Sustainable Development was that it provided a forum for real dialogue, and each of the participants could speak his or her mind freely. Gore was a powerful presence in our meetings, and I think as he looked ahead to his own political future he thought that he could drive this engine of sustainability all the way to the White House. For the White House, including the likes of Georgia-Pacific, GM, and Enron on the council was designed as a way to build mutual understanding with corporate leaders as the White House moved its environmental agenda forward. For Frances and me, it was a great learning experience, strengthening our conviction that we couldn't get where we needed to go on the environment without corporate buy-in. And we wouldn't make any headway with these potential allies if every word that came out of our mouths was negative.

Throughout 1993 and 1994 we continued to meet in this spirit of cooperation and openness. But the latent tensions within the council increased as the midterm elections approached and the political winds began to shift strongly to the right. "The administration had made a lot of missteps in its first two years," said Wesley Warren, who served on Clinton's Council on Environmental Quality and later joined NRDC, becoming our program director in 2005. "Everything from [attorney general nominee] Zoë Baird's nanny and $200 haircuts to the Travelgate firings. Then health-care reform crashed and burned." In the House of Representatives especially, the Democrats had become dangerously complacent, failing to recognize the growing strength of the "angry white males," as the media called them. Many former Democrats had defected from the party during the Reagan years, and younger "Blue Dog Democrats" were calling for fiscal conservatism.

The administration's failed proposal for an energy tax, an initiative that Clinton had put forward without building the necessary support in Congress, had turned into a political liability, another opportunity for Republicans to paint Al Gore as an "environmental extremist." As the congressional elections drew near, we began to get the distinct feeling that the administration's enthusiasm for our issues was waning.

Rodger Schlickeisen, the president of Defenders of Wildlife, spoke for many of us when he said, "We thought we had Gore and were in 'high cotton.' But the administration turned its back on the environment, telling us that we didn't have to worry about it, things would work out."

In November 1994, the Republicans, led by Newt Gingrich of Georgia, gained fifty-four seats in the House of Representatives, winning control of the chamber for the first time in 40 years. The 104th Congress wasted no time in setting a new, radical tone on the environment. The first action of the Republican chairman of the House Committee on Natural Resources was to remove the word "natural" from its name. Congressman Tom DeLay of Texas famously described the EPA as "the Gestapo of government." To balance the budget, both the House and the Senate passed resolutions to sell off assets including national parks, forests, rangelands, and wildlife refuges. Another resolution called for opening the Arctic National Wildlife Refuge (which Senator Frank Murkowski of Alaska preferred to refer to as the Arctic Oil Reserve) to drilling. As in the early Reagan years, some Republicans called for all BLM lands to be returned to private ownership. The House introduced a bill to weaken the Clean Water Act. How could anyone even conceive of such a thing, I wondered, when just twenty-five years earlier rivers had been catching fire and raw sewage was floating down the Hudson? Did this new generation of legislators not care about these things, or were they just too young to remember?

We immediately felt the political earthquake in the Council on Sustainable Development, which was transformed almost overnight from a cooperative partnership to a group of warring factions. Within weeks of the election, lawyers for Georgia-Pacific were helping to write the rules for what we had taken to calling the "Dirty Water Act." I was so outraged by this that I confronted Pete Correll, the head of Georgia Pacific, directly at our next meeting. "How can people serve on a Council on Sustainable Development," I demanded, "and then turn around the next day and try to gut the very environmental laws that are necessary for sustainability? If Georgia Pacific goes out and gets the rules changed to favor them economically, I don't see any reason for us to go on sitting in these meetings."

Interestingly, one of those who took my side in the dispute was Ken Lay of Enron. I found him to be a political moderate all the way through, a quiet, thoughtful presence who always did his best to smooth over differences and keep the dialogue going. I think in part this reflected Enron's heavy investment in natural gas, which Lay correctly saw as an important component of a future, lower-carbon economy. Unlike Georgia-Pacific, Lay's company saw no economic gain from rolling back the nation's environmental laws. As for Correll, he was clearly embarrassed by being called out in public, and it was obvious that neither he nor any of the other corporations wanted to press the fight to a point where we environmentalists would walk out, leading the council to fall apart.

The council did, however, lose momentum, and even Gore seemed to lose interest. Since there was so much opposition to his sustainable development agenda, he seemed to feel that it was not worth spending so much energy running around the country to promote it. The council continued to meet and managed to hash out a final consensus report, with NRDC staff experts going over every single line of the draft and striking out any language that was unacceptable to us. Although the report was phrased in very general terms, and its recommendations were nonbinding, it did reaffirm the core importance of the nation's environmental laws. There was a good deal of hypocrisy on the part of some of the corporations who signed on, since their lobbyists and trade associations had gone right on supporting congressional efforts to eviscerate those laws. Even so, the report was better than nothing, and more important, by the time it was published in the spring of 1996, we had been through the fight of our lives with the 104th Congress—and won our greatest victory.

Newt Gingrich is best remembered for the Contract with America, a crash program of legislative reforms that the Republicans promised to push through in the first hundred days of the new Congress. This artfully written document was full of appealing populist rhetoric about reducing regulations, cutting taxes, balancing the budget, and "getting government off people's backs," all of which sounded reasonable and long overdue. Tom DeLay said that the purpose of the Contract with America was to "make sure that American small businesses and the American taxpayer don't become the next endangered species."

The contract never used the word *environment*, but its provisions added up to a deliberate stealth attack on twenty-five years of environmental protection. It proposed to limit the regulatory authority of the federal government by barring unfunded mandates to states and localities; requiring the government to carry out a "cost-benefit analysis" before issuing any new regulations; and curtailing restrictions on land use by obliging the government to compensate landowners for any financial losses caused by federal regulations. How exactly this was to be accomplished legislatively would be buried away later in a morass of incomprehensible detail and obscure riders to unrelated spending bills.

Patricia and I were driving back one day from our cabin in North Carolina when I turned to her and said, "OK. This is the time to have a fight. Let's get started." We brainstormed as we drove along Interstate 81 from Tennessee, up through the Shenandoah Valley, and on into Pennsylvania, and by the time we got to New York, I had a plan. We needed to do three things simultaneously: unite all the major environmental organizations into a single powerful force; create a strong NRDC advocacy program in Washington to strip away the rhetoric of the Contract with America and reveal its true purpose; and take our case to the country at large, using the media as creatively as we could to build massive grassroots opposition to the Republicans' plans. With the advent of the 104th Congress, much of the environmental movement seemed to think the world had ended; to me, it had just begun.

Time was of the essence, however. The Republicans were vowing to act within one hundred days, and the Clinton administration was in disarray. While Gore tried to hold the line on the legislative agenda—if not the Council on Sustainable Development—the president was less resolute. As Wesley Warren recalls, "There was a contingent at the White House that was telling Clinton he needed to reposition himself in the middle and throw something overboard, and they thought the environment could go."

Thanks to the hugely successful capital campaign that Jack Murray had organized together with board member Adam Albright and Wendy Gordon Rockefeller, the head of Mothers and Others, we had raised an unprecedented $19 million. Our immediate priority was to use some of that money to create our new advocacy center in NRDC's Washington office. Frances took the lead in defining what the center should do, and by January 1995, we had found the ideal person to run it.

Greg Wetstone was a graduate of Florida State University and Duke Law School, my alma mater. He had worked for Democratic congressman Henry Waxman of California and had been chief counsel for the House Subcommittee on Health and the Environment. He knew Capitol Hill inside and out, and he was an avid environmentalist, whose favorite activity was cruising the Chesapeake Bay in the family sailboat.

Greg hit the ground running. As he recalls, "On Monday I was invited to testify at the House Rules Committee. I testified on Wednesday, and I finally got the keys to the NRDC bathroom on Friday."

He was a brilliant strategist, with a laser focus and a no-nonsense philosophy: *Do what needs to be done.* This didn't always sit well with the senior program staff, who had been accustomed to doing their own advocacy and weren't happy about ceding control to a newcomer. But they soon saw the effectiveness of Greg's approach. For me, he was an invaluable guide to the ways of Washington, especially as I worked to unify the efforts of the leading environmental groups in our fight against the new Congress. My hope was that NRDC could provide the kind of intellectual firepower for our side that the conservative

Heritage Foundation and the libertarian Cato Institute were providing for our opponents.

During the first two decades of the modern environmental movement, many organizations had formed and developed independently. There was the usual competition for funds and supporters, but the different groups also had different missions: some focused on wilderness and wildlife and some on outdoor recreation; some were membership organizations, and others promoted their ideas mainly through publications. As early as 1980, Bob Allen had seen the need for better coordination within the environmental movement and pushed us to form the Group of Ten, which included groups both old and new: the Environmental Defense Fund, the Environmental Policy Institute, Friends of the Earth, the Izaak Walton League of America, the National Audubon Society, the National Parks and Conservation Association, the National Wildlife Federation, the Sierra Club, the Wilderness Society, and NRDC.

Under Bob's gentle, humorous guidance, we met regularly and formed a congenial and productive group. But as the 1980s wore on, more and more organizations joined the field. Bob funded a study, authored by former Sierra Club president Michael Fisher, to assess our needs. The result was the much larger twenty-seven-member Green Group. We had fewer things in common, and there was a marked lack of enthusiasm for working together. With the advent of the 104th Congress, this became untenable. It was a classic case of united we stand, divided we fall. Peter Berle, the president of the Audubon Society, was the first chair of the Green Group, and when his term ended in 1995, I agreed to take his place. We realized that we couldn't go on operating as an informal volunteer group, and with the support of Frank Hatch, an NRDC board member and head of the John Merck Fund, we created a proper institutional structure, setting up an office in Washington with a professional administrator and staff.

Meanwhile, Greg Wetstone designed his counterattack against the Contract with America, whose provisions he described as "mind-numbing in their sweep and damaging impact." The key, he decided, was to go through the document sentence by sentence and translate it into clear terms that both lawmakers and the general public could understand.

"It was like jumping into the fire," said NRDC attorney Sharon Buccino. "Greg and I did a 'down and dirty' analysis of the contract, and twenty-five staffers contributed their analysis of what it would do to their particular area of expertise. There were funding cuts for the EPA, changes to the Clean Water Act, and riders tacked on to budget bills that cut funding for various programs. It was a sneaky, back-door way of doing things, and our task was to expose the *nontruth* of these supposed reforms."

In February 1995 we published the results of our down and dirty study: "Breach of Faith: How the Contract's Fine Print Undermines America's Environmental Success." We launched it with the support of Washington's old environmental aristocracy—former Democratic Senator Ed Muskie of Maine, former Senator Robert Stafford of Vermont, a moderate Republican, and former EPA administrator Russell Train, who said the contract would "create a procedural nightmare and endless litigation that would hamstring effective administration of our environmental laws and effectively roll back environmental protection across the board." Which was, of course, its whole purpose.

Greg came up with a brilliant response, drawing on the Republicans' own playbook. In 1993 conservative opponents of Hillary Clinton's plan for health-care reform had made a chart showing how the decision-making process would work. It looked like a map of the New York subway system. Greg prepared a similar chart to show the complexity and expense of Congress's plan for cost-benefit analysis. The legal and bureaucratic labyrinth it would create would magnify the role of big government, not get rid of it. It was an early hint of how the House Republicans might have overreached and how they might eventually be defeated.

There were still a good number of moderate Republicans in those days, and the challenging job of winning over their votes fell to our longtime clean air expert, David Hawkins. Politicians might not generally take what NRDC said at face value, but during his four years as the EPA's assistant administrator for air, noise, and radiation in the Carter administration, David had won a reputation for straight talk among both Democrats and Republicans. Now he provided wavering legislators and their staff with a sophisticated but clear and fact-based analysis of what the effects of the Contract with America would be.

———————

Despite our best efforts, things were not going well, and as spring turned to summer the Gingrich forces were on a roll. All the main anti-environmental provisions of the Contract with America were wrapped up in an omnibus regulatory reform bill, HR 9. Backed by many conservative Democrats, and with the help of a massive lobbying effort by the American Manufacturers Association, the electric utilities, and the plastics and food manufacturing industries, the bill sailed through the House of Representatives. The unholy alliance of young ideologues and traditional industry lobbyists was clearly willing to trade our environment for a buck. Their beliefs were the exact opposite of mine; we seemed to be living in two different Americas. But they were winning.

The high watermark of the Gingrich revolution probably came in July 1995, when President Clinton agreed to perhaps the most environmentally retrograde law enacted over the last two generations—the so-called salvage logging rider. Like a lot of the Republicans' initiatives, it was attached to a totally unrelated spending bill, this one designed to provide financial aid to victims of the Oklahoma City bombing and the civil war in Bosnia. The rider expedited logging on national forest lands and opened up timber sales for areas of forest in Northern California, Oregon, and Washington State that had been placed off-limits a year earlier under Clinton's Northwest Forest Plan—famous (or to others infamous) for its concern to protect the habitat of the northern spotted owl.

The summer of 1995 also marked the turning of the tide. Vice President Gore had told the Green Group that we should not be discouraged: the House Republicans would eventually overplay their hand. There were already some signs of disquiet among Republican leaders in the Senate, starting with Majority Leader Bob Dole, who had introduced a Regulatory Reform Bill that toned down some of the radicalism of HR 9. As Dole positioned himself for the 1996 Republican presidential nomination, the bill drew a lot of attention, especially because of the debate about its provisions on cost-benefit analysis.

The idea sounds innocuous enough: the costs of government regulation should not outweigh its benefits. But most of the regulations that were targeted involved three government agencies: the EPA, the Occupational Health and Safety Administration, and the Food and Drug Administration. How did cost-benefit analysis apply to them? For example, the economic benefits of a particular pesticide are easy to demonstrate; if less of the crop is lost, the producer makes a larger profit. But if the pesticide harms the consumer, how can that be measured in dollars and cents? The harm may take years to manifest itself, and it's always difficult to prove beyond a doubt that a particular chemical was the culprit. Disputes over the burden of proof can tie the matter up in the courts for years. Similarly, if the EPA guarantees that the air is

GREEN GROUP LEADERSHIP MEETING WITH
VICE PRESIDENT AL GORE, 1997

clean, you can easily calculate the cost to manufacturers, utilities, and automakers of installing new antipollution technology, but how do you quantify the economic benefits of improved health, increased longevity, and lower asthma rates in children? The callousness of the cost-benefit advocates was exposed during the debate on the Dole bill. When it was argued that air pollution was the leading cause of premature death in the United States, usually in the elderly, the attitude of the bill's proponents was, "So what? They were going to die soon anyway."

Another vital member of our team at this point was Bobby Kennedy. Bobby had terrific access to senior politicians, and Senate Minority Leader Tom Daschle told him, "We know this is a bad bill, but that's what we're hearing from our constituents. If you want us to stand up to it, you've got to get some activity going. We can't do anything unless you get out your troops."

We did just that. Bobby hit the road, speaking to over fifty thousand people in eighty towns and cities, explaining to them with his usual eloquence how the Republicans' legislation would take away our environmental protections. Greg Wetstone took our case to the media, although that wasn't always easy. Remember that this was the summer of the O. J. Simpson murder trial, and when Greg was interviewed by Greta van Susteren of Fox News, she asked him, only half jokingly, what the Senate bill had to do with O. J.

Again, Greg took a page from the Republican playbook. Arguing for passage of the Dole bill, the Republicans had successfully used the "victim of the system" tactic—publicizing the plight of a sympathetic individual who had been prosecuted for some minor environmental infraction, or whose land had been taken by eminent domain. We needed to put a similarly human face on our demands for environmental and public health regulation.

We saw our opportunity in a proposal in the Dole bill to gut the safety inspectorate at the Department of Agriculture, the purpose of which was to safeguard the nation's meat supply. Presenting his arguments against the cost-benefit policy at a press conference, President

Clinton introduced a lifetime Republican who told the tragic story of his child, one of four who had died in 1993 after eating a Jack in the Box hamburger contaminated with E. coli. The meat-packing industry was a major political force in Dole's home state of Kansas, and the Jack in the Box episode became a big story. Suddenly people were talking not about the Senate Regulatory Reform Bill, but about "Bob Dole's Bad Meat Bill."

As the debate heated up, Bobby Kennedy introduced us to Garry Trudeau, creator of the *Doonesbury* cartoons. With Greg feeding him information about the Dole bill, Trudeau's daily comic strips during the month of August kept up a steady drumbeat on the subject. Bobby gave one of the more devastating strips to his uncle, Ted Kennedy, who waved it in the air during the Senate debate and admonished, "Vote the wrong way on this bill and you'll find yourself in *Doonesbury*." Never underestimate the role of comedy in politics.

The decisive showdown came over the 1996 budget, when the Republican leadership once again introduced a string of insidious antienvironmental riders, nearly sixty in all. "They had nothing to do with the budget," Wesley Warren recalls. "They were attached secretly behind closed doors on behalf of polluters who contributed big money."

Congress presented the president with a "Sophie's Choice": if you want money to govern the country, you'll have to cut spending on your favorite programs. Sign the budget or shut down the government.

This time the radicals had gone too far. Moderate Republicans balked at the confrontation. The public saw a train wreck happening, and they saw that the environmental riders were at the heart of it. As Tom Daschle had requested, the Green Group had brought out the troops over the summer. Eighty-five sacks of mail were delivered to Capitol Hill on the eve of a vote on a new EPA appropriations bill. We had collected a million signatures on petitions demanding the defense of the

RALLY IN SUPPORT OF NRDC'S WORK CHALLENGING 104TH CONGRESS (1995–1996)
Left: Garry Trudeau, Cartoonist, *Doonesbury* comic strip;
Right: Robert F. Kennedy, Jr., Senior Attorney, NRDC

nation's environmental laws. Our switchboard was swamped with calls from people asking what they could do, from well-connected individuals offering to lobby on our behalf in Washington to the young woman in New York who promised to carry a wrench with her at all times so that she could tighten up any leaking fire hydrants that might be wasting water. On November 2, the EPA bill went down to defeat in the House, with sixty-three Republicans deserting the party leadership.

The government *was* shut down that winter after Clinton vetoed the budget bill, and the public overwhelmingly held the Republicans to blame. When the president finally signed the bill in April 1996, all of the worst antienvironmental riders had been dropped.

"These were defensive battles," Greg Wetstone says. "We were fighting to hold on to thirty years of progress. We had educated the public and created a grassroots reaction to 'just say no' to these proposals. And that would give the administration the courage to hold the line and also 'just say no.'"

It was probably the single most important environmental victory in United States history. In five months, we had turned back an apparently unstoppable attack, because public opinion rallied to our side. The 104th Congress had been so extreme, so crude in its tactics, that it had turned the environment for the first time into an issue of burning public concern. "We were ecstatic," Greg says. "Ours was the issue that the new House leadership had lost on." Tom DeLay confirmed this when he told the *Wall Street Journal*, "I'll be real straight with you. We have lost the debate on the environment. I can count votes."

I think the modern environmental movement came of age with the epic events of 1995. We came away from the fight reenergized, having learned a number of lessons that would stand us in good stead during the later presidency of George W. Bush. The coordinated efforts of the Green Group had been vital, and we had made brilliant use of the media. Above all we had seen the power of reaching out to every corner of the country, to grassroots activists, nontraditional allies, and the public at large.

The transformation of NRDC itself was palpable. We were operating at a different level. The fight against the 104th Congress had brought us eighty-five thousand new members. Now it was time for more organizational changes. Although I had been reluctant to change my title, I could see now that the time had come. In 1998, after I'd talked it through with Fritz Schwarz, the board appointed Frances Beinecke executive director, and I became NRDC's president.

The change freed me up from the daily management of the organization. I'd have more energy to devote to the other organizations I cared about, such as the League of Conservation Voters, the Woods Hole Research Center, and the Open Space Institute, which I chaired. I served on the Board of Visitors at Duke Law School and later at Duke's newly established Nicholas School of the Environment and Earth Sciences. As far as NRDC was concerned, I could concentrate on fundraising and political action. I'd spend more time on the road, visiting our other offices, and in Washington, working to consolidate the successes of the Green Group. With Frances taking care of the home base, I knew that we were in the best possible hands as we prepared to meet the challenges of our fourth decade.

The Last
Wilderness

Having talked so much about a paper mill in the Bronx,
diesel buses in New York and Los Angeles, cleaning up
Superfund sites, and fighting the 104th Congress, I hope I haven't given
the impression that NRDC's attention during the 1990s was focused
exclusively on urban pollution and Washington politics. Our passion to
preserve wild places never flagged. What changed was that we applied
the lessons we'd learned from these other programs to come up with
new and more creative ways to save these special places from the over-
exploitation of their finite natural resources.

The Call of the Wild is more than the title of Jack London's book
about a dog in the far north. It is also a call to the past, to a time when
most of the North American continent was wilderness. Wilderness has
always held a special place in the American mind, and whether or not we
experience it directly as individuals, it is part of our heritage. The greatest expanse of wilderness we have left is in Alaska, our "last frontier."

Stewart Udall, who oversaw a notable expansion of the national
park system as secretary of the interior in the 1960s, once said that we
Americans suffer from a "myth of superabundance"—the idea that
we have unlimited resources, that our fish, water, trees, and wilderness
are inexhaustible. Alaska is a prime example of that myth.

Alaska had been a priority for NRDC from our very earliest days. Despite the passage of the Wilderness Act in 1964—one of Udall's greatest accomplishments—no area of Alaska was protected as wilderness. Its vast forests and hidden mineral wealth were a powerful magnet for timber and mining companies, and in 1968 came the greatest threat of all: the discovery by Atlantic Richfield (ARCO) of oil, formed millions of years ago in tropical swamps that lay near the equator before the continents shifted.

After ARCO's discovery, at Prudhoe Bay on the Arctic coast, the issue of land ownership became acute, since getting the oil out would mean constructing a pipeline to the port of Valdez, across hundreds of miles of pristine tundra occupied only by Alaskan native peoples. Udall froze all land transfers in Alaska until the dispute over this vast territory could be equitably resolved. That did not happen during his tenure. It was not until 1971, under the Nixon administration, that the Alaska Native Claims Settlement Act was signed into law. The act opened up some of the disputed territory for the oil industry, which would become the engine for Alaska's economic development. The eighty thousand native Alaskans, meanwhile, abrogated their claims to most of the land in exchange for title to some forty-four million acres and almost $1 billion in compensation.

Some of our greatest environmental legislators—such as Congressman Mo Udall (Stewart's brother), Democrat from Arizona; Senator John Saylor, Republican from Pennsylvania; and Senator Alan Bible, Democrat from Nevada—served in Congress at this time. With the support of Nathaniel Reed, who served as assistant secretary of the interior under presidents Nixon and Ford and later became an NRDC board member, these legislators persuaded Interior Secretary Rogers Morton to champion a provision that was added to the act, requiring an additional eighty million acres to be identified as having the highest value as future national parks, wildlife refuges, and designated wilderness areas. These lands would be given interim protection until 1978. Conservationists, Alaska politicians and residents, and mining, timber, and oil drilling interests fought bitterly over the future of these "national interest lands." Alaska legislators struck back in the Senate. Democrat Mike Gravel filibustered, and Republican Ted Stevens succeeded in significantly weakening the provision in the Energy Committee. As the 1978 deadline approached, NRDC threw itself into the fight.

———————

Alaska was the special passion of our board member Michael McIntosh, who had been the driving force behind the opening of our West Coast office. His family owned the A&P supermarket chain, and his parents sent him to the company's salmon cannery in southeast Alaska to keep him out of the "country club set," as he puts it. He worked on a fishing boat, twenty miles out in the ocean, sixteen hours a day, pulling up nets of salmon. It was grueling work, but he saw mountains, coves, and seas teeming with life and grew to love Alaska fiercely. His parents also gave him, as a graduation present, a lifetime membership to the Sierra Club. These two things profoundly affected Michael and, in turn, NRDC.

In 1977 Mike and his wife, Winsome, invited nine of us to join him on a trip to see the areas that were being proposed for permanent protection. In addition to Patricia and me, the group included Larry Rockefeller and his cousin Ann Roberts, and our good friend Ham Kean. We flew with bush pilots in ancient planes—Widgeons, Otters, and a Grumman Goose—one of which had the words "One More Time" written across the nose. The state was alive with controversy about what should happen to the land, and we were not always welcomed in the communities where we touched down. The Sierra Club had helped organize the trip, and when we flew into the small airport at the town of McCarthy, in the future Wrangell–St. Elias National Park and Preserve, we were greeted with banners announcing "Sierra Club— GO HOME."

From the Wrangells we flew over the soon-to-be-designated Gates of the Arctic National Park in the Brooks Range and met with native

Alaskans in Kotzebue. Then, on our way down to the Kenai Peninsula, our 1940s amphibian Otter was forced down by bad weather. We landed on a sodden runway near the town of Red Devil, on the Kuskokwim River in what is now the Yukon Delta National Wildlife Refuge. We were stranded there for a couple days by pouring rain and bunked in with an Eskimo family, who ran the local bar, grocery store, and "airport." Finally our pilot, Jack, thought we could get out. However, we were not able to rise above the clouds, and as Jack circled around the fog-shrouded mountains looking for a pass, measuring our altitude and location by looking out his window, the hydraulic system failed.

When we finally landed in the river by the town of McGrath, people rushed out of the local bar to see us. We thought they were glad to see that we were safe after our disappearance, but people disappearing in Alaska for a few days was no big deal. Instead they wanted to give us the news: Elvis Presley had died.

Larry Rockefeller came back from the trip inspired by what he had seen. He immediately got in touch with Chuck Clusen, a key figure in the protection of this country's wilderness and public lands. Chuck, a quiet and unassuming midwesterner, was the leader of the Alaska Coalition. Beginning life as a joint effort of the Sierra Club and the Wilderness Society, the coalition had grown into an impressive alliance of state and national conservation groups and was detested by the Alaska congressional delegation and the oil, mining, and timber industries.

Larry asked Chuck—who would join NRDC several years later as our resident expert on Alaska and the national parks system—for his help in forming Americans for Alaska, a diverse group of a hundred leaders in business, labor, and civic affairs, including such prominent individuals as Lady Bird Johnson, Ted Roosevelt IV, Washington State Governor Daniel Evans, and Cathy Douglas Stone, the widow of Supreme Court Chief Justice William O. Douglas. They sent mailgrams to other dignitaries and followed up with phone calls, challenging them to "speak out in our last great chance to save the 'last frontier.'" They were hugely successful, even recruiting leading conservatives such as

William F. Buckley and General Matthew Ridgway, former chief of staff of the U.S. Army. While Chuck's Alaska Coalition kept up pressure on Congress and President Carter, Americans for Alaska played their part by visiting sixty-five senators individually, placing full-page ads in newspapers, and hosting events at the White House with President Carter's secretary of the interior, Cecil Andrus. Their message was that conservation and development were not incompatible; what mattered was to find the correct balance between the two.

In 1978, with Congress still deadlocked over a succession of Alaska bills, Chuck Clusen wrote to the president proposing a novel solution—to protect the "national interest lands" under the Antiquities Act of 1906. The creation of a national park required congressional approval, but the Antiquities Act, which had been passed originally to protect historic Pueblo Indian sites on federal lands in the Southwest, enabled the president to designate an area as a national *monument* by executive order. On December 1, 1978, Carter did this for Alaska, arguing that Congress had forced his hand by its failure to act.

The 1978 midterm elections had moved Congress sharply to the right, and with Carter's defeat by Ronald Reagan in 1980, the scramble was on to come up with a law to protect the Alaskan wilderness permanently before the new administration took office. All parties to the conflict recognized that there had to be a bill of some kind, even if it was not perfect. Thanks to the great leadership of legislators like Mo Udall, John Seiberling, Paul Tsongas, and Alan Cranston, a good compromise emerged: the Alaska National Interest Lands Conservation Act of 1980. It did not give conservationists everything they wanted, but even so it created more than a hundred million acres of new national parks and wildlife refuges and set aside another fifty-six million acres as designated wilderness. After Carter signed the act into law on December 2, 1980, the great environmental writer T. H. Watkins wrote, "With the scratch of the presidential pen that signed it, the act set aside more wild country than had been preserved anywhere in the world up to that time."

**WHITE HOUSE CEREMONY DESIGNATING PRESIDENT JIMMY CARTER
AN HONORARY CHIEF OF THE TLINGIT INDIANS OF SOUTHEAST ALASKA,
FOLLOWING THE SIGNING OF THE ALASKAN LANDS ACT, 1980**
Center of photo: President Jimmy Carter at the podium.
Left to right: Theodore Roosevelt IV; Cathleen Douglas (partially hidden);
Chuck Clusen, Director, National Parks and Alaska Projects, NRDC; Larry
Rockefeller, NRDC Trustee; former Senator Henry Cabot Lodge (R-MA).

The centerpiece of the act, and the most important battleground for
environmentalists since, was the expansion of the Arctic National
Wildlife Refuge (ANWR), first set aside twenty years earlier during the
Eisenhower administration.

Covering some twenty million acres in northeast Alaska, it is the
second largest and the wildest of all our national wildlife refuges. The
coastal plain portion of the refuge is often called America's Serengeti. A

vast continuum of biologically intact arctic and subarctic habitats—from the boreal forests of the interior and the central Brooks Range to the coastal plain and the Beaufort Sea—the refuge is a birthing ground for polar bears and grizzlies, Dall sheep and Arctic wolves, and the endangered shaggy musk ox, a descendant of the prehistoric woolly mammoth. It is also home to huge bird populations including the snow goose, the peregrine falcon, and the gyrfalcon. Above all, it is known by the great herd of 180,000 Porcupine caribou, whose annual migration is probably the most spectacular wildlife phenomenon in all of North America.

Since 1980, the fight to preserve the Arctic refuge has been one of the great symbolic causes of the modern environmental movement. Long coveted by the oil companies, its 125 miles of Arctic coastline remain the last piece of the Arctic littoral in the United States not open to drilling. We cannot afford to lose this fight. It's a threshold question; if the barrier to drilling in the refuge is breached, no part of our wilderness lands will be safe. What will be next? The Canyonlands of Utah? The Greater Yellowstone Ecosystem? It's also an issue where our members have been vitally important. Over the years we have generated hundreds of thousands of letters in support of the refuge, and polls have consistently shown that a majority of Americans oppose opening it up to oil drilling, even when the politicians and petroleum companies have made extravagant (and false) claims about the potential effect on prices at the gas pump.

Not surprisingly, the threat to the Arctic refuge began during the Reagan administration. At first blush, Interior Secretary Donald Hodel, a man with what *Amicus Journal* editor Peter Borrelli called "the demeanor of an undertaker," did not look like an extremist in the mold of his predecessor, James Watt. But he soon showed his true colors when he said that the solution to the hole in the ozone layer was for people to wear hats and sunscreen. In 1987 he set his sights on the Arctic National Wildlife Refuge.

We immediately went on to the counterattack. When the proponents of drilling said that it would lessen our dependence on foreign oil, we showed that it would barely make any difference. According to the U.S. Geological Survey, even at peak production the amount of oil that could be economically recovered from the refuge represents less than eighteen months' worth of the total U.S. supply—and, in any case, it would not reach the market for a decade.

In July 1987, with the oil companies holding up Prudhoe Bay as an example of how new extraction techniques could mitigate the environmental footprint of drilling, we presented a report to Congress showing that the opposite was true. Between four hundred and six hundred oil spills occurred each year on the North Slope and along the Trans-Alaska Pipeline. Contaminated water was being discharged into the tundra, and the wellheads were surrounded by makeshift dumps. There were also airborne emissions of SO_x and NO_x. In all, the violations of state and federal regulations numbered in the hundreds, and there was a complete lack of enforcement by federal agencies. Reporting was strictly on the honor system; the oil companies were left to police themselves.

The catastrophic oil spill from the tanker *Exxon Valdez* in Prince William Sound in 1989 brought home the risks to everyone, and the threat of drilling temporarily abated. After the disaster, we were contacted by Alaskan communities, native Alaskan groups, local environmental activists, and fishermen who were worried that Exxon would not pay for the cleanup. Their fears were well founded. We got hold of a draft agreement in which the federal government would have settled its claims against Exxon for a grossly inadequate amount. We helped torpedo this draft agreement by getting the word out to the press, and Exxon was forced to negotiate a fresh agreement under which it would pay more than a billion dollars to the federal and state governments for cleanup costs and natural resource damages.

After that we won dramatic improvements in the regulatory framework governing the oil industry. The next year, the 1990 Oil Pollution Act was passed, which mandated the use of double-hulled tankers. The emergency oil and hazardous substance fund was increased from $1 million to $50 million, and polluters faced much stiffer liabilities and penalties. In 1991 we spearheaded the successful campaign to defeat another bill in Congress to allow drilling in the Arctic refuge.

Anyone flying over Prudhoe Bay today will see what the Arctic refuge could easily have become—and could still become if we fail to keep our guard up. It is a huge industrial complex covering a thousand square miles of former tundra, with fifteen hundred miles of roads and pipelines, fourteen hundred wells in production, three jetports, and more than sixty contaminated waste sites. In the words of Chuck Clusen, "It is like flying over Gary, Indiana, for a hundred miles."

––––––

The Tongass National Forest, which dates back to the time of Teddy Roosevelt, is the other crown jewel of the Alaskan wilderness. Just as the oil industry coveted the Arctic refuge, so the timber companies looked at the Tongass and saw dollar signs.

In the 1970s and 1980s, the protection of the nation's forests was an issue of transcendent importance to NRDC, and indeed to the entire environmental movement. The U.S. Forest Service predicted that if current logging trends continued, all our unprotected old-growth forest (defined as trees more than two hundred years old) would be gone by 2030. One out of every four logs was being shipped out of the country.

In 1992 we did an internal assessment of forest conservation needs in the United States, identifying the most threatened areas and figuring out the most promising places to work with local partners, as well as the best tools to use for litigation. We decided to focus on the seventeen million acres of the Tongass, which is three times larger than any other of our national forests and contains nearly 30 percent of the world's remaining coastal temperate rain forest.

The Tongass embraces most of Alaska's southeastern panhandle, including the Alexander Archipelago, a five-hundred-mile chain of islands that range from small, rocky reefs to huge, forested landmasses. Like the Arctic refuge, it is an ecological wonderland, some of the richest and most biologically productive land on earth. Left uncut, its old-growth trees will live from two hundred to seven hundred years; the coniferous yellow cedar can survive for a thousand years or more. Thirty thousand grizzly bears live in the Tongass, as well as the world's largest concentration of bald eagles. Both are drawn here by the prodigious runs of salmon.

Yet the Tongass had been extensively logged. Since the 1950s—when the Japanese-owned Alaska Pulp Corporation (APC) and the Ketchikan Pulp Company, a subsidiary of Louisiana-Pacific, were granted fifty-year contracts by the U.S. Forest Service (the only contracts of their kind in the entire national forest system)—the Tongass had lost roughly a million acres of its richest old growth to clear-cutting and forest access roads. We feared that it was headed in the same direction as Prince William Island, farther to the north, which was now known as the "Bald Prince" because hardly a tree had been left standing. Under the two contracts, half a billion board feet of timber were being cut in the Tongass each year, most of it for pulp and much of it for export. But with the economic downturn in Japan in 1993, the demand for Alaskan pulp was severely reduced. A five-hundred-year-old tree producing piano-grade timber could literally be bought for the price of a hamburger. The Tongass, the biggest money loser in the national forest system, cost taxpayers tens of million dollars a year, so it was a perfect time for us to prove that cutting down old-growth forests was economic madness.

We had learned from our earlier visits to Alaska that it was important to come in with a low profile, look for local people who were already organized, and ask if we could offer something—technical and legal skills, or political influence—that might help their cause. Alaskans still tended to think of environmentalists as hippie outsiders, and the offshore commercial fishermen were a tough bunch who largely stayed aloof from the issue. We couldn't march into town and tell them we were going to save their fish. To work effectively on the Tongass, we needed to find the right local partner, a group that would represent people whose jobs were at stake and could be convinced that the fishing industry was a safer long-term source of employment than logging. The group we found was the South East Alaska Conservation Coalition (SEACC), which included a contingent of fishermen who were disturbed by the impact of clear-cutting on salmon streams, notably the erosion that buried the spawning beds under silt.

We began our Tongass campaign in classic NRDC fashion, with lawsuits, lobbying in Washington, and appeals to our membership. The effort was led by Niel Lawrence, our principal litigator on western forests. Law had not been Niel's first career. He had worked for a spell as a car mechanic and had spent a lot of time in the woods in California in the 1970s, watching with horror as the unbroken blanket of trees gave way to clear-cuts. Eventually he made his way to Harvard Law School, where he took a class with Ralph Cavanagh, an energy policy expert in our San Francisco office. In 1980 Niel said he wanted to join NRDC, even if it meant working for minimum wage. Ralph said what he always says: "No problem."

The more Niel learned about the U.S. Forest Service, the more horrified he became at its cavalier attitude to the national forests. Reading the agency's environmental impact statement on a proposal for "salvage logging" in the Marble Mountain Wilderness in Northern California's Klamath National Forest after the wildfires of 1987, he says, "I was staggered at the sloppy thinking. I had never seen an agency with such a siege mentality." In 1990 we took the Forest Service to court to challenge the Marble Mountain logging plan and won. The area remains pristine and roadless to this day.

Despite the economic crisis in the timber industry, and despite the Tongass Timber Reform Act of 1990, which had reduced the scale of the harvest and revised the Ketchikan and APC contracts, the Forest Service seemed determined to go on with business as usual. Together with SEACC and the Sierra Club Legal Defense Fund, we again took the agency to court. In 1993 APC closed down its pulp mill, and the following year the Clinton administration canceled the remainder of its fifty-year contract. Three years later, it was the turn of Louisiana-Pacific, which shut down its Ketchikan mill. That contract, too, was terminated.

Although these two mainstays of the Tongass logging industry had collapsed, the 1997 Tongass Land Management Plan still approved harvesting levels—267 million board feet of timber a year—that made no economic sense. Our drive to save the Tongass was in high gear now, and with a dozen other local and national environmental groups, we formed the Alaska Rainforest Campaign. Together we collected the expert views of biologists, economists, and foresters and filed more than thirty administrative challenges to the 1997 plan. As a result, two years later, it was extensively revised. The logging industry's Alaska Forest Association responded with a lawsuit of its own that overturned the modified plan.

The situation was becoming somewhat reminiscent of the endless unresolved battles over the Alaskan wilderness in the last two years of the Carter administration. Protracted litigation was never going to get to the root of the problem in the Tongass. What we needed was new formal rules for managing the roadless areas in our national forests, and they needed to be set in stone before Clinton left office.

"Roadless areas" are not the same thing as wilderness, although they have their origins in the Wilderness Act of 1964, which led to the creation of an inventory of all roadless areas in national forests that might be suitable for future wilderness designation. The Clinton administration was quite open to the idea of a roadless rule but was determined to lay the groundwork for it through a protracted process of public review and comment. Begun in 1997, the process led eventually to some six hundred public meetings and more than a million and a half comments, the vast majority being in favor of a roadless rule. The intent was to build legitimacy for the idea and safeguard it against any challenges by a future administration. But it seemed to take forever, and the 2000 election was fast approaching.

The battle went down to the wire, and I joined Niel for some furious last-minute lobbying in Washington. Niel made all the familiar arguments in favor of roadless areas: they protected wildlife and sensitive habitat, and rivers and drinking water, and they offered people a place of refuge and recreation. The latest science gave us a compelling new reason to protect the forests: they acted as "carbon sinks," vital assets in the fight against global warming.

In August 2000, in a stroke of good fortune for us, Clinton appointed George Frampton, the former head of the Wilderness Society, as the head of his Council on Environmental Quality. Niel immediately flew to Washington to enlist his support. At the same time I turned to White House Chief of Staff John Podesta, a widely respected public servant and a staunch environmentalist. Niel and I had a great meeting with Podesta, who worked right up to the last minute to make the roadless rule happen.

Eventually we got what we wanted. On January 5, 2001, President Clinton announced a ban on road construction and thus on commercial logging on nearly sixty million acres of U.S. Forest Service land in thirty-nine states. The roadless rule was the most significant environmental legacy of the Clinton administration and one of the biggest steps ever taken to protect our wild places, right up there with Jimmy Carter's Alaska National Interest Lands Conservation Act twenty years earlier. Normally, Congress is in the horse-trading business; you always come away with half a loaf. This time we got it all.

Not surprisingly, President George W. Bush tried hard to overturn the roadless rule, but all his efforts failed, and the Tongass remains.

Mike and Winsome McIntosh, who had first kindled our passion for Alaska, continue to be inspiring leaders of the environmental movement. In 1999 Winsome founded Rachel's Network—named for Rachel Carson—a group of women philanthropists committed to conservation causes. Michael still operates the Boat Company, which he founded in 1980. Each summer, two of Michael's boats take parties of conservationists, funders, and political leaders on a trip through the Alexander Archipelago to witness for themselves the majesty of the Tongass. His philosophy remains simple but profound: "When you cut something that is a thousand years old, you have to ask yourself: Why *do* this?"

Land of the Spirit Bear

In 1993 I received a letter from NRDC trustee Adam Albright. He had just returned from a trip with Conservation International to Clayoquot (pronounced Clak-wot) Sound, a beautiful mosaic of 650,000 acres of dense temperate rain forest and hundreds of small islands on the west coast of Vancouver Island that has many similarities to the Tongass. Although the coastal area where the tourist facilities were located seemed relatively pristine, what Adam found when he traveled into the forested interior was a vast area that was being devastated by logging. When he got back home, Adam wrote me a letter describing the clear-cuts he had seen. A man who loves nature and never passes up the opportunity for a quick swim, he refers to it now as "the Swimming Naked with the Salmon Letter."

Since those were the days before e-mail, I made photocopies of Adam's letter and sent them to a number of colleagues at NRDC. The letter caught the attention of Liz Barratt-Brown, a gifted lawyer in our Washington office. Liz's first assignment after coming to NRDC in 1981 had been to work on the impact of acid rain on the forests of Canada. Since 1991, she had been working with Jacob Scherr in our international program. After the Rio Conference on Environment and Development in 1992, an event that had produced a lot of talk but no binding agreements, she felt frustrated by the slow pace of change. To

Liz, an avid hiker and outdoorsperson, Adam's letter about an imperiled Canadian wilderness seemed a perfect opportunity to strike out in a fresh direction.

Over the next decade, Liz and her colleagues in our West Coast forestry program, notably Niel Lawrence and later Sami Yassa, who joined NRDC in 1990, would transform the way we thought about the long-term protection of our forests. Along the way, they would embrace and further enrich many of the lessons we had learned in the late 1980s and early 1990s. The fight for the Tongass showed that our public forests could be shielded from clear-cutting by federal laws and regulations. But if the insatiable demand for timber continued, the loggers would only move to less protected private forests and to other countries. Although saving wild places like the Tongass would always remain one of NRDC's highest priorities, our forestry team also turned increasingly to market forces as a tool of environmental protection. They appealed to the profit motive, as Allen Hershkowitz had done with the Bronx paper mill project; educated corporations in the economic benefits of efficiency, as Linda Greer had done through her partnership with Dow Chemical; demonstrated that harmful practices would end only when innovation created marketplace alternatives, as Rich Kassel had done in his drive for clean diesel; and unleashed the power of consumer choice and the media, as our pesticides team had done during the Alar episode.

In the case of Clayoquot Sound, this approach was driven in part by necessity. Canada was cutting down its rain forests even more rapidly than was Brazil. For half a century, the provincial authorities in British Columbia had treated clear-cutting as the norm. Forests were disappearing at the rate of an acre per minute, with most of the timber destined for the U.S. market. To make matters worse, the legal avenues we normally pursued in the United States were not available in

Canada. The country had few enforceable environmental laws and no Endangered Species Act, and environmental groups and ordinary citizens could not seek redress through the courts. The only people who could challenge the granting of logging licenses were the First Nations, and no one was consulting them.

Conflicts over logging in Clayoquot Sound had been building since 1979, when MacMillan Bloedel, Canada's biggest timber company, expanded its operations into a particularly sensitive area of old-growth forest that contained some of the country's oldest trees, including fifteen-hundred-year-old red cedars. Pressure on the provincial government mounted steadily until, in April 1993, it unveiled a land use plan for Clayoquot that it claimed would strike a balance between economic, social, and environmental interests. The plan encouraged a high volume of logging for the next five years in order to "maintain investor confidence" in MacMillan Bloedel (in which the British Columbia government was the largest shareholder). The government insisted that 25 percent of the old-growth forests would be protected from cutting—but that was another way of saying that 75 percent could fall to the chainsaw.

The protests that erupted after the plan was announced were unprecedented in Canadian history. Almost a thousand people were arrested during mass demonstrations. There were sit-ins, peace camps, acts of eco-sabotage, and blockades of logging roads. People lay down in front of bulldozers; Wiccan priestesses conducted anti-logging ceremonies; old ladies formed a group called the Raging Grannies. Demonstrators paraded "Stumpy," the five-ton remnant of a four-hundred-year-old cedar from a clear-cut. Greenpeace, which had been involved in the issue for several years, staged events that featured a sixty-foot inflatable chainsaw. The clear-cutting went on regardless.

In June 1993, Bobby Kennedy was invited to visit the Clayoquot Sound by the Nuu-chah-nulth tribal council. The trip that he took to Vancouver Island with Liz Barratt-Brown added an important new element to the campaign, planting the seeds of a friendship between the

First Nations and NRDC that would grow over the next two years into a powerful alliance of local, national, and international groups opposed to MacMillan Bloedel. The tribal representatives told Bobby and Liz that while they had supported a certain amount of logging as part of the local economy, they resented that no one had consulted them about the government's new plan, which directly affected their ancestral lands. Liz immediately bonded with the Nuu-chah-nulth, the local activists who called themselves the Friends of Clayoquot Sound, and what she described as the "Victorian tea ladies who wore yellow armbands saying 'Free Clayoquot from logging.'"

MacMillan Bloedel showed nothing but contempt for the protests. The company vilified the local environmentalists as fanatics who wanted to destroy the island's economy. Outsiders like NRDC were interfering foreign elitists who knew nothing about the local culture. To this Bobby replied crisply that since McMillan Bloedell was a huge multinational corporation, and most of its timber was being sold to buyers in the United States, the fate of Clayoquot Sound could hardly be described as a local matter.

At this point Liz secured a grant from the W. Alton Jones Foundation that brought together all the leading groups involved in the protests for a strategy session. Out of this emerged the Clayoquot Rainforest Coalition, and NRDC signed on as one of four members of its steering committee. (Later, as its reach expanded, the group was renamed the Coastal Rainforest Coalition; eventually it became ForestEthics, which works to this day to protect forests throughout the Western Hemisphere.)

Since MacMillan Bloedel seemed impervious to criticism, we decided to hit the company where it hurt. We would go not only to the places where the trees were being cut, but to the places where they were being sold. The buyers we targeted were powerful institutions that no supplier would want to offend: Home Depot, Scott Paper Company, phone companies like Pacific Bell (which made its phone books from Canadian pulp), and the *New York Times* (which had bought its newsprint from MacMillan Bloedel for years). Ultimately the campaign extended to four hundred companies, with Home Depot as its signature campaign. In the White House, our good friend Kathleen McGinty, the chair of Clinton's Council on Environmental Quality, worked closely with us to encourage Vice President Gore to weigh in on the issue with the Canadian authorities. Dozens of Hollywood stars signed on to the campaign, and we got tremendous media coverage.

Two years into the fight, MacMillan Bloedel caved. The newly hired director of environmental affairs, Linda Coady, acknowledged that it was time for the corporate culture to change. MacMillan Bloedel had been a closed and insular company, but it had learned, Coady said, that from now on it "should not go out into the woods alone." She listened closely to our arguments and worked hard with her bosses to negotiate an agreement that would be acceptable to all parties. Liz Barratt-Brown says she liked and respected Coady for her "flexible approach, open-mindedness, and a willingness to think creatively." The final agreement promised that all but a small part of MacMillan Bloedel's license in Clayoquot Sound would remain off-limits to logging, and sites sacred to the Nuu-chah-nulth would not be touched. A company that had clear-cut over 1.3 million cubic yards of wood a year agreed to turn over its logging rights to a native venture called Iisaak (meaning "respect"). A couple years later, MacMillan Bloedel withdrew from Clayoquot Sound altogether.

"Clayoquot showed how a place-based campaign can spark an international debate," Liz says. "We started at the ground level with local residents and First Nations people and ended up talking to major players in the timber industry, the provincial government, the national government, and then internationally." The Nuu-chah-nulth had taken on an all-powerful corporation, and through the alliances they built, starting with Bobby and Liz's visit in June 1993, they had succeeded in leveling the playing field—and winning.

In 1997 Patricia and I flew to Vancouver Island to see Clayoquot Sound for ourselves. Liz and Bobby came with us, as did several NRDC board members, including Adam Albright and his wife, Rachel. Liz was already working on her next project—an ultimately successful campaign to halt logging on five million acres of the Great Bear Rainforest on the west coast of the Canadian mainland. This is home to the "Spirit Bear," a rare genetic variant of the black bear that Kitasoo tribal legend says was made white by Raven, the creator, as a reminder of the ice and glaciers that once covered the region. (We chose the Spirit Bear as NRDC's new logo in 2000.)

As always, the Nuu-chah-nulth were delighted to see Bobby back on one of his regular visits, and some of the young men challenged us to a game of basketball. They beat the hell out of us.

The Wolf Clan (one of several—there are also Fish, Eagle, and Crow clans) invited us to the funeral for one of their elders, held in a large, windowless corrugated steel building. It took over an hour for three hundred people to file in. As we entered, members of the clan checked us to make sure we had no head covering, jewelry, or chewing gum, which would show a lack of respect for the ceremony. When everyone had been inspected, the doors were closed. It was *hot*. First there was a Christian service that lasted almost three hours. Then the lights were extinguished while the Wolf Clan chanted and made animal noises to release the spirit of the deceased elder. Women cried out laments in a communal grieving, not just for the deceased elder but also for the four young men who had committed suicide in the past months—a distressingly common occurrence in Native American communities, where suicide rates among youth are several times higher than the national average. While the room remained dark, the Eagle Clan took the body away, which signaled the end of the mourning and the beginning of healing. The whole service lasted more than four hours, and it was hard for us to understand much of what was going on.

Afterward we visited several villages for meetings and receptions. They served us iced tea and Betty Crocker pound cakes, and we had long, slow conversations. No one there is in a hurry. As is often the case with native peoples, we heard a constant tension between the desire to protect their ancestral lands and customs and the need for greater economic stability and a future for their young people. The women in particular were vocal, worrying about job losses and the social disintegration of their villages. After we left, Rachael Albright said, "It is heartbreakingly beautiful here—the beauty of the forests and mountains and water and the heartbreak of seeing it damaged. But also the beauty of the people and the heartbreak of seeing the damage their culture endures."

When Patricia and I boarded the small plane to fly back to Vancouver, it was packed to the rafters with sportsmen and their catch. Space in the cabin was so tight that we were asked to hold cardboard boxes of fish on our laps. We flew over broad swaths of clear-cut old-growth forest that were tangled with roots and blowdowns and disfigured by gullies gashed into the earth. It looked like a battleground filled with the corpses of trees. We held the end product of this destruction in our laps. After standing for hundreds of years, sometimes more than a thousand, the trees had ended up as cardboard boxes holding dead fish. They would be thrown in a landfill after the fishermen put the salmon in their home freezers.

———————

After Linda Coady arrived at MacMillan Bloedel, she and Liz Barratt-Brown talked a lot about the concept of sustainable forestry. Obviously no one was going to stop logging. The population was growing, and the demand for timber constantly increasing; it was a $100 billion industry that supported one in every nine blue-collar jobs. But there was a right and a wrong way to do it. By the same token, while the Clayoquot campaign had urged purchasers to avoid *bad* timber, it was just as necessary to show them how to buy *good* timber. These early discussions in British Columbia were a birthing ground for the idea of forest certification, and that is where Sami Yassa entered the picture.

In the early 1990s, Sami, Liz, and Justin Ward were involved in the creation of the Forest Stewardship Council, a coalition of forestry, environmental, and indigenous groups headquartered in Oaxaca, Mexico. The idea was to certify forest products through an independent, science-based, third-party evaluation process that considered issues such as habitat protection, erosion, and impact on water sources.

Sami was a native of New England, and his decision to pursue a career as an environmental advocate had been inspired by hiking in the Green Mountains of Vermont. Like many other NRDC staffers, he had a master's from the interdisciplinary Berkeley Energy Resource Group, the nation's first graduate-level environmental program. An expert on forest ecology and management, he was increasingly concerned about the amount of timber needlessly lost because of the inefficient ways in which it was harvested and used. One in every four trees is lost to waste and inefficiency in the milling process, and about 15 percent of the wood on a residential construction site is never used but ends up, like the salmon boxes, in a landfill. Further amounts are squandered by wasteful homebuilding techniques.

Sami arrived at NRDC in 1990, when scientific understanding of forest ecology was evolving rapidly and a new generation of foresters, as well as some smaller timber companies, were beginning to question the traditional assumptions of the industry. Until then, forestry had operated in much the same way as mining, with a single purpose: extraction of the natural resource for maximum profit. This meant cutting access roads (which can account for as much as 30 percent of the forest acreage affected by logging); high-grading the most profitable trees or clear-cutting the area altogether; and reseeding clear-cut areas with a uniform monoculture of pine or another fast-growing species.

People like Sami saw forests not as the equivalent of mineral deposits, but as complex habitats for innumerable species (including humans)—and they believed that those habitats could be sustained by intelligent harvesting that worked in the same way as fire or wind, destroying some trees while creating the conditions for others to replace them. Seen in this way, conservation and economics were not incompatible. The challenge was to create a viable market alternative to the model of the past, which was destroying our forests at an unacceptable rate. In professional terms, this work was much more creative and rewarding than simply denouncing corporate abuse and boycotting the worst offenders—though it was also much more challenging, especially in the United States, which, with only 5 percent of the world's population, was consuming fully 27 percent of the world's commercial timber harvest.

Since the purchasing power of consumers was the key to changing the timber industry, the first question was how they could know what kind of timber they were buying. That question applied both to the individual shopper strolling down the aisle at the local Home Depot and to Home Depot itself when its procurement managers placed their bulk orders for two-by-fours.

The idea of certifying products produced in an environmentally sustainable way had begun with the Green Seal program in 1989. I had served as one of Green Seal's founding board members, and we began by putting our stamp of approval—and a visible label—on such everyday products as lightbulbs, laundry detergents, house paint, and toilet paper and tissues.

Now the Forest Stewardship Council (FSC) had the vision of certifying and labeling forest products. Debbie Hammel, who was also a Berkeley graduate and had a background in sustainable agriculture, joined our forestry team to help negotiate the FSC's standards. Certification would be for five years, with the possibility of renewal. It was a technically complex task, requiring a detailed understanding of each particular forest environment, since the environments vary considerably. The larger challenge was to carve out enough of a niche for certified wood to affect the market as a whole. The big timber companies were very aware of this, and they responded to the creation of the FSC by setting up a body of their own called the Sustainable Forestry Initiative (SFI). Those are nice-sounding words, but the SFI was a case of the fox guarding the henhouse. It had no claim to independence, and it was largely restricted to forests and big companies in the United States, whereas the FSC proposed to certify wood from forest owners of any size anywhere in the world.

The philosophy of the FSC was to be as inclusive as possible, and over time it grew to be an eclectic mix of about three hundred organizations. This meant that at any given time some members might be urging a boycott of a particular corporation while others were working with that same corporation on the details of a new business plan. That may sound like a recipe for dissension and chaos, but we've found time after time that this kind of loose coalition can be quite effective. Each organization is free to operate in its own way, and no group can be held responsible for the actions of another. The approach also mirrors the message that NRDC has always sent to corporations: work with us and we will help you and praise you; do the wrong thing and we will make your lives miserable. Where timber and paper were concerned, we took that message to one giant purchaser after another: Home Depot, Staples, Lowe's, Georgia-Pacific, Kimberly-Clark, Bowater.

An independent film and video producer named Kirby Walker had become involved with NRDC in the early 1990s. She was passionate about a wide range of issues, including nuclear testing, healthy food, energy, and forestry, and she and her friends organized social evenings where they would make lasagna for a hundred people and invite other young couples to listen to our staff members describe their programs. Sami came to one of these dinners to talk about his work on California forests and FSC certification, and Kirby was eager to know more, since her family owned forestland in the northern part of the state—although she was hesitant to bring that up right away.

"We already practiced sustainable forestry," Kirby remembers. "We knew this land needed to be productive for following generations,

NRDC BOARD RETREAT IN SANTE FE, NEW MEXICO, 2005
Left to right: Kirby Walker, NRDC Trustee; John Podesta, President and CEO of the Center for American Progress, former White House Chief of Staff to President William J. Clinton; Frances Beinecke, at the time Executive Director, NRDC

and we felt we were the best managers in Northern California. We didn't need outsiders to lecture us when we had professional foresters to tell us what to do. We had hired the best ones we could find, and they didn't do this because they hated trees. They loved trees as much as any NRDC staff!"

After long consideration, Kirby decided that it would be useful for her family to meet Sami. He explained to them that we were not hostile to forestry; we just wanted to guarantee that both big and small woodlot owners were preserving their working forests. He was straightforward in admitting that what he was proposing would have little immediate economic benefit. However, because of her family's standing in the community, they would provide an example to others if they took on a leadership role. Sami's patience and intelligence convinced the Walker family of the importance of certification, and as he had predicted, when they took the lead other forest owners in the region followed suit. It took time for the Walkers to make a profit, but today the family is proud to know that it was ahead of the curve.

One of the people Kirby invited to her San Francisco dinners was Bob Fisher, whose father had started the Gap clothing chain. "I heard NRDC's Ralph Cavanagh and David Goldstein talk about energy at Kirby's and thought they were the most brilliant people I had ever heard," he recalls. "Although I didn't understand a word they said."

Kirby introduced me to Bob. He told me that he had grown up on a tennis court, not camping in the wilderness. His awareness of the environment had grown after he started fly-fishing as an adult on western rivers and began to notice the mine tailings and other pollutants left in the streambeds. Several environmental groups were trying to recruit him as a board member. "I realized I was being asked to join the board of these organizations to be the 'token' businessman, but that was fine," he says. "I was determined to prove that businesspeople were not ogres."

I liked Bob, and I pride myself on having a gut instinct for people we can work with. Bob has proved me right since joining the NRDC board in 1992. (Kirby Walker, who had first introduced us, became a trustee the following year.) Bob was not the first businessperson to become a board member, but he was definitely a catalyst for others who joined later. Perhaps most importantly, he brought the kind of business savvy that helped me a lot as I thought about the best ways of building and running an organization that was getting larger all the time.

Bob's determination to show how business could be environmentally friendly ran into a major challenge in 1998 when his family bought 232,000 acres of logged-over land in Mendocino County and created the Mendocino Redwood Company. The land had previously been owned by Louisiana-Pacific, a huge manufacturer of engineered wood and other building products. It was a particularly controversial forest, which included vast tracts of redwoods. The timing could not have been worse. The protection of redwood forests was a burning issue for California environmentalists, and the activist Julia Butterfly Hill was in the middle of her famous two-year-long tree sit in a giant redwood on land owned by the Pacific Lumber Company (PALCO) in neighboring Humboldt County.

Louisiana Pacific had left a legacy of mismanagement, and local groups had been protesting timber cutting on the land for a decade, petitioning for it to be "locked up" in a state park. By the time the Fisher family bought the property, these people were so understandably angry and frustrated that a proposal to operate the forest sustainably was simply not believable to them.

I met with the Fisher family at Gap headquarters, and Sami and I took several trips to the site to meet with the foresters. I warned Bob that this was probably the last place he should start his forestry investment, but the family was determined to go forward. Sami agreed to advise the company and did so for more than a year, with the understanding that NRDC could not support individual companies and instead would work with them to attain FSC certification. The Fisher family agreed to put up the necessary resources to show that a major redwood forest that had been abused in the past could be managed appropriately.

The Mendocino Redwood Company soon became the target of fresh protests. The Gap's headquarters was picketed, and demonstrators marched in front of one of our fundraising events in San Francisco, carrying a redwood stump with signs reading "Gap Sucks" and "Bob Fisher bought NRDC."

The protests eased up, however, when the Fisher family spelled out the details of its future management plan in November 2000: an end to all clear-cutting; the permanent protection of stands of old growth and an end to the harvest of larger, older trees; a 30 percent reduction in the overall level of timber cutting; a 60 percent reduction in the use of herbicides, including a ban on all aerial spraying; and a variety of stream restoration projects to protect fragile steelhead trout and coho salmon habitat.

In 2008 the Fisher family bought another 210,000 acres of working forest in Humboldt County after its owners, PALCO, declared bankruptcy. Fittingly, this was the very land on which Julia Butterfly Hill had staged her celebrated protest, and the Fishers announced that it would be managed under the same FSC standards as the Mendocino Redwood Company.

Bob says today, "In the beginning we spent several million dollars to establish our FSC certification and didn't get much out of it financially. It was a 'flak jacket' while people were getting to know what we were doing. We have a strong family ethic to do what's right for the land, and it has worked out for us in the end. FSC is a badge of credibility. Today we get lots of support from the general public and local citizens living near the forest."

One of the main buyers of timber from the Fishers' Mendocino and Humboldt forests is Home Depot, the biggest home improvement chain in the United States. Winning over companies like this has been vital to the success of the FSC, since home building and home improvement account for more than half of all the timber consumed in the country each year.

In a period of less than two years, Sami Yassa enlisted the support of one big company after another. In 1999 Kaufman and Broad, one of the largest home builders in the country, agreed to reject wood from endangered forests and to give priority to FSC timber, as did Hayward Lumber, a major lumber distributor on the West Coast. That was quickly followed by commitments to sustainability and efficiency from Centex Homes and Pulte Homes, the nation's second and third largest builders of homes and residential developments. These commitments built on the earlier work of NRDC and its partner groups (most of whom had worked closely with Liz on the Clayoquot campaign) in enlisting the support of Home Depot, Lowe's, and Wickes Lumber. All agreed to stop logging in endangered forests and give priority to sustainable timber.

As he made the rounds of home improvement companies, home builders, procurement officers, architects, builders, real estate agents and brokers, and lenders, Sami's technical mastery of the subject proved critical. He wasn't just selling them a general concept; he could also talk fluently about such arcane topics as truss manufacture, cripple studs, stressed-skin insulating core panels, optimum value engineering, and energy-efficient mortgages. These were the kind of things that drove companies' decision making, and Sami showed how they could be both beneficial to the environment and profitable, as well as burnish the corporate brand in a crowded and competitive marketplace filled by increasingly savvy buyers. Just seven years earlier, sustainable wood had been a new and untested idea. Now it was mainstream, and it sent a powerful signal to the timber industry that preserving our forests and wild places was not only the agenda of wild-eyed environmentalists. It was what consumers wanted.

Fourth Decade

2000—2010

One Gem at a Time

CHAPTER

18

For its first quarter century, the modern environmental movement had four central concerns: the quality of the air we breathe, the purity of our water, the land we inhabit, and the untouched places and wild creatures that give us spiritual sustenance and remind us of how the planet once was. They have a common thread: the way in which we used and abused these natural resources was unsustainable. As a new millennium approached, we knew that our vision had to expand beyond these traditional concerns. Science was showing us with ever greater urgency that our destructive footprint threatened the oceans and even the earth's atmosphere and climate, and that the health of all these things—air, rivers, lakes, fields, forests, deserts, mountains, oceans, and atmosphere—was interconnected by the global laws of biology, chemistry, and physics.

At the same time, we were living in an increasingly globalized economy, and as we'd seen in Clayoquot Sound, more and more of the battles we fought would extend beyond national boundaries, and our mastery of U.S. law—while still vital to our work—would not always be enough. Meanwhile, the communications revolution that had begun in the 1990s would challenge us to acquire new skills and identify new ways of energizing our membership, whose numbers had swelled by 2000 to close to half a million.

Our movement had spent much of the 1990s under siege, holding the line to defend the victories won in earlier decades. But as a new century dawned, we could no longer afford to be defined by opposition alone. People didn't want a diet of gloom and doom; they wanted *solutions*. Although we had a new administration in Washington that was every bit as hostile to the environment as the 104th Congress had been, NRDC was convinced that the solutions to our problems could be found through the right mixture of new technologies, enlightened business practices, the power of public opinion, and smart partnerships with allies outside the traditional confines of the environmental movement. What we needed above all was imagination and a willingness to take risks. As Frances Beinecke says, "We had to be opportunistic, to do whatever it would take to win. It's usually not the issues we choose to work on that make us distinctive—it's the *way* we work, our belief in constant experimentation."

———————

Early in 1995, Jacob Scherr, the director of our international program, had received a phone call from a Mexican poet and environmentalist named Homero Aridjis, whom he had met several years earlier during the debate over the North American Free Trade Agreement. Aridjis was calling to ask for NRDC's support for the Grupo de los Cien (Group of 100), which had been formed by Mexican writers and environmentalists to halt the construction of the world's largest salt-making facility, on Laguna San Ignacio in Baja California.

Jacob's first response was, "Laguna what?"

Aridjis explained that Laguna San Ignacio was a vitally important gray whale nursery. A sparkling blue inlet surrounded by desert and sand dunes and backed by towering mountains, it lay at the heart of 6.2-million-acre El Vizcaino Biosphere Reserve, established by the Mexican government in 1988 as the largest protected natural area in Latin America and designated six years later as a UNESCO World

Heritage Site. The only human habitation was a few scattered fishing villages, fifty miles from the nearest paved road. Aridjis told Jacob that Laguna San Ignacio would be devastated by the salt plant, which was being planned by the Mitsubishi International Corporation in partnership with the Mexican government.

Mitsubishi was promising the local people roads, schools, jobs, all the blessings of modernity. The saltworks would cover 116 square miles of tidal flats and mangroves. Powerful diesel engines would suck up 6,600 gallons of seawater per second and pump it around the clock into a vast complex of diked evaporation ponds. From there, the salt would be scraped up by giant earthmovers and transferred to 150,000-ton cargo ships waiting at a mile-long concrete pier, principally for export to the United States and Japan, where the salt would be used in the manufacture of PVC pipe and other plastics. The by-product of the evaporation process would be a billion gallons a year of highly concentrated brine waste, laden with magnesium, bromides, and other toxic chemicals.

This huge industrial complex would be slapped down right next to the lagoon, the last undisturbed birthing ground for the Pacific gray whale. Late each spring, the whales migrated from Baja California to the Bering Sea, returning in winter to Laguna San Ignacio, where they remained for six months to give birth, nurse their calves, and prepare for the next long journey north. The gray whale is one of the oldest known creatures on earth, with an ancestry stretching back thirty million years, but the whaling industry brought it close to extinction. By 1800, the last Atlantic gray whales were gone; by the early twentieth century, no more than four thousand individuals remained in the eastern Pacific. However, their numbers rebounded to around twenty thousand, thanks to the international ban on whaling and the protection of the Endangered Species Act. Then, in a matter of a few weeks in early 1995, the gray whale was removed from the endangered species list, and Mitsubishi announced plans for the saltworks.

Jacob consulted with Joel Reynolds, a senior attorney in our Los Angeles office and a specialist in marine mammal protection. Even though it was obvious that the stakes were very high—we would be taking on one of the most powerful multinational corporations in the world—they didn't hesitate: NRDC would take the case.

Jacob and Joel met with Mitsubishi executives and explained that we were not opposed to salt making per se. Laguna San Ignacio was just the last place in the world where it should be done. (To drive home the point, our board chair, Fritz Schwarz, wrote to the chairman of Mitsubishi asking how he would feel if someone proposed to build a steel mill on the slopes of Mount Fuji.) We would be willing to work with the company to find an alternative site, but if that effort failed, we would launch a public campaign to stop the plant. The meeting was cordial, but there was no hint of negotiation. Mitsubishi simply promised that it would prepare an environmental impact assessment of the project and abide by the results. We knew that this would take years, and we had no confidence that the study would be objective.

———

In March 1997, Patricia and I flew to Mexico with Jacob, Joel, Fritz, and Bobby Kennedy to see Laguna San Ignacio for ourselves. Our group was joined by actor Pierce Brosnan (who had just finished filming a James Bond movie in Mexico), actress Glenn Close, oceanographer Jean-Michel Cousteau, and the renowned nature photographer Robert Glenn Ketchum, as well as a number of leading U.S. and Mexican scientists, environmentalists, and journalists.

On a windy day in Tijuana, we all boarded a World War II—era DC-3. We lifted off from the runway in a cloud of black smoke, only to circle the city and return. With one of its two engines out of commission, the plane was not going to fly that day. Undeterred, we gathered in a small restaurant and ordered beer and *huevos* with beans and hot sauce while we waited for another plane. It was a great opportunity for us to get to know one another.

Three hours later, a second plane was made available, and we flew down the rugged Baja peninsula, with the Sea of Cortez on one side and the Pacific on the other, until we reached San Ignacio, a beautiful small town with a square laid out in front of an old brick chapel. There we climbed into vans and drove for another two and a half hours along dusty, washboard roads, past salt flats, isolated settlements blown brown and stark by the constant wind, and miles of sand and cactus. We finally reached a small encampment where boats waited to take us to the lagoon. Although it seemed as if we had traveled to the back of beyond, news of the arrival of two movie stars had preceded us, and campers in RVs were waiting with their cameras.

What struck us most about Glenn and Pierce was their realistic, unpretentious attitude toward their celebrity. They knew they could help our cause by lending their support, and whenever someone showed up with a camera, they graciously agreed to be filmed. During our stay in Laguna San Ignacio, they gave as much time as necessary to meet and talk with reporters.

They had also come to enjoy a relatively unbothered vacation with their children. Pierce brought his thirteen-year-old son, Sean, and Glenn came with her eight-year-old daughter, Annie, whose best friend, Bobby Kennedy's daughter, Kit, was also with us. The children lent a special excitement to the adventure. When we went out into the lagoon to observe the mother whales with their young, they seemed to prefer the skiffs, or *pangas*, carrying the children, and would ease up alongside them and lift their eight-foot-long heads out of the water to be petted (or kissed!). It probably didn't hurt that Glenn sang "Amazing Grace" to lure the whales to the boat.

The trip, and others that followed each winter, inspired enormous media attention and led to the formation of the largest environmental coalition in Mexico's history—and perhaps the largest coordinated international environmental campaign anywhere, ever.

More than fifty Mexican groups became involved, and as the effort gained momentum, polls showed more than 70 percent opposition in Mexico to the saltworks.

But taking on Mitsubishi was not easy. Mitsubishi is one of the biggest corporations in the world, with 185 separate companies in 85 countries making cars, electronic appliances, cameras, and petrochemicals. We also discovered that Mitsubishi owned banks—one held the mortgage for the new green building we were planning to open in Los Angeles, so we had to cancel the loan and boycott the bank, too. This was a scary moment for me, but I was convinced by Alan Horn, the president of Warner Brothers and an important NRDC board member, that banks were just another business and that we would be able to find another one for the mortgage. Which we did.

The campaign against Mitsubishi took off beyond anyone's expectations. Linda Lopez, in our membership department, and our longtime consulant Stephen Mills issued appeals that produced an overwhelming response. Under their guidance, our membership operation had been revolutionized. Mitsubishi and the Mexican government were deluged with more than a million letters, postcards, and e-mail messages (a powerful new weapon that we discovered in the course of this campaign and that would be central to all our campaigns in the future). Our partner organization, the International Fund for Animal Welfare, published a series of full-page newspaper ads, one of which ran in the *Wall Street Journal* over the signatures of fourteen mutual fund managers who declared that "Mitsubishi's poor environmental record is not a sound investment." At the same time, Joel Reynolds engaged the renowned marine biologist Roger Payne to review the project and its potential impacts on Laguna San Ignacio and, if he considered it appropriate, to draft a statement of concern for widespread circulation. Cosigned by Payne and thirty-five of the most distinguished scientists in the world, including nine Nobel laureates, the statement said that the saltworks "would pose an unacceptable risk to significant biological resources" and urged cancellation of the project. It appeared in the *New York Times*, the

International Herald Tribune, the *Los Angeles Times*, and the Mexican daily *La Reforma*. The Mexican environment minister complained to Jacob Scherr, "I can't go anywhere in the world without people asking me about Laguna San Ignacio."

In the midst of all this, Mitsubishi started a PR offensive of its own, taking out a full-page ad in the *Los Angeles Times* that showcased the company's nearby saltworks at Ojo de Liebre as a "partnership with nature." Inconveniently for Mitsubishi, however, Baja fishermen had just found the floating corpses of almost a hundred endangered black sea turtles. After an investigation of the incident, the Mexican government found that the turtles had been killed by a spill of concentrated brine from Mitsubishi's existing plant at Ojo de Liebre.

Multifaceted campaigns like this are hugely expensive, and this one cost NRDC millions of dollars in the end. It could never have happened without the support of committed friends like Anne Earhart, the president of the Marisla Foundation. Anne's philanthropic strategy was to look for people with passion and give them whatever they needed to get the job done. She had been traveling to Laguna San Ignacio with her children for years, camping in the desert and going out to see the whales. "I love this land of high winds, desert, and mangroves, with water alive with whales, porpoises, and pelicans," she says. "To be with an animal that has chosen to come up and look you in the eye is a transcendental experience. Mothers offer their young for me to touch, rather than protecting them. It is magic." Her daughter Sarah feels the same way. She has worked as a guide at Laguna San Ignacio, and her master's thesis is an analysis of the impact of ecotourism on the local people.

The welfare of the people of Laguna San Ignacio was a high priority for our campaign. In 1999 we hired Ari Hershowitz, a scientist who was fluent in Spanish, having spent his childhood in Latin America, where his parents were teachers. Ari's first assignment was to go down to Laguna San Ignacio. His task was to go to each of the towns, villages, and settlements to see what jobs people had and what kind of money they made, and hear their views about the proposed saltworks.

He stayed with a family in the village of Punta Abreojos, which had been a whaling center until the 1940s. After the whaling ban, the village had developed a thriving, sustainable lobster and abalone fishery, and the fishermen took great pride in their traditions. He found that they were worried by the prospect that the loading docks and ship traffic from the Mitsubishi plant would destroy their livelihood. They also complained that the Mexican government had left them out of the discussions about the future of Laguna San Ignacio, and Ari made sure that from this point on their voices would be heard. Their unified opposition to the salt-works turned out to have a huge impact on the eventual outcome.

The climax came on March 2, 2000. We had a board meeting scheduled that day, and it was a nail-biting affair. I reported on the status of the campaign. Mitsubishi was about to deliver its environmental impact assessment, five years in the making and more than three thousand pages long. The Mexican government, Mitsubishi's partner in the project, would be holding a press conference later in the day. The outcome was uncertain, and the trustees were nervous. As Jacob left the meeting to catch his flight to Mexico City, our board chair, Fritz Schwarz, took him aside and said, "We're way out on this one, Jacob, so let's win."

In Mexico City, President Ernesto Zedillo came to the podium and to everyone's surprise began speaking about the natural wonders of Laguna San Ignacio. It turned out that he had decided to visit the site himself with his wife and children just a few days earlier. Like us, they had taken a *panga* into the lagoon to see the whales and their calves close up. Within minutes, a lone gray whale had swum over to the family's boat. The president's wife had leaned over the side to kiss its head; Zedillo had taken a picture of the moment. "This is a place that has had minimum interference from humans, one of the few places like that left on the planet," he told the press conference. "Taking into account its natural and world importance and its singularity, I have made the decision to . . . propose a permanent halt to the project."

As Jacob tells the story, the saga of Laguna San Ignacio was framed by two phone calls, five years apart. "The first call was from Homero [Aridjis] asking for help. The second came as I was sitting in the plane waiting to take off for San Diego on my way to the *laguna*, worrying about our prospects for stopping the saltworks. Just as I was turning off my cell phone, it rang. Mitsubishi had abandoned its plans. I was so happy that I turned to the woman sitting beside me and exclaimed, 'This is the greatest day of my life! Mitsubishi's out!' She thought I was crazy."

As Homero Aridjis said, "It was a victory of nature over commerce." We had shown that it was possible to take on a powerful foreign corporation in another country and give it a good whipping. "It was a case study in how to do a grassroots campaign in the era of globalization," Joel Reynolds told the *Los Angeles Times*. At the same time, he acknowledges, though our strategy may appear brilliant in hindsight, there was a lot of improvisation along the way: "We just did what we could as each new challenge emerged."

The story does not end there, for we wanted to make a lasting contribution to the lives of the local people. Our members have made sure that this will happen. Since 2000, they have contributed over a million dollars to install solar electricity, buy easements to protect the land surrounding the lagoon, build classrooms, and put computers in the village schools. We have also set up partnership programs between children in Baja and middle-school students in the United States. Over the past decade, ecotourism has continued to provide a substantial source of income for the local fishermen.

As we reflected on the Laguna San Ignacio campaign, a number of things became clear to us. First, the role of our members had been absolutely critical; nothing aroused their passion more than the fight to save pristine places and charismatic wild creatures. Second, many more San Ignacios out there needed similar protection. And third, we needed a permanent capacity to fight for them; it didn't make sense to gear up a new campaign from scratch each time one of these places was threatened. So Frances Beinecke worked with Jacob to create a permanent program to protect threatened wild places in the Americas. We launched the initiative in March 2001, and Jacob came up with the name: BioGems. Since then we have designated more than thirty BioGems, from the Arctic to Patagonia, with a dozen or so on the "active list" at any given time.

At about the same time as the creation of the BioGem initiative, Frances was talking to Allen Hershkowitz, who was emerging, exhausted, from the long drama of the Bronx paper mill. She suggested that he should take some time off to write a book, which he did (*Bronx Ecology* was published by Island Press in 2002). And since he already knew so much about the paper industry and recycling, it might be a good idea for him to go to the source, to see where all that paper came from in the first place.

When the book was finished, Allen began to visit the forests of the Cumberland Plateau in eastern Tennessee, at the southern edge of the Appalachians. Larger than the state of Connecticut, the plateau is one of the most biologically rich temperate hardwood forests in North America, a once pristine expanse of red oaks, tulip poplars, beeches, buckeyes, sugar maples, and black walnuts, as well as mockernut, pignut, and shagbark hickories—170 tree species all told. Together with the neighboring Great Valley and Cumberland Mountains, it is home to the highest concentration of endangered species in the United States, including many rare fish, salamanders, bats, mussels, rodents, crustaceans, and migratory birds. "The forest was so lush and teeming with life," wrote Alex Shoumatoff in NRDC's magazine, *OnEarth*, "I half expected to see monkeys flinging themselves through the trees."

Allen found that the Cumberland Plateau was also one of the world's biggest sources of pulp for glossy magazines, throwaway catalogs, and toilet paper. Leaders of the Dogwood Alliance, a local coalition of religious, student, and community groups, told him that 156 chip mills and 103 pulp mills had been built in the thirteen southeastern states since the late 1980s, the great majority of them to meet the soaring global demand for pulp and paper from buyers as far away as Japan. A fourth of the world's paper and wood products were coming from these southern forests, where four million acres were being cut down each year and converted into plantations of loblolly pine, planted in monotonous rows and in some cases genetically engineered for maximum productivity and profit. This process required the aerial spraying of huge amounts of fertilizers and herbicides—the latter to prevent native hardwood species from growing back. In the most heavily logged areas, the bird population had declined precipitously. Herbicides had destroyed the undergrowth, leaving no cover for wildlife. Exposed streams had warmed up so much that the fish were at risk.

As Allen flew back and forth across the plateau with members of the alliance, he was horrified by the sight of clear-cuts stretching away as far as the eye could see. In other places he saw entire mountaintops sliced off by giant machines to expose their coal seams—a practice the industry euphemistically refers to as "cross-ridge mining." With 90 percent of the land in private hands, the Cumberland Plateau was largely unprotected by government regulation.

The Dogwood Alliance told Allen that the largest landowner on the southern part of the plateau was Bowater, the biggest U.S. manufacturer of newsprint and a leading producer of the glossy coated paper stock used for magazines and catalogs. He also heard about the work of Jonathan Evans, a plant ecologist with the Landscape Analysis Laboratory at the University of the South in Sewanee, Tennessee, who had been mapping forest change on the Cumberland Plateau since 1994. Using satellite imagery and aerial photography, Evans and his colleagues had studied an area of more than six hundred thousand acres and found that about 12 percent of it had been converted to pine plantations. He was particularly aware of the extent of clear-cutting by Bowater, since the company's property abutted land that belonged to the university.

Like NRDC, the Dogwood Alliance believed in influencing corporate behavior through pressure from consumers, and it had had some success in persuading Staples to phase out products from endangered forests. They told Allen that Bowater had ignored all their requests for a meeting. Perhaps NRDC could have greater success.

Allen could see that Jon Evans's work was the key, for he had not only compiled satellite images and aerial photographs of the forest but overlaid these with tax maps that recorded the ownership of each piece of property. The images in his database had been created at three-year intervals, starting in 1997 and then repeated in 2000 and 2003, and they showed the steady loss of forest canopy. Where there were patches of clear-cut, they all belonged to a single owner: Bowater. We decided that we had all we needed to take action.

In January 2004 I wrote to Bowater chairman and CEO Arnold Nemirow to request a meeting to discuss the company's logging operations on the Cumberland Plateau. No response. I followed up with a second letter in early February, this time saying that if we received no answer we would alert our membership—as we had in the case of Laguna San Ignacio. Still no response. On February 29 (it was a leap year), we sent a call for action to our members and online activists, who now numbered seven hundred thousand, telling them that Bowater was clear-cutting forest of rare ecological importance and replacing it with single-species pine plantations to make toilet paper, newsprint, and shopping bags. We also designated the Cumberland Plateau one of our BioGems.

The response was astounding. Fully 5 percent of our members and activists sent e-mail protests to Nemirow. Thirty-five thousand messages in one day. Next morning, there was a Federal Express delivery on my desk from Nemirow, requesting a meeting to discuss our "false allegations."

We met at the offices of Fritz Schwarz's law firm, Cravath, Swain, and Moore, in Midtown Manhattan. At our insistence, Danna Smith, the executive director of the Dogwood Alliance, also joined the meeting. Nemirow, who was accompanied by Rick Hamilton, a thirty-four-year Bowater veteran and head of the company's forestry operations, told us categorically that we were wrong. "There are no clear-cuts," he said. "None. Withdraw your allegations and stop your campaign."

The serious atmosphere of the meeting and the conviction of Bowater's claims made me hesitate. Allen says that I gave him a look that said, "You'd better be right on this, Hershkowitz. After the Bronx paper mill, this is a career moment for you." However, I felt confident enough to answer, "We think you're wrong." If Bowater would agree to a second meeting, we would present our evidence.

Three weeks later, Rick Hamilton and members of his team met us at the Landscape Analysis Laboratory at Sewanee. We showed him the tax maps that Jon Evans had assembled and pointed to the numbered lots that we wanted to discuss. He and the Bowater lawyers confirmed that these were indeed the company's property. Then we showed him the aerial and satellite images of those lots, one at a time, at three-year intervals. In 1997 the land was fully forested; in 2000 it was thinned; in 2003 it was clear-cut.

After the ninth series of slides, I said to Hamilton, "That's a lot more than none."

He said, "That's puzzling to me."

After the twentieth series, Hamilton turned to an aide and asked, "Have we been clear-cutting up there?" The aide muttered, "Well, a little."

After the sixty-fourth series, Hamilton said, "Okay, I apologize. I did not know this was happening."

After that meeting, Hamilton was gone, placed on "indefinite medical leave."

The door was open now for serious negotiations about Bowater's future operations. Nemirow said he was willing to review the company's practices and make sure they met stronger environmental standards.

I said that we would call a halt to the protest letters, although the information we had posted on our web site would remain there. I developed a genuine respect for Nemirow, and our talks, which went on for fifteen months, were always conducted in an atmosphere of good faith.

Only once did we hit a serious bump in the road. About two-thirds of the way through the negotiating process, Nemirow produced a leaflet from the Dogwood Alliance that had arrived at Bowater's offices that morning. The leaflet called for further protests against the company, and he was understandably upset. By this time, our team had been joined by Sami Yassa and another colleague from our San Francisco office, Debbie Hammel. I could see the look of alarm that flashed between Sami and Allen. Clearly, Dogwood's latest protest was a violation of the terms of our negotiations and had the potential to blow the whole process out of the water. I said to Nemirow, "Well, you have to understand how upset these people are. These are hard-fought issues, and the members of a coalition don't always work in sync with one another. The important thing is for us to move forward." As Allen remembers it, Nemirow gave a smile and wink, set the leaflet aside, and said, "All right, let's continue." It confirmed my view of him as a man of great intelligence and class.

In June 2005, Bowater, NRDC, and the Dogwood Alliance signed a memorandum of understanding committing the company to a management plan that complied in all but name with the protocols of the Forest Stewardship Council. This included a phaseout of the conversion of natural forest into pine plantations, limits on the use of chemicals, and the preservation of tens of thousands of acres of special biological significance. Two years later, Tennessee Governor Phil Bredesen announced that the state would buy 124,000 acres of Bowater land for permanent protection under public ownership.

———

If there are no giant corporations like Mitsubishi or Bowater tearing the heart out of our wild places, does that mean they are safe? Not at all, as you can see by looking at the most iconic of all such places, Yellowstone, one of our first BioGems.

Each year in early spring we host a trip to the nation's first national park for NRDC board, staff, and donors. One of the most frequent participants is Josie Merck, a board member and an artist with a passion for wildlife. Over the years, Josie has painted many of these "critters," as she calls them, inspired by the naturalist E. O. Wilson, who once said, "Humanity is excited not because we are so far above other living creatures but because knowing them well elevates the very concept of life." Nowhere is this more apparent than in Yellowstone's beautiful Lamar Valley—which, like the Arctic coastal plain in Alaska, is often compared to Africa's Serengeti. On our visits there, we admire the great herds of elk and bison and hope we will be lucky enough to catch sight of some of the gray wolves that were reintroduced into the park in 1995 and 1996, as well as the most charismatic of our wild creatures, the grizzly bear, which emerges at this time of year from hibernation.

Before the settlement of the West, grizzlies roamed from the Great Plains to the Pacific and from Canada to Mexico. But like the bison and the wolf, the grizzly was systematically exterminated—for sport, to protect livestock, or simply because it inspired so much fear in people. There had once been as many as a hundred thousand grizzlies in the lower forty-eight states, but by the 1970s only about a thousand survivors clung on in Yellowstone and other wild corners of the northern Rockies, hemmed in by the relentless spread of roads, logging, off-road vehicles, oil and gas drilling leases, and suburban sprawl. Not only does each individual bear need a range of two hundred to four hundred square miles, but the grizzly has the lowest reproductive rate of any mammal in North America. With bear numbers and habitat in rapid decline, the situation was desperate, and in 1975 the five remaining grizzly bear populations in the lower forty-eight states were listed as threatened under the Endangered Species Act. The entire northern Rockies ecosystem was at risk, since the health of everything from beavers and bighorn sheep to

YELLOWSTONE 2008
Left to right: Peter Lehner, Executive Director, NRDC; Steve Gehman,
naturalist and founder of Wild Things Unlimited

songbirds and cutthroat trout is related to the health of the grizzly, its
keystone species.

NRDC became the go-to organization on grizzly bears when we
hired Louisa Willcox as our senior wildlife advocate. Although Louisa
had grown up and gone to school in the East, she had worked on conservation issues in the Rockies for more than twenty years, including stints with the Greater Yellowstone Coalition and the Sierra Club.
She had crossed paths with NRDC's Johanna Wald many times, and
in 2002 she called Johanna to see if we would be interested in hiring
someone to work on grizzly bear protection. Sure, Johanna said—but
on the condition that Louisa raised her own salary for the first year.
Given the reputation she had built through her work on grizzlies, this

was not too difficult, and a generous grant from Dianne Stern, whose husband, David Stern, National Basketball Association commissioner, was a longtime NRDC supporter—kick-started our new program.

This was something different for us. We were not known for our work on wildlife issues, and we had never had a field office of the kind Louisa set up in a converted barn at her home in Paradise Valley, Montana. "Fort Doug," she called it—the Doug in question being her husband, Doug Honnold, a lawyer for Earthjustice (formerly the Sierra Club Legal Defense Fund). He acted as lead attorney on many of the cases we would subsequently fight on behalf of wolves and grizzlies. Louisa was a born grassroots campaigner, whose mantra was to work "on all fronts, at all scales." Though this was a new approach for us, it was increasingly in tune with the philosophy that Frances Beinecke described—constantly experiment, and do whatever it takes to win.

Such a strategy was especially necessary in the case of grizzly bears, Louisa believed. With the protection of the Endangered Species Act, the Yellowstone population had rebounded from a low of perhaps 140 to around 500 to 600 animals. That was still a precariously small number for a species so vulnerable to development. The life of each individual bear counted, and protecting the species involved everything from lobbying in Congress to prevent new oil and gas drilling leases to teaching owners of vacation homes not to leave dog food out on their porches. It also meant working with the patchwork of eighty different state and federal agencies that had jurisdiction over grizzly bear habitat in the Greater Yellowstone Ecosystem. "Miss a beat," Louisa says, "and the bears will die."

Then in 2007, shockingly, the Bush administration announced that the number of grizzlies in Yellowstone had grown to the point where the species could be taken off the endangered species list. This reasoning was absurd—the numbers had climbed precisely because the bear enjoyed this federal protection, and delisting it would turn the problem back over to the states. In practice, that meant that Montana, Wyoming, and Idaho would manage the grizzly as a game animal; "protecting" it would simply mean limiting the numbers that hunters were allowed to kill. As Doug Honnold said, "it would be like taking patients in an emergency room and stabbing them a few more times." We immediately challenged the delisting decision in federal district court.

However, lawsuits alone were not going to solve this problem. Louisa had been deeply impressed by the response of NRDC's members to the threats to the gray whale in Laguna San Ignacio and realized that they were key to this fight too. Yellowstone and the rest of our national parks and wilderness areas would never have been created in the first place, she reasoned, without the passionate support of people in other parts of the country. Although NRDC had not historically been a wildlife organization, no single issue moved our members more, whether the animal at risk was a curious, friendly whale or a ferocious grizzly bear. "People understand that these animals have a functional role in the landscape that ultimately is tied to them," she says. "Their health and the animals' health are interconnected, and we will not survive as a species unless we come to understand that principle at a deeper level."

But how interested was the Bush administration, not to mention ultraconservative politicians in Montana, Wyoming, and Idaho, in the views of NRDC members from outside the region? When the grizzly was taken off the endangered species list—and even more so when the administration announced that it intended to do the same thing with the Rocky Mountain gray wolf—Louisa saw the importance of proving that these animals also had support at the local grassroots level. In the case of the wolf, this was especially difficult. Almost extinct when it was listed as endangered in 1974, the gray wolf had come back strongly, and the U.S. Fish and Wildlife Service now puts the population at 1,645 animals. Wolves are fierce predators, and conservationists had sometimes underestimated the impact that this enlarged population would have on valuable livestock. We knew this was a reality we could not ignore, and Louisa has worked assiduously to build bridges to sympathetic local ranchers. These are not technical issues that can be worked out in an office in New York or Washington. They involve dialogue and problem solving among what Louisa calls "real people in real-time situations. Like, what am I going to do about this wolf around my cow pen? *Now*."

————————

Grizzly bears, too, evoke strongly negative feelings among people in the northern Rockies, and encounters carry a high risk of violence in which the grizzly is usually the loser. As long as they have enough to eat, grizzlies usually prefer to keep their distance from humans. But since they are few in number and split up into several distinct, geographically isolated subpopulations, they are intensely vulnerable to any abrupt shock, such as the disappearance of an important food source. That is what has happened, as the greatest environmental challenge of our time—climate change—has hit the Yellowstone ecosystem with sudden, brutal force, bringing a threat to the grizzly that no one anticipated when the decision was made to remove it from the endangered species list.

As the time for hibernation approaches, Yellowstone's grizzlies move to higher altitudes in search of the large, nutritious nuts of the whitebark pine, on which they gorge in order to build up the body fat they will need to survive the winter and give birth to healthy cubs in the spring. During a bad year for pine nuts, grizzly mortality may be three times as high as during good ones, because the search for alternative foods brings them into closer contact, and conflict, with people.

While more common species of pine, such as the ponderosa and the lodgepole, have long been susceptible to infestation by the mountain pine beetle, the whitebark, a hardy species that grows only above about eighty-five hundred feet, has been largely protected, because at these altitudes the beetle cannot survive the harsh winter temperatures. Around 2002, however, that began to change.

When the U.S. Forest Service provided data to support the delisting of the grizzly in 2007, it estimated that of the million acres of whitebark around Yellowstone National Park, about 16 percent had been lost to pine beetle infestation—a significant amount, perhaps, but not enough to constitute a serious threat. We were convinced that the problem was much worse and that the data the agency had relied on was too crude to give an accurate picture.

At the same time as our challenge to the grizzly delisting decision moved forward in the federal courts, we decided to file a petition arguing that the whitebark pine itself should be protected under the Endangered Species Act, in part because, as a slow-growing, high-elevation, and relatively immobile species, it was uniquely vulnerable to climate change. We had the necessary in-house expertise to do this, thanks to the creation of NRDC's new science center, opened in late 2006 with the support of physician and board member Tom Roush. Directed by conservation biologist Gabriela Chavarria, the center created two-year postdoctoral fellowships for scientists from a variety of disciplines, with the aim of providing expert technical support for our advocacy programs. The whitebark pine petition was coauthored by one of our first science fellows, geneticist Sylvia Fallon.

To find out how much of the forest was really affected by the pine beetle, we put together a unique collaboration among federal agencies, scientists, geographic information system experts, conservationists, amateur citizen scientists, and a Colorado-based company named EcoFlight. During the summer of 2009, members of the team flew over and photographed every acre of the Greater Yellowstone Ecosystem in EcoFlight's six-seater Cessna to map the full extent of whitebark pine loss. Our findings were devastating: about 60 percent of the trees were dead or dying. Some experts have predicted that the pine will be functionally extinct in another five to seven years, with devastating long-term effects on the grizzly bear and the ecosystem as a whole.

On September 21, 2009, as this book was nearing completion, Judge Donald Molloy of the District Court for the District of Montana finally ruled on our lawsuit: the Yellowstone grizzly should be returned to the endangered species list, since the decision to remove it had failed to take into account the impact of climate change on the bear's food supply.

Cause for celebration, yes—but only up to a point. The grizzly will never truly be safe, Louisa Willcox says, until we develop a comprehensive, science-based plan to stitch together and protect all the scattered fragments of the bear's habitat, from the northern Rockies all the way up into Canada. And the public who live and enjoy recreation in that habitat must find a place in their hearts to share the land with an animal that has nowhere else to go. This work will not be over any time soon.

Water, Water Everywhere

Joel Reynolds, the director of our marine mammals program and one of the leaders of our successful campaign against Mitsubishi in Laguna San Ignacio, grew up in a family of musicians. "Noise interests me," he says. In 1994, when he heard that Walter Munk, a professor at the Scripps Institution and the father of modern oceanography, was planning to install transmitters on the floor of the Monterey Bay National Marine Sanctuary to blast powerful acoustic signals from California to the coasts of Asia for up to ten years, as a means of measuring water temperature, he was curious to learn more.

When he discovered that Munk's study, known as Acoustic Thermometry of Ocean Climate, or ATOC, might have a harmful effect on as many as 750,000 marine mammals, he sent a letter to the National Marine Fisheries Service requesting a hearing before the necessary permit could be issued. Munk was furious and called me, demanding to know why on earth an environmental organization would stand in the way of an important project designed to advance scientific understanding of global warming. I checked the facts with Joel and gave him my full backing. After several months of negotiations with Munk and his team, we reached an agreement: the ATOC source would be moved to a less sensitive location, fifty miles west of the Monterey sanctuary. Sound transmissions would be limited to those necessary to determine, as part of a two-year study, what the impacts would be on whales, dolphins, elephant seals, and other marine mammals that might be at risk.

In the course of these conversations, Munk expressed his frustration at being subjected to this kind of scrutiny, since he considered the noise from his experiments to be negligible compared to other forms of manmade ocean sound. For example, he told us, the U.S. Navy had been testing new sonar technology off the coast of California that would generate noise at a thousand times greater intensity and over a staggeringly wide area of the ocean. That piece of information was the genesis of NRDC's groundbreaking global campaign to control ocean noise pollution—a campaign that continues to this day and is still spearheaded by Joel, joined in 1999 by senior policy analyst Michael Jasny.

Sound travels five times more rapidly through saltwater than through air, and marine mammals depend on acoustics for everything from navigation, migration, communication, and the detection of food to the identification of potential mates, the avoidance of predators, and the maintenance of social relationships. As any scuba diver knows, the ocean is a rich and complex acoustic environment, filled with clicks, grunts, buzzes, and whistles. Increasingly, this natural symphony is being overwhelmed by a cacophony of human-generated noise from the rumbling of giant oil supertankers and commercial shipping, the blasts of massive air cannons from seismic survey vessels, and the sonar signals of submarines. Joel calls it "acoustic smog."

From the mid-1980s, evidence began to accumulate that such extraordinarily intense noise could kill or physically injure marine mammals and disrupt their social and territorial behavior. At first, the causes were unknown. But a pattern began to emerge after a series of mass strandings of marine mammals in various parts of the world. Scientists found a correlation between these events and naval sonar exercises, some of which involved a new kind of sonar that flooded thousands of square miles of ocean with sound designed to detect enemy submarines at long range. In one notorious incident in 2000, whales of four species stranded on beaches in the Bahamas after a nearby exercise by a U.S. Navy battle group. Two years later, in the aftermath of NATO maneuvers off the Canary Islands, necropsies on dead whales revealed bleeding around the brain, emboli in the lungs, and lesions in the liver and kidneys—symptoms of severe decompression sickness, or "the bends." Beaked whales, a mysterious, deep-diving species found all over the world, seemed especially vulnerable, accounting for more than 80 percent of all the animals stranded.

In 2002, after extensive discussions with the U.S. Navy and a lengthy administrative permitting process, Joel and staff attorney Andrew Wetzler filed the first in a series of lawsuits focusing on the navy's use of sonar and challenging a long-range, low-frequency active (LFA) sonar system that had been approved for deployment over three-fourths of the world's oceans. The court promptly issued an injunction against the use of this sonar, relying on a variety of federal laws: the National Environmental Policy Act, which could always be invoked to demand an environmental impact analysis of any large federal project; the Endangered Species Act; the Coastal Zone Management Act of 1972; and the Marine Mammal Protection Act, also passed in 1972 to give special protection to these animals "because of their cultural and ecological significance, their potential vulnerability, and the exceptional difficulty of measuring the impacts of human activities on marine mammals in the wild."

These cases were never easy, since legitimate concerns about national security always weighed heavily on the minds of judges. But we won consistently, and in several instances, including the LFA case, the court imposed an injunction against the use of sonar and then ordered the navy to meet with us to work out a satisfactory agreement that committed it to adopt reasonable safeguards.

Starting in 2005, our lawsuits turned to mid-frequency active (MFA) sonar, which is deployed on two-thirds of the United States' fighting ships. The first of these suits produced a settlement in which the navy agreed for the first time to prepare environmental impact statements for all future training exercises and to fund almost $15 million in new research into marine mammals and marine ecology. Our second MFA-related suit, in 2006, took aim at one of the navy's largest multinational war games—called Rim of the Pacific (RIMPAC) and conducted in Hawaiian waters every two years. Sonar had become a politically explosive issue, and at the eleventh hour, Defense Secretary Donald Rumsfeld issued the first exemption to the navy from the requirements of the Marine Mammals Protection Act to allow the war games to proceed. To the navy's surprise, the court nevertheless went ahead with a temporary restraining order, relying on the National Environmental Policy Act and citing "considerable convincing scientific evidence demonstrating that the navy's use of MFA sonar can kill, injure, and disturb many marine species, including marine mammals." With diminishing options, the navy agreed to additional sonar safeguards. Based on those assurances, the RIMPAC exercises were allowed to proceed.

In March 2007, together with the California Coastal Commission, we filed the most significant lawsuit of all. *NRDC v. Winter* challenged a two-year series of major training exercises off the coast of Southern California. This time, according to the navy's own estimates, the use of MFA sonar would cause a biologically significant impact (or "take," in the language of the Marine Mammal Protection Act) on 170,000 marine mammals of thirty different species, including five endangered whale species. More than four hundred animals would suffer permanent injury. Judge Florence-Marie Cooper of the District Court for the Central District of California described the measures that the navy proposed to take to mitigate the risk as "woefully inadequate and ineffectual," and she ordered a set of six additional safeguards.

The navy not only appealed the ruling, but at the same time went to the White House for help. Citing national security concerns, President Bush exempted the California exercises from the Coastal Zone Management Act, and the White House Council on Environmental Quality waived the requirement in the National Environmental Policy Act for an environmental impact statement—both firsts. When the district court found the intervention of the White House illegal, and the U.S. Court of Appeals for the Ninth Circuit agreed, the navy wasted no time in petitioning the Supreme Court for review. At the end of June, the court, now presided over by Chief Justice John Roberts, agreed to take the case.

The normal standard of judicial review is that a higher court can overrule a lower one only if its findings were "clearly erroneous." But in its November 2008 judgment, the Roberts court never mentioned that well-established principle. Instead, by a five-to-four margin, it simply substituted its own view of the facts for that of the district court, over-ruling the trial judge's careful balancing of the public's legitimate interest in protecting the environment and the navy's legitimate interest in securing our national defense. Writing for the majority, Roberts ignored the district court's analysis of the scientific record and the range of harm likely to result from unmitigated sonar training, and accepted at face value the navy's claim that no harm had ever come to a marine mammal in forty years of sonar exercises in the region. He found that two of the six mitigation measures imposed by the lower courts on the navy unduly infringed on its ability to carry out effective training and vacated that part of the injunction.

Even so, four of the restrictions did remain in place. Most important perhaps, the Supreme Court reaffirmed the fundamental rule of law, even as it applies to the military, acknowledging that, "of course, military interests do not always trump other considerations." The bottom line was still the one eloquently expressed by the district court: that deference to the navy must always be tempered by "the established principle of every free people . . . that the law alone shall govern, and to it the military must always yield."

We're extraordinarily proud of what we've accomplished over the past decade to protect these magnificent creatures of the oceans. In a long historical survey article in the *New York Times Magazine* in July 2009, writer Charles Siebert said that NRDC's sonar litigation marked "a turning point" in the long, fraught relationship between humans and whales. I don't feel that he was exaggerating.

Marine noise pollution is only one of the innumerable threats to the health of our oceans. We had worked for many years on the environmental problems affecting coastal areas—opposing oil drilling on the Outer Continental Shelf, pressing for passage and implementation of the Oil Pollution Act in the wake of the *Exxon Valdez* spill off Alaska, and documenting the pollution of beaches from things like raw or inadequately treated sewage and polluted runoff from city streets and farms that leads to bacterial contamination and can make people sick. After medical waste began washing up on beaches in the Northeast in the late 1980s, we had pushed successfully for uniform standards—first at the state level and eventually in federal law—for monitoring beach water quality and deciding when beaches should be closed for public health reasons. (We still publish an annual report each summer, *Testing the Waters*, which looks at water quality at beaches on oceans, bays, and the Great Lakes—the 2009 edition was our nineteenth.) As a result of all this work, Sarah Chasis had become one of the nation's leading experts on coastal policy, and in 1992 she was the first recipient of the Coastal Steward of the Year Award from the National Oceanic and Atmospheric Administration.

Even so, we had never given much thought to the rest of the oceans. Perhaps we accepted the general view that their bounty was inexhaustible and that human activity could never do them any serious harm. Or perhaps it was their sheer size—70 percent of earth's surface. Most of the deep ocean was still unknown to science; only recently have we learned that it contains the greatest reservoir of biodiversity on the planet.

In those days, NRDC's senior staff gathered at Beaverkill, near our home in the Catskills, for an annual retreat. During these gatherings we held "visioning sessions" to brainstorm big new ideas. At the 1993 meeting, I asked, "What are we doing about the world's fisheries?"

Sarah remembers her initial reaction. She looked across at Lisa Speer, who had worked a lot in Alaska and had joined NRDC in 1983 from the National Audubon Society, replacing Frances Beinecke when she went on maternity leave. (For years, Lisa jokes, people referred to her as "the new Frances.") Both raised their eyebrows.

"Fish?" Sarah thought. "What could we possibly do about global fisheries?"

But I was convinced that fisheries had to be the next big thing for us. My views in those days were greatly influenced by the world-renowned oceanographer Sylvia Earle, who joined our board in 1994. Over lunch one day, Sylvia described the oceans as a four-billion-year-old legacy we were squandering with pollution and overfishing. I was surprised when she told me that the world's annual fishing catch had peaked in the mid-1980s, and that by 1995, 22 percent of marine fisheries were depleted and 44 percent had been fully exploited. The biggest fish—in other words, the most prolific breeders—were especially badly hit. By the end of our meal, I never wanted to eat fish again.

If we were to get involved in this huge issue, we would need to find a niche, one that would not duplicate what other groups were doing. I encouraged Sarah and Lisa to pick up on one of the recommendations of the 1992 Rio Earth Summit—the need for an international treaty to govern fishing for migratory species on the high seas. When coastal fisheries were depleted, fishing fleets moved onto the open ocean, which was essentially lawless—to the point where clashes between different countries' fleets sometimes escalated into physical violence.

Much of the discussion at the United Nations was essentially about allocation: who should get how many fish? Our role would be to push for the treaty to embrace conservation goals, and we thought we could be most effective if we devoted our efforts to influencing the U.S. government, knowing that as a major coastal nation concerned with protecting fisheries in both its own and international waters, its views would carry a great deal of weight. Our mantra: Instead of deciding how to divide the pie, let's protect the pie. While Sarah represented the views of NRDC at the UN, Lisa was invited to join the official U.S. delegation. Representatives of nongovernmental organizations were able do this as long as they did not publicly diverge from the official position. Sarah and Lisa double-teamed the problem.

This was a new world for us, and it was quite an education. Sarah and Lisa attended a lot of meetings, but some were restricted to official UN delegates. Late one evening, they were waiting patiently outside a conference room to get the report from one of these closed sessions. When a smartly tailored delegate from the European Union came out, Sarah asked him if the meeting was over.

"Not yet," the man answered, hardly glancing at them. "Why, are you waiting to clean the room?"

"I decided it was time to change my dress and makeup," Lisa said.

———

Joking aside, Sarah and Lisa were discouraged by the initial lack of progress toward an agreement. Even though there were many friends of the environment in the Clinton administration, the United States did not want a binding treaty affecting all high-seas fisheries, and no one in the White House seemed to be paying much attention to the issue. Sarah decided that it was time to embarrass the administration into action. She mentioned the foot-dragging to Jessica Mathews, who had worked with Gus Speth at the World Resources Institute and now ran the Washington office of the Council on Foreign Relations and wrote a weekly column for the *Washington Post*.

Mathews wrote a scathing piece, blasting Clinton and Gore for their failure to exercise leadership on such a vital global issue. The very next day, the United States came out in favor of a binding treaty, marking a critical turning point in the negotiations. The result was the UN Fish Stocks Agreement, an extremely progressive document that set binding conservation standards for the management of both "highly migratory" fish (such as tuna) and "straddling" stocks (such as cod), which migrate between one country's economic exclusion zone and another. The Senate ratified the treaty in 1996, making the United States just the third country to do so.

The negotiations over the Fish Stocks Agreement, which lasted almost three years, had been an invaluable education for us on the range and complexity of the crisis facing the world's oceans. With the assistance of more than fifty advisers—scientists, conservationists, government officials, and fisheries experts—we harvested the data we had gathered in a 1997 report, *Hook, Line, and Sinking*, which summed up the main threats and put forward a set of detailed recommendations. By relying completely on government sources, we avoided fights over the quality of our data and were able to get endorsements from influential senators, fishery managers, and commercial fishermen. The report helped to create momentum to implement the newly reauthorized Magnuson-Stevens Fishery Management and Conservation Act, the nation's main fisheries law.

Despite the new treaty, overfishing was still the central problem, because fishing boats had the technology and the geographical reach—thanks to electronic navigational equipment, sonar, gigantic plastic nets for trawling the seabed, eighty-mile longlines of baited hooks, and huge refrigerated factory ships—to devastate in just a few seasons stocks that would take many decades to replenish. As the advertising slogan for one fish-finding device said, "Now the fish have nowhere to hide." Worse, this orgy of overfishing was being driven by worldwide government subsidies to the tune of more than $50 billion a year, which encouraged unsustainably high catch rates. At least a fourth of all the fish caught (not to mention the albatrosses, sea turtles, dolphins, and other species accidentally netted and hooked) were unwanted bycatch, which was thrown back into the water, usually dead or dying. Vital coastal and reef habitat was being destroyed by pollution and bottom-trawling, while many fish and shellfish were becoming unfit for human consumption as a result of bacterial pollution or contamination by man-made toxics such as pesticides, PCBs, and airborne mercury.

We were also getting our first glimmerings of the long-term impact of climate change on the oceans. We already knew that they were warming; each month seemed to bring fresh revelations about the bleaching of coral reefs, the melting of the polar ice caps, and the acidification of the oceans as a result of their absorption of atmospheric carbon dioxide, which poses a serious threat to species that need calcium to form their shells and exoskeletons. As Sylvia Earle pointed out in her introduction to *Hook, Line, and Sinking*, almost nothing was being done to remedy or even understand all these problems: each launch of the Space Shuttle cost more than the United States was spending annually on scientific ocean research.

By the end of the decade, alarm over the condition of the oceans had become widespread among scientists, environmentalists, and policy experts. But the general public remained almost totally unaware of the crisis. In 1998 we'd organized a successful consumer campaign called Give Swordfish a Break, in which we partnered with a nonprofit ocean communications group, SeaWeb, and the Wildlife Conservation Society. This caused a splash in the media after dozens of top chefs, major hotel chains, cruise lines, airlines, and restaurants refused to go on serving this particular threatened species. Eventually, the United States lowered its quota and closed swordfish nursery areas in its coastal waters, and international quota restrictions were established. Swordfish stocks rebounded spectacularly. Although this served as the prototype for many later consumer-oriented campaigns on sustainable seafood, there are limits to what such campaigns can accomplish on a problem of this magnitude. If you think it is hard to convince people that global warming is real, try persuading them that the oceans are running out of fish.

Josh Reichert, the managing director of the Pew Charitable Trusts' Environment Group, recognized that if the public was to be moved to demand action, the crisis facing the oceans had to be publicized much more widely. When legislation to form a U.S. Commission on Ocean Policy stalled, he formed the Pew Oceans Commission, inviting me to become one of its eighteen members. It was a stellar group that included elected officials of both parties, outstanding scientists, leaders of conservation groups, representatives of the fishing industry, even the first American woman to walk in space. Our mandate did not extend to the oceans as a whole, but only to a two-hundred-mile band around the U.S. coastline—the nation's "exclusive economic zone." Even that, however, covers a vast area of 4.5 million square miles, more than the total landmass of the United States. The idea was to show that if the United States could manage its marine resources sustainably, that model could be replicated elsewhere.

The commission met for the first time in June 2000, with Republican Governor Christine Todd Whitman of New Jersey in the chair. After just a couple meetings, however, she was appointed by President Bush as the new administrator of the Environmental Protection Agency, and another Republican governor, George Pataki of New York, was asked to join the commission. President Clinton's former chief of staff, Leon Panetta, a good friend to NRDC, took over the chair. This was one of the best things that has happened to our oceans. Leon had grown up in Monterey, California, the setting for John Steinbeck's novel *Cannery Row*, and he had represented a coastal constituency in

Congress for sixteen years. He cared passionately about these issues and showed amazing diplomatic skills in holding together a consensus among a very diverse group of people.

The commission was a great experience. Sarah Chasis was absolutely critical in pushing the environmental agenda throughout the whole process, and she and I traveled the length and breadth of the country, visiting coastal communities from Maine to Hawaii and Alaska to New Orleans, where we consulted with local officials and activists, commercial and sports fishermen, and marine biologists. Pew commissioned syntheses of scientific studies of everything from the creation of ocean "dead zones" by nutrient runoff to the prevalence of invasive species in U.S. coastal waters.

Reichert's idea had been to put the oceans crisis on the map for policy makers and the public, and he succeeded beyond anyone's expectations. Legislation to create an oceans commission had been languishing in Washington for years, but only after the Pew initiative was announced did Congress finally pass the Oceans Act of 2000, which created a commission of its own. Unfortunately, although the legislation was introduced in 2000, the U.S. Commission on Ocean Policy was not set up until the following year—by which time a new administration was in office. Not surprisingly, while the mandate of the new body overlapped with ours, the members appointed by George W. Bush did not much resemble those who served on the Pew commission, tilting heavily in the direction of the navy, shipping interests, and the offshore oil industry. There were no leading environmentalists or fishermen on the U.S. commission. Nonetheless, it had an able chair in Admiral James D. Watkins, and the scientific evidence of the degradation of the oceans that had been gathered for the Pew report, which came out in 2003, was so powerful that the congressionally created commission came up with findings that were very similar to ours. Both commissions concluded that there was a need for immediate action to reverse the decline of our oceans.

"America's oceans are in crisis, and the stakes could not be higher," the Pew report began. It sounded an urgent alarm about overfishing, unwise coastal development, land-based sources of pollution, and climate change. It emphasized the critical connection between economic and ecological sustainability—collapsing fisheries meant the loss of thousands of jobs and billions of dollars. Above all, it spotlighted the lack of a coherent set of laws and regulations for managing human activities that affected the oceans. Instead, what passed for an oceans policy was a patchwork of narrow, fish-by-fish, crisis-by-crisis measures. The Pew report called for a new "oceans ethic" and a coherent, comprehensive national policy on fisheries management, habitat protection, coastal development, and pollution control.

Panetta and Watkins worked hard to harmonize their recommendations, leading to the establishment of the Joint Ocean Commission Initiative in 2004, which they cochaired. Although few steps were taken to implement the recommendations of the two commissions during the remaining four years of the Bush presidency, the important thing was that a template now existed for an enlightened U.S. oceans policy once his successor came into office.

———————

It would be wrong to say that the Bush record was 100 percent negative. Just two weeks before leaving office, he dusted off the 1906 Antiquities Act—the same law that Jimmy Carter had used thirty years earlier to protect public lands in Alaska—to create three new "marine monuments" in U.S. waters in the Pacific Ocean. Bush's executive order put almost two hundred thousand square miles of biologically unique habitat off-limits to mining, drilling, and commercial fishing, the largest area of our oceans ever protected by law.

The protection of critical habitat will be an integral part of our effort to save the world's oceans, and Sarah and Lisa's colleague Karen

Garrison, a senior policy analyst in our San Francisco office, has worked with great success since the late 1990s to promote marine protected areas (MPAs). She describes these places as the underwater equivalent of our national parks and wilderness areas.

The term "marine protected areas" is actually a catchall for three different levels of safe haven for fish. Think of the concept as being similar to the zoning of land: in marine *conservation* areas, fishing is generally allowed, but specific species are off-limits; marine *parks* ban commercial fishing, but permit recreational fishing; and marine *reserves* prohibit all fishing—they are described as "no-take" areas.

The United States has lagged behind the rest of the world in creating MPAs. New Zealand's first reserve was established as long ago as 1970, and one-third of the Great Barrier Reef in Australia and one-fourth of the coastline of South Africa are now protected. Many American fishermen have viewed these areas with suspicion, seeing a threat to their livelihood or their passion, and there was heated debate about such reserves in the Pew commission. From years of studies in other countries, Karen believed that this mistrust was understandable but unfounded. Protected areas had consistently been found to contain up to four times as much marine life as unprotected ones in similar habitat—and significantly more large fish, which are prime targets of commercial fishing. Large fish are the key to rebuilding depleted populations and keeping them productive, since a full-grown female may produce a hundred times more eggs than a smaller fish of the same species. Other studies have shown that rebuilding depleted populations can triple a fishery's economic value. Fully protected areas also "keep all the parts," protecting intact ocean ecosystems that are the foundation of healthy fisheries and bring a whole host of other benefits.

Karen's efforts have centered on California, whose coastal waters provide critical breeding, spawning, and nursing habitat for myriad species, including many that are important to the state's multibillion-dollar fishing industry. Karen's signal accomplishment has been California's 1999 Marine Life Protection Act, the result of legislation that NRDC sponsored and Karen helped shape. Given the initial hostility of the fishing industry, few people would have thought she had much chance of success. But Karen is a skilled coalition builder, and the act eventually passed without opposition because she was able to organize a statewide united front of supporters while persuading commercial fishermen to remain neutral.

The law called for the creation of an interconnected string of protected areas up and down California's 1,100-mile-long coastline. From a biological point of view, the idea is somewhat akin to Louisa Willcox's dream of joining up the isolated pockets of grizzly bear habitat in the northern Rockies. California's proposed MPAs contain a variety of different habitats and are connected by ocean currents, which carry fish, eggs, and other ocean species from one area to another. A well-designed network can achieve much greater ecological benefit than managing individual areas that are isolated from one another.

The California law was the first of its kind in the United States and helped inspire President Clinton to issue an executive order the following year calling for federal agencies to use their full authority to expand and strengthen marine protected areas across the nation. The idea is spreading, Karen says: "Underwater parks have been created now in biological gems of the ocean off Florida, Alaska, and the Northwest Hawaiian Islands, and around some other islands in the Pacific."

The challenge of coalition building did not end when the California law was passed in 1999. The plan called for MPAs to be created successively in four coastal regions. Each part of the state required its own scientific and economic analysis, and each had its own unique character. Karen and her allies have reached out to potential sympathizers at public meetings, beach festivals, dive clubs, local business groups—anywhere they could build support for the idea.

The process got off to a rocky start. In 2004, facing budget pressures, Governor Arnold Schwarzenegger announced that he was putting plans for the marine protected areas on hold. The public outcry that this provoked, together with an offer by foundations to underwrite the cost of public participation and scientific support, persuaded the governor to reverse course. Since then, the process has moved ahead successfully thanks to clear scientific guidelines and rigorous evaluation; strong public participation; leadership from the governor and a task force of policy experts; and forward-looking members of the state Fish and Game Commission, the final decision maker. Public support has also been instrumental, coming from aquariums, recreational fishermen, divers, surfers, and beach-goers, as well as from Environmental Entrepreneurs (E2), a group of business leaders closely associated with NRDC.

The first of the four regions, the Central Coast, stretching from Point Conception, just north of Santa Barbara, to Año Nuevo, near Santa Cruz, was operational by 2007. Next came the North Central Coast, from Año Nuevo to Point Arena, 120 miles north of San Francisco. The plan is for the whole chain of MPAs, including the South Coast and North Coast, to be completed by 2011.

In building support for the protected areas, Karen has been able to defuse some of the doubts of fishermen by pointing to the Channel Islands National Marine Sanctuary, off the coast of Santa Barbara. This network of twelve fully protected reserves had been created as a voluntary initiative while the Marine Life Protection Act was first getting under way. We had designated the islands and their rich underwater kelp forests as one of our BioGems and supported the voluntary process on the ground. The resulting network of marine reserves provides an important advance indicator of how the MLPA areas will work. A five-year review of the protected areas in the Channel Islands by biologists and economists showed what Karen had already seen in studies of such areas in other countries: the sanctuary was helping to restore the health of the ecosystem, strengthening biodiversity, and increasing the numbers and size of fish—and the economic losses feared by fishermen had not materialized.

We are not under any illusions that marine protected areas alone are going to resolve the crisis of our oceans. But what sets them apart is that they are one of the only measures designed to *restore* life in the ocean to its former abundance. Everything else is designed to mitigate its destruction, and that work goes on, day in and day out, rarely grabbing the headlines. Sarah Chasis, Lisa Speer, and the rest of our oceans team continue to work in time-honored NRDC fashion, strengthening laws that most of the public has never heard of, like the Magnuson-Stevens act—bringing lawsuits to make sure it is properly enforced and closing loopholes when it comes up for reauthorization—and lobbying for stricter international rules on destructive fishing techniques, like the landmark 2007 agreement to ban bottom-trawling in sensitive areas of the Pacific, in which Lisa was deeply involved.

In October 2008, Patricia and I joined an NRDC delegation to the World Conservation Congress in Barcelona, Spain, where Lisa Speer and Frances Beinecke were to take part in a seminar on conditions in the Arctic. The first speaker was Prince Albert II of Monaco. He told the audience that his interest in the Arctic had first been stirred by the polar expeditions that his grandfather, Albert I, had led at the end of the nineteenth century. Now, he said, even though he was the monarch of a small, wealthy state on the Mediterranean, he realized that his country, like all others, would be irreversibly changed by the vicious cycle of events under way in the Arctic: the melting of the polar ice cap, whose white surface reflects solar radiation back into the atmosphere, and the absorption of more sunlight by the dark water, leading to further melting of the ice, which in turn will lead to ever higher ocean temperatures, rising sea levels, and the disruption of ocean currents and the world's weather. Only five nations have sovereign rights over the Arctic. Therefore, it will take a coordinated global effort to turn back the crisis that is unfolding in the Arctic—and in the oceans as a whole.

I have no doubt that we have to raise public awareness of the crisis of the oceans to the same level that we have finally reached over global warming. The two problems are inseparable. The oceans have already absorbed about half of all the carbon dioxide we have emitted since the Industrial Revolution, and no one quite knows how much more they can take. Nor does anyone know how many of the changes that are under way can be reversed.

We do at last have the promise of a new era in national oceans policy. In March 2009, Jane Lubchenco, one of the nation's leading oceanographers, a member of the Pew commission, and a longtime friend of NRDC, was appointed to head the National Oceanic and Atmospheric Administration, and three months later President Barack Obama announced the formation of a task force to design our first comprehensive national oceans policy. Although we have a tremendous amount of work to do, we have the right framework to build on. As Sylvia Earle says, "We have one chance to get it right, now and forever."

The Rule of Law

I've tried to tell the story of NRDC decade by decade. But the reality is that life doesn't always fit neatly in those chronological boxes, especially not the kind of work we do. Part of our philosophy, our organizational DNA if you like, has always been that when we take on an issue, we dig in for as long as it takes to win, whether ten years or even twenty, and our staff know that we will back them with the resources they need.

There are so many of these decade-spanning stories that it's hard to know which ones to single out, but I've chosen two. Each shows a different facet of how our work as lawyers has evolved over the four decades since we set out as a small band of young litigators trying to create and enforce a new kind of law. One story is about the kind of lawyering that is aimed at federal and state agencies and administrators charged with protecting the public interest, and often involves complex and protracted negotiations. The other is about straight-ahead litigation, the kind that brings polluters before a judge and draws on the full range of trial skills, from discovery and deposition to the cross-examination of witnesses. Each of these cases involves a storied river with an important place in American environmental history—one that originates in the High Sierra of California, and another that rises in the great north woods of New England. Both ended in landmark victories.

———————

In 1982, with the help of NRDC board member Michael McIntosh, we had set up what we called our citizen enforcement project. Mike was outraged by the environmental failures of major corporations, which he considered a moral crime. He wanted them to face the justice system, and the main tools he wanted us to use were the citizen suit provisions of the Clean Air Act and the Clean Water Act.

From the start, our caseload focused heavily on protecting the nation's most important watersheds. During that first year alone we filed a dozen separate river-related lawsuits, and over the next decade

FRANCES BEINECKE, AT THE TIME PROGRAM DIRECTOR OF NRDC, PADDLING ON THE GREAT WHALE RIVER, QUEBEC, CANADA, 1992

we brought more than a hundred actions against corporations in twenty-three states, obtaining millions of dollars in penalties to pay for cleanups. Almost all these cases involved violations of permits granted to the companies under the Clean Water Act for the discharge of pollutants.

The most satisfying part of the work was bringing to book corporations that thought they were too big to have to obey our environmental laws. For example, we won landmark settlements in 1987 against Bethlehem Steel, for its pollution of the Chesapeake Bay, and in 1990 against Upjohn, the pharmaceutical giant, for contamination of the Quinnipiac River in Connecticut. Each of these cases in turn brought the largest penalties won in a citizen suit under the Clean Water Act.

Then, in 2007, we won the last in a string of victories against Texaco, for illegal discharges into the Delaware River—nineteen years after our suit was originally filed.

"Texaco had a refinery on the Delaware that was discharging oil and grease into the river, containing very toxic compounds," remembers senior attorney Nancy Marks, who worked on the case with our litigation director, Mitch Bernard. "There were thousands of violations. But Texaco dug in its heels, and there were three separate trials, in 1991, 1998, and 2000. However, we just wanted them to do the right thing—and we would not give up until they did." Millions of dollars from the final settlement went to local environmental groups recommended by our partners in the litigation, the Delaware Audubon Society.

In 1998 NRDC honorary trustee Frank Hatch sent Frances a batch of clippings from the *Portland Press Herald* in Maine, his home state, describing mercury pollution in the Penobscot River. Our first reaction was that this didn't feel like a case for NRDC. Our Clean Water Act litigation involved current, ongoing violations, and this was largely a historical problem involving mercury discharges dating back to the 1960s and 1970s.

We had also wound up the original citizen enforcement project in 1994, feeling that we had picked off most of what Nancy calls the "low-hanging fruit." After successfully suing so many major corporations, we had created a major deterrent, and the number of "end-of-pipe" violations had declined sharply. The focus was now on "nonpoint source" pollution, for example, from agricultural or stormwater runoff. In a sense, the citizen enforcement project had fallen victim to its own success.

Despite our initial skepticism about the Penobscot case, we owed it to Frank to find out more, and in 1999 Nancy went up to Maine for the first time. The local organizations she met with did little to encourage us: the Natural Resources Council of Maine seemed to see it as a hopeless case; the Penobscot Indian tribe, who lived farther upriver, did not see that they had a stake in it; and the trout and salmon fishermen did not want to rock the boat. None of these groups seemed to feel that there was any point in going up against a big corporation. That was precisely what Nancy found most appealing. Moreover, neither the EPA nor the state environmental agency seemed to be doing much on the case.

Besides, this was not just any river. The Penobscot was an icon to many environmentalists, historically home to the United States' largest runs of Atlantic salmon, which were blocked by dams, paper mills, and pollution. Henry David Thoreau had paddled the Penobscot, and the river rose on the slopes of Mount Katahdin, where the great naturalist had written of his transcendent experience of "the fresh and natural surface of the planet as it was made for ever and ever."

Back in New York, Nancy recommended that we take the case, and Mitch agreed. Since the problem did not fall within the scope of the Clean Water Act, we decided to bring suit under the Resource Conservation and Recovery Act. Like the Clean Water Act and other environmental laws, RCRA has a citizen suit provision. It also has a second and rather different provision based on the common-law idea of nuisance. RCRA says that if you have disposed of any kind of hazardous waste, *present or past*, "which may present an imminent and substantial endangerment to human health or the environment," you can be sued in federal district court. Even so, RCRA was normally used to clean up specific industrial sites, not fifteen miles of riverbed, so it felt like a long shot. But we would give it a try, and the Maine People's Alliance, to whom Frank Hatch had introduced us, eventually agreed to join NRDC as coplaintiffs. Once we had won the alliance's confidence, Nancy says, the partnership became one of the most productive we'd ever had.

The Mallinckrodt Corporation is not a household name like Texaco, but it is a powerhouse in the pharmaceutical and chemical industries. In 1967, when it went under the name of the International Minerals and Chemical Corporation (IMC), the company had built a chlor-alkali plant on a 240-acre site in Orrington, Maine, on the banks of the Penobscot. The plant used mercury as a catalyst in the production of chemicals for the paper industry. IMC/Mallinckrodt operated the facility until 1982, after which it was owned by two other companies until it was eventually closed down in 2000. (The last owner was a small corporation named HoltraChem, explaining why it is sometimes referred to as the HoltraChem/Mallinckrodt case.)

As soon as the plant was built, IMC/Mallinckrodt began discharging mercury-contaminated sludge from its sewer straight into the Penobscot. Later it stored more in unlined landfills on the riverbank. Until 1972, these actions were perfectly legal, since the Clean Water Act had not yet been passed. Also, for reasons that are not well understood, large amounts of mercury from industrial processes are lost into the environment, and Mallinckrodt could not account for the loss of more than a hundred pounds of mercury from the plant each day.

When mercury is released into the environment, it ends up in the sediments at the bottom of rivers, lakes, and oceans. There it is converted by microorganisms into its organic form, methylmercury. This is the most toxic form of mercury, and its concentration in animal tissue increases exponentially as it moves up through the food chain, through a process known as biomagnification. By the time it accumulates in larger fish (the main source through which it reaches humans), it can be millions of times more concentrated than it is in the surrounding water.

Mercury is the only metal known to biomagnify, and it is this unique property that makes mercury such a serious threat to human health and the environment. Methylmercury attacks the central nervous system, the kidneys, and the immune and reproductive systems. It is especially toxic to the brain of fetuses and young children.

Since the 1970s, both the EPA and the Maine Department of Environmental Protection had been ordering Mallinckrodt to study the extent of contamination downriver of the Orrington plant, but the company had merely been going through the motions. In the words of the judge who eventually heard the case, "The decision to forgo more vigorous efforts was deliberate." In recent years, however, the EPA had dropped the ball, and by invoking the power that RCRA gave the courts to intercede where federal regulators were failing to do their job, our lawsuit made the agency look bad—even though that was not our intention.

We brought our suit against Mallinckrodt in April 2000 and went to trial in March 2002. Like so much of our litigation, it was a case of David versus Goliath. Mallinckrodt came to trial with a battery of lawyers in the courtroom and many more backing them up in Chicago. For most of the case, we had two—Mitch and Nancy. On one occasion, the judge put us on forty-eight hours notice for a court appearance. Mallinckrodt protested that this was impossible: it would not give the company time to rent out the entire hotel for its team of lawyers and their Xerox machines. Mitch said, "Well, I guess we could use a new box of pens." But this apparent weakness can also be our strength. With unlimited resources, a big corporation can often be tempted to overplay its hand. When a big team of lawyers is involved, the principal litigators usually have only a digested version of the facts, and much of the important detail remains with the paralegals and junior associates at the base of the pyramid. Our lawyers have to have an encyclopedic personal knowledge of the case, which makes them much more agile in court, especially on cross-examination.

This is a big part of Mitch's genius as a litigator, and he is one of the best in the country. "Nothing is left undone with Mitch," Nancy says. "Every single angle that can be explored is explored. No one works harder or is more strategic." Both Nancy and Mitch believe that the key to winning a trial is telling a clear, convincing story based on ironclad facts, and that most judges, regardless of their political leanings, will ultimately rule objectively if the facts are persuasive. All three judges who found in our favor in the Texaco case, for example, were Republican appointees, and Judge Gene Carter of the District Court for the District of Maine, the judge in the Mallinckrodt case, was a conservative who was not expected to be especially sympathetic to environmental causes.

Cases like this are notoriously difficult to prove and often come down to a battle of expert witnesses. Mallinckrodt produced a phalanx of PhDs with laser pointers and charts and graphs, much of it junk science based on a chain of questionable assumptions. We had just one "demonstrative exhibit"—a large, beautiful map of the Penobscot Bay, which we put up on an easel at every possible opportunity to keep the judge's mind focused on what was ultimately at stake. We also had two scientific experts. Our most important witness was aquatic biologist Robert Livingston, who understood that the crux of any RCRA case is what the law means by *"may present imminent and substantial endangerment* to human health or the environment." Livingston showed beyond doubt that the Penobscot was seriously contaminated with mercury; that dangerous levels of methylmercury were present in fish and shellfish; and that anyone eating these would be at risk—even if they did not get sick for years. Mallinckrodt split hairs about the meaning of *may* and *imminent*.

The judge said he found Livingston's testimony "particularly credible and persuasive" and ordered Mallinckrodt to pay for a thorough study of the mercury contamination of the Penobscot, leading to a detailed plan for its cleanup if the study showed this to be necessary and feasible. In 2007 the U.S. Court of Appeals for the First Circuit upheld the ruling on appeal. Circuit Judge Bruce Selya summed up the court's reasoning in simple terms: "Dr. Livingston testified, in effect, that the presence of a great deal of smoke justified looking for a fire.

Mallinckrodt excerpts only his isolated statement that he has not actually seen a fire yet." That interpretation of RCRA "imminent and substantial endangerment" clause explains why the Mallinckrodt case is seen as a landmark in environmental law.

During the years that the case wound its way through the courts, we decided to build up our team of specialized litigators so that we could take on more cases of this kind. We now have six full-time litigators, all with great trial skills, and three litigation fellows, divided among our offices in New York, Washington, San Francisco, and Los Angeles. At any given time, they may have a couple dozen cases on the active docket.

Mitch and Nancy clearly love the intellectual challenge of litigation, and I identify with that, having once been a prosecutor in the U.S. attorney's office. "One of the things I like about litigation is that it's a great leveler," Nancy says. "Even though we are always out-resourced by the big corporations, we don't lose many cases. But we do lose some. Mitch always says that if you're not losing cases, you're not stretching enough. You shouldn't just be doing the slam dunks."

On the opposite side of the country lies the San Joaquin, the second longest river in California. It rises among the snowfields of the Sierra Nevada, close to Yosemite National Park. Three hundred fifty miles downstream, it joins the Sacramento River to form the largest estuary on the West Coast. John Muir, founder of the Sierra Club, likened the estuary, or delta, with its immense oak forests and wetlands and its teeming wildlife, to the Garden of Eden.

Yet by the late twentieth century, Californians were barely aware of the San Joaquin, for it no longer existed as a real river in any meaningful sense. The problems began with a huge hydroelectric dam on the upper river in the early 1900s. The wholesale reengineering of the San Joaquin got under way when the U.S. Bureau of Reclamation decided that "surplus water" from the river should be exported to other areas as part of the massive Central Valley Project, launched in 1933 to transform arid areas into productive agricultural land and shield California's farmers from economic ruin in the aftermath of the Great Depression. Starting in 1940, the bureau built major dams on both the Sacramento and the San Joaquin. It was the 319-foot-high Friant Dam near Fresno that ripped the heart out of the San Joaquin.

The dam rerouted 95 percent of the flow of the river into two big irrigation channels, watering about a million acres of cotton, corn, fruit, almonds, alfalfa, wheat, and other cropland up and down the eastern slopes of the San Joaquin Valley. Fresno County became the richest agricultural county in the United States, and the San Joaquin became, as the *Amicus Journal* once put it, "both tub and toilet" for California's agribusiness boom. Below the Friant Dam, more than sixty miles of the river ran bone-dry in all but the wettest years. What flows did emerge farther downstream were often heavily polluted by agricultural runoff and municipal sewage outflows.

Meanwhile, the Sacramento–San Joaquin Delta too had been grossly deformed. Giant pumps installed in the 1950s and 1960s reversed the flow of the lower reaches of both rivers to channel water southward to the California Aqueduct. Although the delta provides water for twenty-three million people, including part of the drinking water supply for almost two-thirds of California's population, it was so polluted that tens of millions of dollars had to be spent each year on purification plants. The loss of the freshwater inflow from the San Joaquin had wiped out one of the richest salmon fisheries on the West Coast. Old-timers can still remember when the sound of thousands of Chinook salmon thrashing their way upstream at the site of the Friant Dam would keep people awake at night.

In 1988 the original water contracts at the Friant Dam came up for renewal, and the U.S. Bureau of Reclamation, which managed the dam and the diversions, said that the contracts would be renewed automatically, on the same terms as before: every drop of water from the upper river would go to the same powerful contractors, primarily farmers on the east side of the San Joaquin Valley. Hal Candee, who had been hired to work in our San Francisco office a few years earlier, thought differently. Marc Reisner, who sadly died of cancer in 2000, had provided the blueprint for Hal's work in his classic book, *Cadillac Desert*. "Marc's argument was that the West was a heavily subsidized and tremendously expensive 'hydraulic society,' based on dependence on dams and aqueducts that destroy some of America's greatest natural resources," Hal says. "An advantage of not growing up in California was that I could not accept that just because the San Joaquin had been dried up for forty years, it had to stay that way."

Many environmentalists thought that we were crazy to fight for the river, saying that it was impossible to turn back so much history. Farmers and valley towns had depended on this water for more than forty years and would not willingly give it up. NRDC's response was that it did not have to be a zero-sum game. The responsibility of government agencies was to serve the public interest; how could that be squared with an arrangement that benefited only one party? If the San Joaquin could be managed more efficiently—if for example just 10 percent of the water could be saved through conservation measures—perhaps you could have prosperous farms *and* a healthy river. That had been done for other important California rivers like the Tuolumne, the Stanislaus, and the Merced, all of which still maintained year-round flows and returning salmon—albeit in reduced numbers.

The first step in *NRDC v. Rodgers* was a familiar one for us: file a NEPA suit in district court demanding an environmental impact assessment—including an examination of alternative ways of meeting the farmers' demand for water—before the new contracts were issued. This time, working with a coalition of fourteen groups that contained sports and commercial fishermen as well as environmentalists, we added some new twists. In 1992 we amended our complaint to charge that the Bureau of Reclamation was failing to comply with California's Fish and Game Code, which said that dam operators had to release sufficient water to sustain healthy fish populations farther downstream.

This was in line with a recent Supreme Court ruling that if a federal agency planned a water diversion, it had to obey state laws.

The Department of the Interior, of which the Bureau of Reclamation is part, retorted that it was exempt from this ruling and had no obligations to the fish. The farmers' right to the river was nonnegotiable, it asserted, and the bureau had no real role in the matter. It was merely acting as a "trustee" for the water.

These were the opening shots in a two-decade battle to restore the San Joaquin, and the dispute over federal versus state authority became the crux of the case.

Looking back at it, I think that it was the kind of case that only NRDC, of all environmental groups, could possibly have taken on. It involved courtroom skills and negotiating savvy, legislative action and lobbying in Sacramento and Washington, and the ability to build and hold together a large and diverse coalition. This meant creating a stellar team to work on the case over its twenty-year lifespan, and that's what we did, with people like senior scientist and San Joaquin River project manager Monty Schmitt, senior policy analyst Barry Nelson, and attorneys Jared Huffman (now a California state assemblyman), Kate Poole (2008 California Lawyer of the Year), and Michael Wall, head of our San Francisco litigation team.

Outside supporters, too, such as our pro bono counsel Phil Atkins-Pattenson of Sheppard Mullin in San Francisco, play an essential role in a case of this complexity. And we needed serious financial backing to be able to follow through on a twenty-year commitment. In this instance, that came from people like George A. Miller, a retired businessman and philanthropist who found it incomprehensible that public water was being given away for a pittance for a private purpose. The Bureau of Reclamation was selling irrigators an acre-foot of water—enough to meet the needs of a family of five for a year—for just three dollars.

By the end of our first decade of work on the San Joaquin, we had won a series of court rulings culminating in a unanimous decision in 1998 by the U.S. Court of Appeals for the Ninth Circuit. The judges agreed with all our main arguments, ruling that the Bureau of Reclamation was subject to California's Fish and Game Code and that its renewal of contracts for water from the Friant Dam was a violation of the Endangered Species Act. The contracts were rescinded. The Friant water districts tried to appeal this ruling to the Supreme Court, but their request was denied.

Court rulings do not end a case like this, however; they simply send it to the next stage, which is the complex technical negotiations to determine how the decision is to be implemented in practice. How much water would have to be released from the dam in order to restore salmon to the river? Would that amount be consistent with federal law? At this point, Congress had also gotten involved in the dispute, passing the 1992 Central Valley Project Improvement Act. The act ordered the Bureau of Reclamation to remedy the environmental harm caused by the New Deal—era project and stated that the preservation of fish and wildlife was no less important than the provision of water for irrigation. However, the act stipulated that any new federal plan to release water from the Friant Dam had to be "reasonable, prudent, and feasible." What did that mean for this case, which had been brought under state rather than federal law?

The negotiations between NRDC and the Friant water users dragged on for four years and ultimately involved a court-appointed mediator. Both sides commissioned expert studies to estimate how much water it would take to restore the salmon. Our view was that any release schedule had to be flexible. The purpose of the exercise was to restore salmon to the river, so if the amount of water released turned out to be insufficient to accomplish that, it was logical to us that the releases would have to be increased. This reflected a doctrine known as "adaptive management." But all our proposals—and even those of the mediator—proved unacceptable to the Friant water users, who said our plan would dry up the Central Valley. The talks collapsed.

The case then returned to the courts, and Senior District Judge Lawrence Karlton did the judicial equivalent of banging our heads together. He declared flatly that the operation of the dam was illegal and that all the river's "historic fisheries" had to be restored. If we failed to agree on how this could be accomplished, he said, the court would impose its own solution through a "remedies trial." He would prefer us to solve the problem with a scalpel, he said, but if necessary he would do so with a meat cleaver. He scheduled the historic trial for Valentine's Day, February 14, 2006.

As that date approached, the case suddenly became more politically complicated when California Democratic Senator Dianne Feinstein intervened personally in the dispute. The Friant water users had approached her with a plan that they maintained would protect their needs while leaving enough to satisfy the environmentalists, and she prepared to introduce legislation that would have resulted in the termination of our lawsuit.

In September 2005 Hal got an urgent call from Feinstein's staff, who said that she was about to introduce a rider to a Senate appropriations bill. "It will end your case, but it will protect the river," they said.

"Can I see the bill?" Hal asked.

"You have one hour."

Hal was greatly disturbed by what he read. He called back and told the senator's office, "This rider would override both federal law and the California state constitution."

"That's not our intent," he was assured.

"But that's what will happen."

The bill was put off a month, and in the end Feinstein agreed to set aside her rider if we would go back to the negotiating table with the farmers. We agreed, but on two conditions: first, the settlement had to be driven by the parties to the case, not by elected officials; and second, none of the parties would "go behind or around" the negotiations with any new legislation. The talks had to be held in good faith. Feinstein agreed. We soon went back to the court with the water users and the government and promised that this time the talks had a very good chance of success. The judge agreed to postpone the trial.

"We could have had a complete victory in court, but then there would have been winners and losers," Hal says. "Asking the farmers to give up a percentage of their water was no small deal. We needed to find a way to mitigate some of their losses. We wanted to take the long view and find a win-win solution."

It took another year of negotiations and technical studies, but in the end we did just that. The details are too complicated to get into here, but they involved a series of proven, cost-effective techniques such as recharging groundwater, more efficient management of the Friant Dam, conservation, the integrated or "conjunctive" use of groundwater and surface water, and recapturing water downstream and returning it to the farmers. These measures, combined with a negotiated restoration plan, were enough to satisfy both sides, and in September 2006 we announced our landmark agreement, overcoming decades of disputes and bitterness. It set in motion one of the largest and most important river restoration projects in the nation's history. It would end up costing $800 million, but this would be split between the federal and state governments and the water users. Our economic analyses predicted that some of the cost would be recouped in time by income from increased recreational use of the river, healthier fisheries, and economic benefits to the Sacramento—San Joaquin Delta.

On March 30, 2009, after two more years of tweaking the legislative details of the settlement in Congress, President Obama signed the San Joaquin River Restoration Act into law. And six months later, on October 1, engineers opened the gates at the Friant Dam, and for the first time in more than sixty years, water flowed down the dried-up channel of the San Joaquin—a small, symbolic step toward the restoration of one of America's great rivers.

We're Having
a Heat Wave

What NRDC and the environmental movement ultimately will be remembered for is what we did to deal
with the climate crisis. There is no longer any serious scientific debate
about the problem or its cause—global temperatures are rising to
alarming levels because of the increase in carbon dioxide (CO_2) and
other "greenhouse gases" in the atmosphere, most of them as the result
of human activity.

George Woodwell of the Brookhaven National Laboratory and the
Woods Hole Research Center, one of our earliest board members, was
the first person I knew who gave the clarion call about climate, back in
the 1970s. His fellow member Dean Abrahamson shared George's concern. It was almost three decades before Al Gore's movie, *An Inconvenient
Truth*, and George and Dean were still voices in the wilderness. Their
warnings had a lasting influence on how NRDC has approached the
issues of climate change, airborne emissions, and energy policy.

George told Congress in 1979, "If we wait to prove that the climate
is warming before we take steps to alleviate the carbon dioxide buildup,
the effects will be well under way and still more difficult to control.
The climatic change problem is totally entwined in the energy problem;
where we get our energy from and how efficiently we use it."

PRESIDENTIAL CAMPAIGN, HUDSON VALLEY, NEW YORK, 2000
Vice President Al Gore and John Adams

George described the earth as a living system that is a product of biotic evolution. If we chronically disrupt the delicate but stable balance of this naturally self-regulating system, our world will be fundamentally altered. The essential issue is carbon, a chemical element, and CO_2, the ubiquitous, invisible, and odorless gas produced when two oxygen atoms bond to a single carbon atom. CO_2 is naturally emitted in a multitude of ways, including something as simple as leaves falling to the ground in the autumn and rotting. Atmospheric carbon is also absorbed naturally by those same trees when they put forth new green leaves the following spring.

Since the Industrial Revolution began, the burning of fossil fuels that stored carbon in the earth for millions of years has altered this balance by steadily increasing the concentration of CO_2 in the atmosphere. Scientists measure this concentration in parts per million, or ppm. At the time of the Earth Summit in Rio de Janeiro in 1992, the level of atmospheric CO_2 was 356 ppm; by 1997, the year of the first binding international treaty on climate, the Kyoto Protocol, it was 363; as I write this at the end of 2009, it is 387 and rising. Climate scientists say that a sustained level of more than 350 ppm is likely to bring lasting and irreversible change to life on the planet as we know it, and there is a growing consensus that we need to reduce our CO_2 emissions by 80 percent by 2050 if we are to hold climate change within acceptable limits.

There is no silver bullet for solving the climate crisis. The challenge, says Ashok Gupta, one of NRDC's first professionally trained economists, is to remake our energy economy through a variety of "wedges," which together will add up the huge slice of emissions reductions that we need to achieve in the next forty years. He ticks off some of the elements: finding alternatives to petroleum for transportation, in the form of electric vehicles and plug-in hybrids; radically reducing the use of coal and exploring all possible technological options for burning it more cleanly—including burying harmful emissions safely through a process called carbon capture and storage; and developing renewable energy sources such as wind, solar, and biofuels (at least those whose production does not create as many environmental problems as they solve). Yet other approaches include working for state-level reforms in energy policy where there is an absence of federal leadership; establishing smart growth and energy-efficient building codes; and encouraging conservation and "demand-side management," such as reforms in the way utilities generate and sell electricity.

"Utility regulatory reform—who wants to talk about that at a cocktail party?" jokes Ashok's colleague Dale Bryk, an expert on the subject. But this dull-sounding topic is one of the keys to solving the climate crisis. In 2006 we published a study of the prospects for energy reduction for each of the climate "wedges." By far, the greatest potential was in a package of "end-use efficiency" measures including appliance standards, building code enforcement, and utility reforms. These were measures that NRDC had begun to pioneer a quarter of a century earlier in California. They marked the true beginning of our climate program, although they happened a full decade before we hired our first formally designated climate scientist.

It all started in 1979 and 1980, when we made two new hires in our San Francisco office. One was Ralph Cavanagh, a fast-talking, youthful-looking graduate of Yale Law School, who was often referred to as NRDC's "Wonder Boy." The other was a physics PhD from Berkeley named David Goldstein. David has his own unique personality, though it is very different from Ralph's. He speaks slowly with a dry wit that captures the essence of a situation. His mantra, frequently repeated by his NRDC colleagues, is "Bite an issue in the ass and don't let go for ten years."

After graduation, Ralph decided that he was cut out to be a negotiator, not a litigator, and that he wanted to devote himself to the regulatory reform of utilities. His colleagues wondered how he could dedicate his professional life to something so arcane and complex, which would tie him up in the labyrinth of federal and state bureaucracy, but Ralph was one of the first people in the country (and NRDC was the first environmental organization in the country) to see that utility reform and efficiency were the "low-hanging fruit" in the long process of weaning ourselves away from our dependence on fossil fuels. More than half the carbon dioxide emissions from the entire U.S. economy are tied directly to the natural gas and electricity distributed by the nation's utilities. This was also a sector we knew quite well from the work that Dick Ayres, David Hawkins, and others had done in the 1970s on clean air and acid rain, so we already had some in-house expertise for Ralph to draw on.

We knew that the United States had always been an egregiously wasteful user of energy; Japan and Germany were both twice as energy efficient. For decades, our utilities had operated on a business model of sustained growth and low risk, a kind of natural monopoly whose strength was based on economies of scale. The more energy a utility produced, the more profit it made and the more the consumer benefited from lower prices. Since profits were tied to the amount of electricity sold, the utilities projected ever increasing demand and built more and more new power plants to meet it. Each new plant produced energy more cheaply than its predecessor, so the customer was kept happy.

At least in theory. By the mid-1970s, however, the flaws in the traditional business model were starting to show. Artificially cheap energy had led to increased demand, which led to increased production—but new power plants were beginning to show serious cost overruns, and eventually that burden would be passed on to the consumer in the form of higher electricity bills. Demand would then drop, and the utilities would compensate by raising prices further. In the language of economists, we were creating a crisis of overcapacity.

The need for a new approach was glaringly apparent in the Pacific Northwest, where the majority of the regional power supply came from a string of thirty hydroelectric dams on the Columbia River and its tributaries, owned by the Bonneville Power Authority (BPA), which sold the electricity through dozens of local utilities. It was the cheapest power in the country, and demand was doubling every decade. The system was unsustainable.

To keep this runaway train rolling, the BPA was proposing to finance a string of twenty-six new power plants, some nuclear and others coal fired. Even before Ralph arrived, we had led a regional coalition opposing the plan. BPA administrator Donald Hodel (later to become President Reagan's secretary of the interior, replacing James Watt) was enraged, saying that we were infringing on the personal choice of consumers. "Over the past several years," he said, "the environmental movement has fallen into the hands of a small, arrogant faction which is dedicated to bringing our society to a halt. I call this faction the Prophets of Shortage. They are the antiproducers, the antiachievers. The doctrine they preach is that of scarcity and self-denial." The *Wall Street Journal* editorial page also weighed in, naming NRDC as the main culprit in the energy crisis facing the Pacific Northwest.

With construction delays, cost overruns, and the fact that it would be ten to twelve years before the new plants came on line, Ralph saw the BPA's plans as economic lunacy, as well as having serious environmental consequences in the form of new threats to air quality and nuclear safety and waste issues. In 1980 he proposed an extended moratorium on the construction of any new power plants and posed two simple but profound questions: did utility profits necessarily have to depend on the amount of electricity generated, and did demand have to increase at the same rate as population and economic growth? The answer to both questions was no—if you built in efficiency, which a number of serious academic studies at the time were beginning to recommend as a strategic choice for energy planners. The measures Ralph suggested included better insulation of homes, the elimination of excessive lighting in commercial buildings, and the use of waste heat from industrial processes to generate electricity. While our lawyers would continue to hammer the utilities for their environmental sins, Ralph took a different, complementary approach. He didn't talk about climate change or clean air; he appealed to the enlightened self-interest of utility executives in "least-cost planning."

By 1983, regional planners had come around to our way of thinking and formally adopted conservation as *the* dominant energy source in the Northwest. All new plant construction would be deferred indefinitely. At the same time we won a landmark ruling in the U.S. Supreme Court upholding the right of states to reject new nuclear power plants on economic grounds. These were huge steps forward. As the great environmentalist and energy expert Amory Lovins of the Rocky Mountain Institute says, new power plants generate megawatts; avoiding the need for them creates "negawatts."

To test the conservation idea in practice, Ralph proposed a novel experiment: a pilot efficiency program designed to reach every residence in a selected locality. This would rigorously evaluate the impact on electricity consumption and project how long it would take for the cost savings to balance out the investment in new generating capacity, while indicating the extent to which a representative sample of individuals could be persuaded to add major energy conservation measures to their homes.

The largest utility in the Northwest, Pacific Power and Light, agreed to give it a try, in partnership with BPA and a small electricity cooperative. The location chosen was Hood River County, Oregon, just a few miles from the giant Bonneville Dam on the Columbia River. This was a diverse, ethnically mixed community, part urban and part rural, with a population of about fifteen thousand that was not necessarily predisposed to green ideas. The projections of what conservation could accomplish on a larger scale would therefore tend to be on the conservative side.

Within two years, about 85 percent of households had signed up for intensive energy audits and major construction work using state-of-the-art techniques. Work crews insulated attics, walls, and floors, sealed leaks, and installed double-pane storm windows and heat exchangers. Contractors were closely monitored for their efficiency and cost-effectiveness. It was the biggest experiment of its kind attempted anywhere in the world.

The project's construction phase lasted for two years, from 1983 to 1985. Residents were thrilled with the results. So were we, and so were the BPA and Pacific Power. Billboards went up in the streets proclaiming Hood River County "the Nation's Conservation Capital." The project had demonstrated that the cost of reducing demand could be lower than the cost of adding capacity, and that relatively simple efficiency measures could be introduced much more rapidly than building a new power plant. Ralph's main point had been proved. Just as important, the tone of the debate had been significantly altered. Instead of engaging in confrontation and litigation, traditional adversaries had discovered that they could sit down together and find a solution that made everybody happy. In 1985 the BPA gave Ralph Cavanagh and NRDC its Administrator's Award for Exceptional Public Service, one of several we received for our work on Hood River.

———

NRDC had worked out that the average household, using currently available technologies and without changing lifestyle, could cut its energy use by 70 percent or more. Part of this could be accomplished by retrofitting homes, as had been done in Hood County. Another huge chunk of savings would come from redesigning household appliances, most of which were energy hogs. Enter David Goldstein.

At the Lawrence Berkeley National Laboratory, David had been a graduate student of California's great energy efficiency visionary, physicist Art Rosenfeld, who oversaw innovations such as the solid-state power source that eventually gave us compact fluorescent lightbulbs and a computer program called DOE-2 that models the energy performance of buildings and now saves the country about $10 billion a year in electricity and natural gas costs. For David, he was an inspiring mentor.

David started, as Ralph had done, by breaking down a huge abstract problem into a deceptively simple question: how much energy does it take to wash your clothes?

"Energy is not a meaningless blob," David says. "It is a sum of appliances, buildings, cars, and industrial machines. This energy has to come from somewhere. We could stop some of the 'bad' sources, but if we didn't do something about demand, energy would still come from somewhere, and we probably would not like that somewhere."

To answer his "washing machine" question, David started doing what he calls "combat research," relying on academic research and published papers by efficiency-minded designers. California provided more fertile ground for this work than any other state. Thanks in large part to Art Rosenfeld's work, the California Energy Commission had created the first statewide efficiency standards as early as 1976, beginning with refrigerators, freezers, and air conditioners. After coming to NRDC in 1980, David worked closely with the commission as it—and later the U.S. Department of Energy—expanded and strengthened these regulations to include stoves, clothes dryers, space heaters, pool heaters, dishwashers, lighting fixtures, and many other appliances.

Like Ralph (and for that matter like Linda Greer with Dow Chemical or Sami Yassa with Home Depot), he spent less energy focusing on companies that were evading the law and concentrated instead on those that were causing unintended harm to the environment by conducting business as usual, but would be willing to change if they were shown innovations that would be equally or more profitable.

At first David ran into the same kind of skepticism from appliance manufacturers that Ralph had initially encountered from the utilities. "They insisted that their job was to respond to customer need, and they didn't want anyone telling them what to do," he recalls. "They were doing things the same way they always had and were making profits. So why change?" Ralph's work with the Hood River project offered one important answer to this question: if utilities and customers both bought into the idea of energy efficiency, that would go a long way toward creating a ready-made consumer market for improved appliances. Beyond this, David's expertise as a scientist, and his understanding that inefficient products were usually the result of inefficient—and thus more expensive—manufacturing processes, helped break down the manufacturers' stereotype of environmentalists as antibusiness and antitechnology.

As his efforts on California's regulatory reform continued, he found the companies more and more willing to work constructively with him on developing tighter standards. Eventually this work led to the National Appliance Energy Conservation Act of 1987, which covered twelve common household appliances and would slash consumer energy bills by an estimated $25 billion by 2015.

With more and more utilities on board and a tougher regulatory system in place, David looked for a high-profile, market-driven incentive for manufacturers to revolutionize their technologies. The idea crystallized in a meeting he had with Pacific Gas and Electric. Two dozen utilities would join together to fund a $30 million prize for the smartest and most environmentally friendly new refrigerator, which at the time was the most energy-profligate appliance in people's homes. Technically the initiative was called the Super Efficient Refrigerator Program, but everyone referred to it as the Golden Carrot.

The winner, announced in 1993, was the Whirlpool Corporation, whose design would use at least 25 percent less energy than federal standards required, as a result of a more efficient motor, a redesigned compressor, new high-tech defrost controls, and other innovations. It would also eliminate the use of freon as a refrigerant and chlorofluorocarbons as insulators, both of which were destructive to the earth's atmospheric ozone layer. (NRDC attorney Dan Reicher, who had just left to work in the Clinton administration, later suggested that the president should refer to such technical advances as the "Fridge to the Future.") After refrigerators, the Golden Carrot program would move on to washing machines and air conditioners.

For his work on energy efficiency, David would eventually receive the MacArthur Foundation's "genius" award in 2002.

———

In the thirty years since Ralph Cavanagh and David Goldstein came to NRDC (both are still with us today), California's population has increased by twenty million, but its per capita demand for electricity has remained stable and is now more than 40 percent below the national average. With the exception of a two-year crisis in power supplies in 2000–2001, which resulted from a mania for deregulation and the temporary, ill-considered abandonment of Ralph's philosophy of decoupling utility profits from production levels, energy efficiency remains at the top of what utilities and regulators call the "loading order" for meeting the state's demand for electricity.

Tightening standards for energy-efficient appliances is also still high on our agenda. That means keeping pace with constant technological innovation and changing market conditions, and thinking about the entire range of appliances—from giant corporate server farms and data centers to the humble everyday AC adapter (think of how adapters are warm to the touch—that's all wasted energy). "For instance," says Ashok Gupta, "computer game consoles are incredibly big energy consumers. We did a study showing that a single console can use twice as much energy as a refrigerator. And they are left on all the time. So what do we do? We use the market. When we showed Walmart the results of our study, it insisted that the manufacturers find more efficient ways to power the product."

California, meanwhile, continues to be a national leader in appliance regulations. Its latest advance, announced in November 2009, is the toughest set of efficiency standards in the world for televisions, a process in which Ralph and David's colleague, senior scientist Noah Horowitz, was deeply involved. The standards will reduce electricity costs by more than $8 billion and avoid the need for a new 500-megawatt power plant.

"We've made a lot of progress," David Goldstein says. "From six people working on energy, we now have over sixty, and we've changed the world. Now that I'm fifty-seven years old, people are finally listening to me—even though I'm saying the same things I said when I was twenty-seven."

———

If the federal government had followed California's lead, George Woodwell's direst predictions would not have been fulfilled, and our national energy and climate policy would be in a very different place today. Unfortunately that did not happen.

Like David Goldstein, our first climate scientist, Dan Lashof, had a PhD from Berkeley. He arrived at NRDC in 1989 from the Environmental Protection Agency, where he had worked on one of the agency's earliest reports on climate change. This laid important groundwork for the newly established Intergovernmental Panel on Climate Change, a body set up by the United Nations Environment Programme and the World Meteorological Organization to provide governments with authoritative scientific data on the world's climate. The IPCC issued its first periodic assessment in 1990.

Dan began work with Dick Ayres, Jacob Scherr, David Hawkins, and others on what we called at the time our Atmospheric Protection Initiative. This was a major effort to coordinate the work of lawyers and scientists from eight different NRDC programs, and it involved a host of issues, including not only global warming but acid rain, energy, and ozone depletion. (NRDC had in fact been a major force in the push for an international treaty, the 1987 Montreal Protocol, which banned CFCs not only from refrigerators but from all industrial uses, as the main contributor to the recently discovered "ozone hole" over the Antarctic.)

Our first public effort on climate change as such was a 1989 pamphlet called *Cooling the Greenhouse*. The program moved into high gear a couple years later with the approach of the 1992 Earth Summit in Rio de Janeiro. This was the first time in history that governments had come together to discuss a binding treaty on climate change. Six thousand delegates flocked to Rio from 170 countries, including more than a hundred heads of state—the largest number assembled in a single place at the same time. More important, and in contrast to the Conference on the Human Environment in Stockholm twenty years earlier, Rio swarmed with representatives of nongovernmental organizations, indigenous groups, and women's organizations.

David Doniger in our Washington office called administration officials to underline the importance of President George H. W. Bush attending the summit in person. Although the president did end up going to Rio, he resisted any talk of binding limits on CO_2 emissions, as well as refusing to sign on to the important treaty on biodiversity that was drafted at the summit. As far as global warming was concerned, the United States was missing in action, and the language in the "framework convention" on climate that came out of Rio remained purely aspirational.

After Bush left office, the Clinton administration put together an action plan within its first year that promised to meet the emissions reduction targets laid out in Rio. Part of this would be accomplished by raising corporate average fuel economy (CAFE) standards, forcing the auto industry to make more fuel-efficient cars. Dan was invited to join an advisory committee of government officials, environmentalists, and automakers that would hammer out new CAFE standards, but, he said, all they did was talk. He got the uneasy feeling that the goals set forth in Rio were never going to be achieved unless emission limits were made mandatory.

The organizers of the Rio summit felt the same frustration. In 1995, following the publication of the second and much more alarming assessment report on climate from the Intergovernmental Panel on Climate Change, the UN insisted on a follow-up conference that would write a binding "protocol" to the Rio framework convention.

Four of us flew to the meeting in Kyoto, Japan, in November 1997—myself, Dan Lashof, Jacob Scherr, and our Washington advocacy director, Greg Wetstone. Our old colleague David Doniger, who at this point was the director of climate change policy at the EPA, had been personally involved in drafting proposed language for the protocol. We went to Kyoto with high hopes, though with no certainty about the outcome.

Although it was exciting to meet with so many world leaders who were strongly committed to solving the climate crisis, the talks soon bogged down in serious disagreements. Many involved developing countries such as China, which complained that in their struggle to bring hundreds of millions of people out of poverty it was unfair to be hamstrung by limitations on the use of energy that had never been imposed during the industrialization of the West. With the process close to a standstill, Vice President Al Gore flew in and made an impassioned speech urging the participants to bridge their differences. The point of the meeting, he stressed, was not to write a treaty that would solve this massive problem overnight, but to keep moving in the right direction. He urged the U.S. delegation to be as flexible as possible in working for a consensus plan "with realistic targets and timetables, market mechanisms, and the meaningful participation of key developing countries." After two all-night negotiating sessions in a row, a deal was finally reached.

"When we flew back from Kyoto, we were all excited," Dan remembers. "This had been the real stuff, and we were going home with a treaty that had teeth. However, as soon as we got back, things unraveled."

In retrospect, perhaps we were naive to expect more. Clinton talked a good line on Kyoto, but he never invested any real political capital in it, in part because of the unrelated distractions that led to his impeachment in 1998. Above all, he never laid the necessary groundwork to get it through Congress. "It should have been foretold when the Republicans took over Congress that Kyoto would fail," says David Doniger. "There was a knee-jerk skepticism of the science, coupled with the fact that the Republicans identified it with Al Gore's future. If they refused to ratify the treaty, that would hurt Gore as the nominee for president in 2000."

———

The failure of the United States, the world's biggest single emitter of greenhouse gases, to ratify the Kyoto Protocol almost killed it. Certainly it crippled the protocol's effectiveness. With the road to an international climate treaty blocked, we needed a fallback strategy. It was time, as David Hawkins would say, "to change the facts on the ground."

The brilliance of David's plan was its simplicity. It involved thinking outside the box, as David often does. If Kyoto was crippled by the United States remaining on the sidelines, what other ways were there to reduce CO_2 emissions and set an example for the rest of the world?

David's answer was something he had worked on for a quarter of a century and knew better than anyone: the Clean Air Act. After all, he reasoned, while CO_2 didn't cause acid rain like sulfur dioxide and nitrogen oxide, or damage your central nervous system like mercury, it was still an airborne pollutant, and much of it came from the same source— the burning of fossil fuels. David and Dan Lashof decided to work with David Doniger at the EPA to craft a plan to cap CO_2 emissions from coal-fired power plants. Vermont Republican Jim Jeffords, with Dan's help, had already introduced four-pollutant, or "4P," legislation in the Senate in July 1999. As the November 2000 election approached, Al Gore threw his weight behind the idea.

To everyone's astonishment, Republican candidate George W. Bush stole Gore's thunder by saying that he too endorsed the idea. David Hawkins had always reasoned that since the utilities were going to have to deal with regulations on carbon emissions eventually, they might as well do it now, and bipartisan agreement on the issue seemed to make it a done deal. But when Bush was elected, everything changed.

Right after the election, businessman and Hollywood producer Steve Bing gave us the largest single grant NRDC had ever received, to set up our new Climate Center. David Hawkins would be its director. Dan Lashof, who by now had gained a reputation as the "master translator" of the arcane details of climate change for congressional staff and the media, would be its science director. David Doniger, returning to NRDC after his stint with the Clinton administration, became the policy director. From the energy program, Ralph Cavanagh and David Goldstein brought their expertise on efficiency, and Ashok Gupta added his knowledge of economics and energy policy and his brilliant skills as a negotiator.

In March 2001, the new climate team gathered for the first time in the DeWind Conference Room, named for our former chair. Despite our qualms about the new administration, things looked promising. The president's new EPA administrator, former New Jersey Governor Christine Todd Whitman, was conferring that day with European officials about the U.S. commitment to reduce CO_2 emissions. Then the news came on TV: Bush had reneged on his promise to back the 4P idea.

After that, the blows came thick and fast. On May 17 Bush announced the recommendations of the secret energy task force chaired by Vice President Dick Cheney: no mandatory reductions in power plant emissions; billions of dollars of taxpayers' money for the fossil fuel industry; a cumulative increase of forty billion tons in U.S. carbon emissions by the year 2020; and a 50 percent cut in the renewable energy budget. Although Bush is often thought of as a creature of the oil industry, the giveaways to the coal industry were even greater, and within months the president had announced his intention to reform the Clean Air Act with his infamous "Clear Skies" initiative. "It was a classic wolf in sheep's clothing," says John Steelman, the program manager of our Climate Center. "Not only did it rule out CO_2 as a pollutant, it gave the utility companies twenty years to address the other three pollutants—SO_x, NO_x, and mercury."

Senator Jim Jeffords (who had changed his affiliation to independent) soldiered on for several months with his proposed Clean Power Act. At 9 a.m. on September 11, 2001, David Doniger was in a Senate Environment Committee meeting room discussing the details of the bill when the call came to evacuate the building. The World Trade Center and the Pentagon were under attack. "We evacuated climate legislation as well that day," David says. "Nothing could be done with the Bush administration on environmental issues. The 'Little Ice Age' had begun for the environmental community."

Yet we had been down this road before. The extremists in the Republican Party had overreached in the mid-1990s, and David Hawkins for one felt that they might have overreached again. "The only silver lining," he says, "was that now every single White House reporter was able to connect the dots on global warming. It was not just a science story anymore." The battle over carbon was on.

California Dreaming

Our strategy on climate change after 2001 can be best described as one of total encirclement. Since the Bush-Cheney White House was impervious to reason and science, we decided to work around it on all fronts—with state legislators and governors; with business and financial leaders, from individual visionary entrepreneurs to the giant Wall Street banks that make multibillion-dollar investment decisions; and with the American public and the mainstream of popular culture.

We would take three messages to these audiences. First, stopping global warming is urgent and nonnegotiable if we want to ensure the survival of the planet as we know it. Second, federal limits on carbon emissions are inevitable sooner or later, and by designing economically and technologically smart programs that put individual states, businesses, and investors ahead of the curve, we can create a bandwagon effect. Third, the key to achieving the progress we want is incremental change, based as far as possible on consensus and, where necessary, on compromise.

To many environmentalists, urgency and compromise may sound incompatible. My answer to that is simple: although the search for consensus has always been a hallmark of NRDC's work, climate is fundamentally different from every other environmental challenge we have faced. Pesticides, diesel soot, smokestack emissions, logging—these things and many others I have described in these pages are threats that grow incrementally if left unaddressed. But climate change—as the melting of the polar ice caps and the warming of the oceans show us dramatically—creates feedback loops that will take us within just a few decades to a point of no return. Imagine a car that is speeding downhill out of control. You have to start applying the brakes immediately, even if this does not slow you down as much as you would ideally like. The later you put your foot on the brakes, the worse the shock of stopping. Wait until it's too late, and the car will already be over the cliff.

———————

We started off with the old saying in mind: "As California goes, so goes the nation." If it were an independent country, California would have the world's sixth- or seventh-largest economy, roughly equal to France, and we were sure that whatever steps the state took to slow carbon emissions would serve as an example for others. California offered us many other assets: it had a long tradition of environmental activism; in an economy dominated by the high-tech boom, it was home to many of the country's most imaginative entrepreneurs; and if we wanted to reach the mainstream popular culture, this was the place to do it.

The November 2000 elections brought us a brave California assemblywoman (now senator), Fran Pavley, who left her position as an eighth-grade teacher to run for public office. One of the first bills she proposed was to cut CO_2 emissions from automobiles, which were the largest single contributor in the state to global warming, accounting for 40 percent of all emissions. Her Clean Cars Bill, designated Assembly Bill (AB) 1493, said that CO_2 was a pollutant as defined by the Clean Air Act, and required automakers to reduce emissions from all new cars and light trucks sold in California by 30 percent by 2016. No one in the world had passed such a law, and its implications were staggering. Detroit did not make such a special product line for sale in California, and if the state passed AB 1493, it would invite a predictable challenge in the federal courts by opponents arguing that both clean air standards and fuel efficiency standards are set and enforced in Washington, not Sacramento.

Fran came to us for help, having met NRDC's Annie Notthoff some years earlier, when Fran had been a member of the California Coastal Commission. Annie had started work in our San Francisco office in 1981, and I think of her as a poster child for how far we have come during those three decades. In the beginning, she worked ten hours a week, doing a bit of everything around the office, so that she could also pursue her master's degree in urban and regional planning at UC Berkeley and raise her two young children. Today she is our California advocacy director and one of the most effective environmental campaigners in the country. To help flesh out the details of AB 1493 and plan a strategy for getting it through the legislature in Sacramento, Annie introduced Fran to our resident auto industry expert, senior policy analyst, Roland Hwang, and to a newly founded group that has been critical to NRDC's success during our fourth decade: Environmental Entrepreneurs, or E2.

E2 was established by two Californians, businessman Bob Epstein, a cofounder of the leading database company Sybase, and biologist and medical researcher Nicole Lederer. The group's philosophy is simply expressed: what is good for the environment can also be good for the economy.

After Sybase went public in 1991, Bob gave money to a number of environmental organizations and began a search for the most effective partner. He also wanted to see how each group worked with major donors. He says he found NRDC the most thoughtful and respectful, and I give our membership director Linda Lopez a great deal of the credit for that. Bob also looked at our management philosophy and liked our focus on teamwork. "NRDC is a place where you leave your ego at the door," he says.

In terms of skills and strategies, Bob wanted four things in a partner: legislative ability; litigation and enforcement skills; scientific expertise; and an understanding of business. We had the first three, and though we had taken some steps toward the fourth, we still had a ways to go. Bob thought he could help us in that area, and in 1999 he joined our board. Nicole also became a trustee in 2002.

In 2001, however, when Fran Pavley presented her Clean Cars Bill to the legislature, E2 had no experience in lobbying. Bob hadn't even been to Sacramento in almost a decade. But these "neophytes," as Fran calls them (counting herself among them), quickly became a force to be reckoned with.

AB 1493 was fiercely opposed by both the oil industry and the automobile manufacturers, who spent more than $5 million fighting its passage. They put out a steady stream of misinformation about the bill, saying that California would limit the number of cars per family and raise gas taxes, and that the price of cars would skyrocket. They whipped up opposition on conservative talk shows. In response, we and our partners created a series of "there they go again" ads showing that the automobile industry was using the same kind of scare tactics it had tried before to fight seat belts, catalytic converters, and unleaded gas. No, our ads said, the sky would *not* fall if the bill passed. There was no economic or technological reason why more efficient cars could not be built by the deadline set by AB 1493.

In the end, Fran Pavley won. A statewide poll by the Public Policy Institute of California found that 81 percent of Californians favored her bill, including a remarkable 77 percent of SUV owners, and almost every daily newspaper in the state came out in support. San Francisco Senator John Burton got the bill through the senate, and in July 2002 Governor Gray Davis signed it into law.

Getting AB 1493 onto the California statute books was only the first of two battles, and the second one would be much more challenging. General Motors and DaimlerChrysler quickly filed suit against the state of California and the California Air Resources Board, charging that only the federal government could regulate fuel economy. President Bush's EPA agreed that the California bill was in effect an attempt to set a gasoline mileage standard. What was California to do? To answer that question, we would have to go to court—and eventually the critical question of whether CO_2 could be regulated as an air pollutant would go all the way to the Supreme Court.

Since the passage of Fran Pavley's Clean Cars Bill, E2 has gone on to become a force in California and national politics. In the tradition begun by Alice Sandler (Ross's wife) and Adele Auchincloss back in the 1970s, Bob and Nicole began to invite friends and business colleagues to their homes or to the NRDC San Francisco office to learn about our work in regular "Eco Salons." E2 has spread to twenty-seven states and holds similar events in many major cities. Delegations travel regularly to Washington to make their case to lawmakers that the move to a low-carbon economy represents a tremendous opportunity for American businesses. One group that addressed leaders of the House of Representatives in 2008 included a leading venture capitalist, the CEO of a company that does green housing retrofits, and the CEO of a biofuels company in Hawaii. That's a fairly typical assortment of E2 members and suggests why the group has gained so much credibility in the business community: more than simply supporting a cause, it puts its money where its mouth is.

———

Steve Bing's support for the creation of our Climate Center in 2001 was one of the first tangible signs of the roots that NRDC had begun to put down in another influential California community—the entertainment industry. At the beginning, the board and staff had some reluctance about this—a "just let us do our work" snobbishness that reminded me of the arguments about becoming a membership organization a quarter of a century earlier. Aware of the need to proceed with caution, we put our trust in the advice of a handful of people who had the right mix of high-level connections in Hollywood and a serious commitment to the environment, and also understood the strategic importance of California to national policy on global warming.

Our most important early supporters were Peter Morton, cofounder of the Hard Rock Cafe chain of restaurants, and Alan Horn, the head of Castle Rock Entertainment and later the president of Warner Brothers. Peter was especially prescient in his early concern about the problem of urban runoff—the polluted water that flows from sources such as overloaded storm drains and paved streets and parking lots. The problem was especially serious in Los Angeles, since so much of the runoff ended up in the waters off the recreational beaches of Santa Monica Bay.

David Beckman, who had started off at NRDC working with Gail Feuer, headed up our new four-person Los Angeles water program. "Storm water runoff is not the sexiest of issues," David acknowledges, "but it is vitally important. As cities grow, all the permeable surfaces are paved or built over so that the rainfall mingles with urban pollution and flows directly into the ocean. Nationwide, this is our single fastest-growing source of water pollution."

"With climate change and expanding cities," David continues, "we need to keep our water, not throw it away." So together with Nancy Stoner and Kaid Benfield in our Washington office, he is now working to develop the concept of "green infrastructure," a collection of strategies such as capturing water in cisterns, creating rooftop gardens, and "creating" water by reusing it, that help the urban environment to operate more like a natural landscape.

Meanwhile, Alan Horn, who is now NRDC's vice-chair, gave me the grand tour of Hollywood, introducing me to studio heads, leading directors, and other important industry insiders such as Steve Bing. Of all the people to whom Alan introduced me, no one was more important than Laurie David, who took our relationship to mainstream popular culture to a new level. Laurie, who joined our board in 1999, had worked on *The Late Show with David Letterman* and was married to Larry David, creator of *Seinfeld* and *Curb Your Enthusiasm*.

"I had been at weekly dinner parties with the biggest names in Hollywood," Laurie says, "but I was in awe at the brilliance of the staff and board members at NRDC. I knew I had to hit the books and read every article in order to get up to speed."

At one NRDC meeting, Laurie came up to me and asked, "How do you not get overwhelmed with all the problems in the world? I want to do something, but I don't know what."

"Laurie," I said, "There's only one issue: global warming. It's the mother of all our problems."

After that, she says, she focused on global warming "like a mad woman."

Laurie started with her friends, inviting them to her home to learn about fuel-efficient cars and persuading them to switch to hybrids. That was just the beginning. She told us that we wouldn't get where we needed to go unless we reached the housewives, the women who buy clothes, the people who watched her husband's show. Before long, Larry David had a fictional TV wife who was an NRDC board member, and his plot lines were revolving around things like driving Toyota Priuses and worrying about the pesticides used on golf courses.

Laurie knew plenty of other women in Hollywood who felt the same way as she did about the environment, and she worked with Elizabeth Wiatt, the wife of James Wiatt, head of the William Morris Agency, and six others to create the NRDC Action Forum, which worked closely with E2 to hone its lobbying skills. The Hollywood women took their first trip to Washington in 2001, spending two full days with members of Congress, advocating energy efficiency and protesting Bush's "Clear Skies" initiative. The nation's capital had never seen anything quite like them.

With the help of friends like these, one thing led to another with almost dizzying speed. Once or twice a year there were movie premieres to benefit NRDC. Star-studded evenings of song and comedy, called Earth to L.A.!, brought in precious funds for our work and brought us to the attention of ever-wider audiences. Of all these glittering events, perhaps the one that most clearly sticks in my mind is the 2003 Turn

Up the Heat concert at the Staples Center in Los Angeles. Steve Bing had persuaded the Rolling Stones to perform a benefit concert for NRDC, and President Bill Clinton had agreed to appear on stage to proclaim his personal commitment to the fight against global warming. I have to admit, for Patricia and me to be standing up there while fifty thousand people rocked under enormous NRDC banners and Mick Jagger jumped about all over the stage was nothing short of mind-boggling.

Meanwhile, the TV networks and cable channels were busy producing specials on climate change featuring Laurie and Bobby Kennedy. Even Fox News got in on the act. Then Laurie learned of Al Gore's famous slide show on global warming and suggested he turn it into a movie, which she co-produced. Almost before we knew it, *An Inconvenient Truth* had won the Academy Award for best documentary feature of 2006, NRDC was greening the Oscars themselves, and NRDC board member Leonardo DiCaprio was up there on stage urging people to support our work.

FREE ROLLING STONES CONCERT TO FIGHT GLOBAL WARMING, ORGANIZED BY STEVE BING, STAPLES CENTER, LOS ANGELES, FEBRUARY 6, 2003
Rolling Stones with John Adams, Frances Beinecke, Steve Bing, and David Hawkins

DiCaprio had first come to talk to me in 2000, at Gore's recommendation. When he asked me at our first meeting how he could be most helpful, I advised him to model himself on Robert Redford—which he has done, immersing himself in the issues, producing his own documentary on global warming, and joining the NRDC board.

Over the past decade, dozens of the top stars in Hollywood and the music industry have offered us their support. Sometimes it's a matter of hosting a special event; sometimes it's writing a generous check. But Leonardo is one of a small, select group of individuals from the entertainment industry—people like Meryl Streep, Glenn Close, Pierce Brosnan, and Sigourney Weaver (Frances Beinecke's roommate at Yale)—who have formed a deeper and more lasting bond with NRDC.

I can't think of anyone who has shown us more of this unobtrusive, long-term loyalty than the singer-songwriter James Taylor. James became a board member in 1992 and offered to promote NRDC's work through his summer tour that year. Our son Ramsay and his University of Wisconsin classmate Mike Goldberg followed the tour across country for twenty-four thousand miles, burning through three rental cars in the process. At each stop, they set up NRDC information booths, enlisting local volunteers to hand out brochures in exchange for free tickets. At the end of the evening, Ramsay and Mike would break down the booth again and drive on through the night to the next concert, taking turns sleeping in the car. In the process, James became a good friend. He hosted our twenty-fifth anniversary event in 1995, and when I eventually stepped down as president of NRDC at the end of 2005, he came to the party and serenaded us with his best-known song, "Carolina in My Mind," noting our mutual ties to North Carolina.

As we navigated these new and unfamiliar worlds, we relied constantly on the wise counsel of Bob Redford. In 2006, at a brainstorming session at his Sundance Institute in Utah with Laurie David and our new communications director, former *New York Times* reporter Phil Gutis, Bob came up with another inspired idea. He said that if we were really interested in getting our message across to ordinary Americans, there was no better place to do so than at a baseball or football game. Allen Hershkowitz mentioned that through his work on the Cumberland Plateau he had been introduced to the owners of the Philadelphia Eagles football team, who were interested in using recycled paper for their game-day programs and yearbooks. After a few more planning sessions, Allen was off and running with an innovative initiative to green the National Football League, National Basketball Association, National Hockey League, and Major League Baseball.

In the spring of 2008, the legendary Fenway Park, home of the Boston Red Sox, went green. The hot dogs were organic, volunteers collected all the trash to be recycled, and the stadium generators were supplemented by solar panels. On April 22, Earth Day, I was asked to throw out the first pitch. I had played baseball all my life and tossed thousands of balls to our kids. But Fenway Park, in front of thirty thousand people? I needed a little practice, so Patricia and I went to the Boston Commons in the late afternoon, and she, using my old catcher's mitt, warmed me up for the big pitch. We wondered what people must be thinking as they strolled through the park, seeing these two older people tossing a baseball back and forth. We'd come a long way from our founding conference in Princeton more than three decades ago. Our small idea had hit the big time.

———

With all the energy and talent available to us in Los Angeles, and with so much of our program work focused on California, we had decided it was the right time to build an NRDC office that would be the first major green building in the city. As in New York, I saw the location as vital. We had first set up shop in one of the finest art deco buildings in downtown LA, out of a sense of commitment to the neighborhood and its mix of communities. But we soon realized that downtown was not an inviting location for the visitors, reporters, politicians, and members we wanted to attract to our workplace. We moved twice, settling eventually on Santa Monica.

We chose this location because it was easy to get to, with friendly neighborhoods and walkable streets. We found a fifteen-thousand-square-foot building a few blocks from the ocean and the Santa Monica pier. It was close to public transportation and the weekly farmers' market, and there were no tall buildings around it. However, the layout was odd—long and narrow with high windows. It had once been an acupuncture school.

After a nationwide search, we settled on the architectural firm of Moule and Polyzoides, and Elizabeth Moule set about designing a building that would meet LEED standards. Our board chair Fritz Schwarz and board member (and future chair) Dan Tishman felt that we should go all the way and get LEED Platinum certification, the highest possible rating for a green building.

The old 1917 building was gutted to its skeleton, and 90 percent of the tear-down material was recycled. Central light wells flooded the offices with light and allowed for natural ventilation. We put solar panels on the roof and installed a water recycling system that results in a 60 percent savings. To reduce the use of timber, the walls were made of a mix of fiber and cement. The modest amount of new wood we did need was cut from FSC-certified forests, and the furniture was made from recycled materials. Reporters who came to visit noted the small details like the hemp carpets, bamboo flooring, and conference room chairs upholstered in recycled seat belts.

The only problem with going for LEED-Platinum status was the cost. Instead of a building costing a couple million dollars, we were looking at closer to nine million. The entire NRDC board pitched in to bridge the financial gap, with Steve Bing and our other new Hollywood friends in the lead. Peter Morton, Alan Horn and his wife, Cindy, Elizabeth Wiatt, and Jill Tate Higgins (a cofounder of E2 in Southern California) all donated conference rooms. The first floor, which is open

NRDC *INFORMANT* MOVIE BENEFIT, 2009
Left to right: Frederick (Fritz) A. O. Schwarz, Jr., NRDC Chair 1993–2008;
Daniel R. Tishman, NRDC Chair 2009–present

to the public, houses the David Family's Environmental Action Center, Leonardo DiCaprio's E-Activism Zone, and the Gil Friesen and Janet Rienstra Green Building Alcove.

We inaugurated our new offices in November 2003, with a name that could not have been more appropriate—the Robert Redford Building.

Meanwhile, the serious work of fighting global warming through state legislation went on, and once again Fran Pavley was at its center. Her first major bill had addressed the problem of CO_2 emissions from *mobile* sources—automobiles. This one, the California Global Warming Solutions Act, or AB 32, dealt with *all* sources, notably power plants, factories, and transportation, and its ramifications were even greater.

"California really stepped up the pace in 2006," says Annie Notthoff. "The governor and the legislature were competing to be the top warrior on global warming. Our San Francisco energy 'brain trust'— Ralph Cavanagh, staff scientist Devra Wang, and senior policy analyst Sheryl Carter—came up with two path-breaking bills that year. One was AB 32, sponsored by Fran Pavley and Assembly Speaker Fabian Nunez, and the other was Senate Bill 1368, backed by Senate President Pro Tem Don Perata."

AB 32 was not ours alone; NRDC worked on the initiative with others, including Karen Douglas of the Environmental Defense Fund. "But SB 1368 was an NRDC creation from start to finish," says Annie. "Ralph wrote an idea on a pad and gave it to Devra and Sheryl. They turned it into legislation."

AB 32 required California to roll back global warming emissions to 1990 levels by 2020, which would slash statewide emissions by 30 percent relative to what they would have been without any caps. The law would serve as a prototype for other states and eventually the nation to emulate. To meet the emissions target, the law could rely not only on tough regulations but on incentives and market mechanisms such as a "cap and trade" system that would operate much like a stock exchange for carbon. The basic idea of cap and trade is to set an overall ceiling for emissions, with each power plant or other source being given (or purchasing) a certain number of "allowances." Those who come in under their emissions limit can trade their allowances, or credits, with others who do not. As a result of AB 32, California would be in a position to link up with other similar cap and trade programs. Businesses would be able to buy and sell allowances with others in the state and in a global marketplace—with other states adopting similar measures or even with international programs such as the European Union's carbon-trading system.

This carbon market would act as an incentive for new, clean technologies and create a pot of money for the state to invest in efficiency measures and in renewable energy sources such as wind and solar power. SB 1368 would go a step further, preventing more long-term investments in power generation with high rates of greenhouse gas emissions. "Under this law, California utilities are not able to make any investments in power plants that would emit more CO_2 than a natural gas plant," Sheryl Carter explains. "So a proposed coal plant built in the traditional way would not be able to get financing. Utilities will be looking instead at efficiency as the quickest, cheapest, and best long-term solution. And efficiency is something that can be done in increments, starting immediately."

E2, with five years of experience under its belt, threw itself into the lobbying effort for AB 32 and SB 1368. The group started off with a 2006 position paper, "Solving Global Warming One State at a Time," which laid out the economic advantages of the bill. Meanwhile, E2 delegations worked the halls of the legislature in Sacramento, neutralizing the arguments from the bill's opponents that the measure was "anti-business."

Nicole Lederer recalls, "When the California Chamber of Commerce and the oil industry argued that the bill would bring California's economy to its knees, we said, 'We *are* business and we support this bill.'"

"We made it our business to know how every member would vote, what objections there might be, and who might best address them," says Bob Epstein. Every time they met with a member of the assembly or senate (and there were 124 meetings in all), E2 followed up within twenty-four hours. The reports they sent to the speaker's staff and to Fran Pavley showed that reductions were possible, that they would have a positive economic effect, that there was business support, and that environmental justice issues were addressed. It was critically important to us that the allowance trading system would not have the unintended effect of leaving the dirtiest plants in the poorest areas.

Negotiations went on all summer, with August 31, the end of the legislative session, as the deadline. After Republican Governor Arnold Schwarzenegger announced his support for the bill at a press conference, Annie Notthoff and the E2 team took copies to every office they had visited over the previous six months, explaining how that particular legislator's suggestions had been incorporated and confirming his or her support. Within twenty-four hours, AB 32 was approved by a combined vote in the senate and assembly of seventy to forty-six, and the governor signed it into law on September 27, 2006. SB 1368 followed soon after.

By the time AB 32 became law, we had already taken major steps toward creating a similar system in the Northeast. Back in the late 1980s, Ashok Gupta and Kit Kennedy, a Harvard Law School graduate and a tough-minded but pragmatic negotiator, had launched a new program to make the same progress on utility reform, demand reduction, and appliance efficiency in New York State that we had made in California. After George Pataki became governor, I joined Ashok and Kit at many meetings with him to discuss the virtues of energy efficiency and persuade him that consumer demand could be met without the need for environmentally ruinous new generating capacity.

In the Pacific Northwest, our concern had been new coal-fired and nuclear plants; in New York, it was a massive hydroelectric project on James Bay in northern Quebec. The idea was for the state to buy power from the Canadian company Hydro-Quebec, generated by new dams that would flood Cree ancestral land. As in the Clayoquot Sound case, we were unable to bring a lawsuit in the Canadian courts, so we used the power of what Ashok calls our bully pulpit, rallying our members to protest the destruction of part of the largest untouched wilderness area in North America for the sake of producing expensive and unneeded electricity. In 1992 Pataki's predecessor as governor, Democrat Mario Cuomo, accepted that energy efficiency was a better option and canceled the multibillion-dollar purchasing agreement.

In 1997 we hired Dale Bryk to join the New York team. She did not start off with a background in energy issues, but she was a quick study and shared both Kit's formidable negotiating skills and her boundless energy. By 2003 Dale had helped develop the first mandatory cap on CO_2 emissions on electricity generation in the country. There was no hiding that the switch to a lower carbon economy would involve some short-term pain before the economic benefits kicked in, so we worked closely with Pataki to bring in a consortium of other New England and Mid-Atlantic states to strengthen the plan and ease the transition. As our regional work expanded, so did our climate team, with the addition of Theo Spencer, whose main focus is opposing conventional coal plants, and Nathanael Greene, who has become one of the country's leading experts on biofuels.

Building support for this initiative involved a lot of retail-style lobbying with individual utilities, state and elected officials, and potential backers in the corporate sector. This was an uphill battle at first, Dale says. "People come to the table with a worldview that is very hard to shake." But after watching Dale in action, you would have to conclude that her motto in life is "Never take no for an answer."

One of her first projects was to make sure that New Jersey included increased spending on energy efficiency in a new state law on utility restructuring. Although we had local partners, we didn't have much of a presence in the state capital, Trenton. Dale decided that the challenge was to find the one key policy maker who would champion the issue. This led to an introduction to Paul DiGaetano, the Republican majority leader in the state assembly.

"We met in a little family Italian restaurant near Trenton where everyone knew DiGaetano," Dale remembers. "When he came into the restaurant, I was showing Ashok, whose parents are Indian, pictures of my trip to Tibet. I'm sure DiGaetano wondered what the two of us, an Asian and a woman in sandals, could possibly understand about New Jersey energy policy and New Jersey politics. With grand Italian style, he ordered us a big meal and then asked, 'What's your pitch?' I didn't think he'd get it, but I said we wanted him to put somewhat complicated language into the New Jersey restructuring bill that would increase spending on efficiency."

"I think we can make this happen," he answered. And he did—more than a billion dollars were allocated to energy efficiency in New Jersey over the next decade.

From this story, Dale concludes: "There are tons of people who support our work but don't have the power to make it happen. You need a leader who will find consensus among all the groups, and that leader can be from an advocacy group, politics, or even business. Assemblyman DiGaetano was that person."

For the next five years, we played an instrumental role in developing the framework for a multistate agreement. In December 2005, Connecticut, Delaware, Maine, Maryland, Massachusetts, New Hampshire, New Jersey, New York, Rhode Island, and Vermont announced the Regional Greenhouse Gas Initiative. The plan took effect in 2009, and by 2019 it will reduce CO_2 emissions in these ten states by 10 percent. Economists also estimate that the combination of a carbon cap and efficiency will lower household electricity bills by about $100 a year, showing again that consumers do not have to choose between the environment and their pocketbooks.

California's AB 32 and SB 1368 remain the linchpin of a system that is spreading nationwide by leaps and bounds. Half the country has now moved in the right direction on greenhouse gas emissions, and the rest will surely follow. New Mexico and Arizona were the first to follow California's lead. Then came the Western Climate Initiative, a grouping of seven states (including several traditionally "red" ones) and three Canadian provinces, followed by the Midwestern Regional Greenhouse Gas Reduction Accord, with nine more states and three Canadian provinces as either members or observers.

The Midwestern initiative was a big part of the reason we opened an NRDC office in Chicago in 2007, our first permanent presence in the heartland. The office's director, Henry Henderson, and his colleague Andrew Wetzler compare the challenge to the earliest days of NRDC, since the national concern about the environment that began in the 1970s never really reached the Midwest.

"We inherited a range of economic arrangements that were very successful in the nineteenth century—a coal-based grid and a car economy, coupled with intense agricultural production," says Henry, who served for six years in the 1990s as the first commissioner of Chicago's Department of Environment. "Our regulators are supposed to be advancing environmental standards, but in fact they protect dirty energy because they have an instinctively protectionist approach."

Given this stuck-in-time quality of environmental politics in the Midwest, the work of the Chicago office is strongly focused on litigation. "Mitch Bernard's litigation team is a game-changer," Henry says, "although of course we have a range of other resources that we can also bring to bear—NRDC's name, our science center, our energy team, and our advocacy ability. It used to be that no one in the Midwest could take on a big fight on these issues, but NRDC has changed that."

Taking on the bad guys in our time-honored fashion is only one side of the coin, however. Henry and his colleagues, like those in our other offices, are also pushing hard on the economic benefits of a green economy. Henry has worked with Michigan Governor Jennifer Granholm, for example, to show that a cap-and-trade system would mean new jobs for her state; the emphasis is on quality of life issues. It's not easy. We are on a new frontier here, and one that can sometimes be hostile. But Henry reflects all the excitement and enthusiasm I remember from our earliest days at NRDC. "There are big challenges," he says, "but this is our job, and we take pleasure in it. We have the righteous audacity that changes things. We are not extremists; we are just very determined."

The China Syndrome

No matter how much progress we make at home, the climate crisis will not ultimately be solved without the participation of China, or without U.S.-China cooperation. Over the past three decades, China's journey from a centrally planned to a market system has produced an economic miracle that has raised more than two hundred million people out of poverty—but with horrifying environmental consequences. About three-fourths of China's energy is generated by coal. To meet its soaring demand for energy, China now consumes more coal than the United States, the European Union, and Japan put together, building the equivalent of one new five-hundred-megawatt coal-fired power plant every ten days. Just a few years ago, experts were predicting that China would overtake the United States as the world's largest emitter of CO_2 by the year 2020; it actually happened in 2006. How China balances its demand for economic growth and energy with the world's urgent need to reduce carbon emissions is the greatest environmental challenge of the century.

What can an international group like NRDC do about such a monumental problem, let alone in a country with almost no history until recently of nongovernmental organizations and a long-standing suspicion of interference by outsiders? Not much, perhaps—unless you happen to hire someone like Barbara Finamore.

Barbara had worked with Tom Cochran on our nuclear program in the early 1980s. Soon after that, she moved to Moscow with her diplomat husband and took time off to have three children. In 1990 the family moved again, this time to Beijing, where her husband became head of the internal political section of the U.S. Embassy. Barbara took a job as a consultant with the United Nations Development Programme, working on a "sustainable development blueprint" for China as a follow-up to the 1992 Earth Summit in Rio de Janeiro. Almost no information about environmental issues was available locally, and she had to go around to seventy different government agencies to find out what they were doing and what their needs were (not an easy job for an American in those days, so soon after the violent suppression of the Tiananmen Square democracy movement). Then she had to bring forty separate reports together and compile them into a single document that would be China's contribution to Agenda 21, the country-by-country sustainable development plan that emerged from the Rio summit. When the job was done, it struck her that she probably knew as much about sustainability issues in China as anyone.

At this time, China did not yet have a legally recognized environmental NGO, or nongovernmental organization (the first one, Friends of Nature, would not be registered until March 1994). Barbara met a number of people who were at least beginning to ask the right questions. In particular, she was impressed by a professor at the China University of Politics and Law, Wang Canfa, who asked if she would teach some one-day classes on U.S. and international environmental law. Barbara remembers that the level was, to put it mildly, basic. "The students asked questions like, 'What is the Constitution?' and 'What is Congress?' But I was totally taken with Wang Canfa. One day he asked me, 'What do they do in the United States to stop people taking to the streets in protest at their environmental conditions?' I said, 'We have lawsuits.'"

Barbara began to wonder for the first time whether we might have a role to play here. People like Wang Canfa were essentially in the same position as the founders of NRDC in 1970. If China was to thrive economically and overcome its environmental problems, it was going to need laws, lawyers, independent advocates, and technical expertise in everything from public health to energy policy. We had been working in those areas for more than thirty years. Perhaps we could harvest that experience for the benefit of those in China who were working to accomplish the same goals.

By 1995 Barbara was back in Washington. Tom said she could have her old job back on the nuclear program, but by now China had become a near obsession. "I felt like Cinderella," she recalls. "NRDC said that if I did my chores [meaning litigation], I could do whatever else I wanted, just as long as the funding could be found." Even as early as this, Barbara was thinking about climate: she understood that although China's soaring energy needs and CO_2 emissions were a big part of the problem, China would also be a big part of the solution. However, she knew that a U.S. organization could not walk in and start telling China what to do. The initiative had to come from the Chinese side.

She brainstormed ideas with her NRDC colleagues. Dan Lashof had made a trip to China with President Clinton's energy secretary, Hazel O'Leary, where they discussed plans for an "efficiency power plant," in which half the planned generating capacity would be offset by a corresponding demand-side reduction. That proposal did not get off the ground, but Barbara was excited by the concept and talked to Ralph Cavanagh and David Goldstein to learn all she could about energy efficiency.

She still needed to identify what she called "the who, the what, and the where." Already familiar with Beijing, she decided to venture farther afield and asked Rob Watson, our green buildings expert, to accompany her. Rob had been deeply skeptical when Barbara first suggested that NRDC get involved with China. He had just come back from Russia and knew that you didn't dabble in a country of this size. Besides, we had no funding. However, he did agree to go with her to explore the possibilities in the ancient city of Chongqing, on the Yangtze River.

Barbara thought Chongqing was promising because it had just been declared an independent municipality, which gave it the same level of authority as a provincial government. It was slated for massive urban and industrial development, and the Three Gorges Dam, the largest hydropower project in the world, was under construction nearby. "The city officials welcomed us, but we were like aliens to them," Barbara says. "They had no idea what an NGO was, who we were, or what we were proposing. When we started talking about efficiency power plants, they thought we were crazy! Finally we were just reduced to saying, 'What do you need? We're here to help.'"

After listening to a description of Rob's work, the officials said they would be interested in a green retrofit of one of the hotels in the city. But this turned out to be a big misunderstanding; they had taken Barbara and Rob for investors who were offering to pay for the project. The miscommunication was cleared up when one of our local advisers introduced Barbara and Rob to Timothy Hui, a radio announcer at the time of the Tiananmen protests who had quit his job rather than limit his reporting to the official version of events. When Timothy's expert translation had cleared up the confusion, Barbara and Rob proposed instead to help the city design an energy-efficient building code. The officials enthusiastically agreed.

Buildings account for 50 percent of all energy consumption, and building-related activities for 42 percent of greenhouse gas emissions. When a country is growing and urbanizing as fast as China, a tremendous opportunity exists to get it right from the start and preempt future environmental problems.

Patricia and I saw the dramatic changes for ourselves during two trips we made to Chongqing with Barbara, the first in 2002 and the second five years later. On our first visit, the steep streets rising up the hillsides from the Yangtze River were packed with people bustling around the small shops. Coolies (from the Chinese word *kuli*, or "bitter strength") ran through the narrow alleyways with everything from bok choy to cinder blocks hanging from the poles they balanced on their shoulders. Few buildings rose more than ten stories, although the smog was so severe that we could see no higher than the fifth story from the sidewalk. It was a place of no shadows; air pollution blocked out the sun.

On our return visit in 2007, Chongqing had been transformed into a city of skyscrapers and broad streets packed with cars. The small stores had been replaced with shopping centers, modern hotels lined the boulevards, and four-lane highways radiated out from the city hub. Chongqing, like all of China, had become a vast construction site. The one thing that had not changed was the pollution.

The Three Gorges Dam, built to provide energy for this burgeoning megacity and beyond, was only a year away from full operation, and on our second trip down the Yangtze the ship floated over the homes, mines, and villages we had visited five years earlier, now resting silently in the murky depths. More than a million people had been relocated, most of them transferred into modern high-rises. Today the municipality of Chongqing is home to more than thirty million people.

Devising the Chongqing building code was a true learning experience in how to work in China. The city drew up a code according to our recommendations, but when Barbara and Rob returned to go over the draft with officials, they were told that such a document could not possibly be shared with foreigners, so it had already been submitted to the legislature. However, the most significant outcome was that the Chongqing code caught the attention of the Ministry of Construction, which decided to expand its provisions to the entire Yangtze River Basin region, one of China's three main climate zones.

After those first overtures to the officials in Chongqing, one thing led to another. Back in Washington, Barbara was browsing through the *Federal Register* one day in preparation for a lawsuit when her eye fell on a notice asking for volunteers to work on a showcase green building in Beijing, a collaboration between the U.S. Department of Energy and China's Ministry of Science and Technology. The project had grown out of Rio's Agenda 21 but had never been funded. Barbara wrote up a proposal, and it was accepted. Rob put together a consortium of companies, which he called ACCORD21, to work on the project and provided years of technical and professional guidance.

The 130,000-square-foot Agenda 21 building in the Chinese capital was inaugurated with great fanfare in 2004. Housing two departments of the Ministry of Science and Technology, it also serves as the secretariat of Agenda 21, which Barbara had worked for back in the early 1990s. China's first LEED-certified building (it received the coveted LEED Gold certification), it uses 75 percent less energy per square foot than other comparable government buildings and 60 percent less water. For our work on the project, China's Ministry of Construction gave us its first Green Building Innovation Award.

There are many difficulties involved in working in China, but in comparison to the United States during the Bush years, there was also one great advantage. As China's environmental situation worsened, government officials increasingly acknowledged the problems they were facing. And as they learned more about NRDC, there was a real willingness to listen to us and draw on the expertise we could offer. As a result, we were able to build productive relationships with officials at all levels—local, provincial, and national.

Excited by the success of the LEED-certified Agenda 21 building, the Beijing municipality signed an agreement in 2006 for a green retrofit of all government and large commercial buildings in the city, some three hundred in all, asking us to provide technical assistance along the way. Similar retrofits were carried out in Shanghai, and buildings in that city have adopted an energy labeling and rating system for prospective buyers and tenants that is based on David Goldstein's work. We also worked closely with Beijing and International Olympic Committee officials to make sure that the Olympic Village for the 2008 Games set ambitious standards for energy efficiency. This complex too was awarded LEED Gold certification.

Many of our ideas about green buildings and smart growth have become part of Chinese national policy. We helped the government develop its first national energy efficiency standards for buildings, and these were incorporated into China's eleventh Five-Year Plan (2006–2010), which calls for all new buildings to lower their energy use by 50 percent, rising to 65 percent in four large municipalities: Beijing, Shanghai, Tianjin, and Chongqing, which have a combined population of more than seventy-five million people. We are also working with the Agenda 21 secretariat to promote low-carbon urban planning in two midsize pilot cities, Zunyi and Tongling, stressing the smart growth principles of compact, mixed-use development that will minimize vehicle travel, protect natural land, and enhance the social and economic vitality of these communities.

———

Our work in Chongqing had presented its share of frustrations, but it also led to a chance encounter that connected directly to the work we were doing on climate in California and produced results that have been nothing short of spectacular.

Barbara attended a conference in Chongqing organized by Asia-Pacific Economic Cooperation, the intergovernmental body that promotes economic growth, trade, and investment in the region. The topic of the meeting was demand-side management, or DSM, a term that refers to the package of economic and technical measures utilities can employ to encourage a more efficient (and environmentally sustainable) use of electricity by consumers—essentially what Ralph Cavanagh and David Goldstein had been working on for years in California.

At the Chongqing conference, Barbara happened to meet the head of a new DSM center in the coastal province of Jiangsu, one of the most prosperous provinces in the country. The Jiangsu center was involved in education and training, and did not yet have any projects that would apply DSM principles to a real-life situation. But the Jiangsu officials came back to us some time later to see if we would help them develop one. What prompted this sense of urgency was the wave of blackouts that hit China in 2002 and 2003. Utilities were operating the system around the clock at almost 100 percent capacity and taking stopgap emergency measures such as ordering factories to work only at night or to close down for a week at a time. Even so, the skyrocketing demand for energy had brought the power grid close to the point of collapse.

In 2004 NRDC signed a memorandum of understanding with the Jiangsu provincial government—to our knowledge the first agreement of its kind between a government entity and a foreign NGO in the country's history. The Jiangsu officials realized, as we did, that China's use of energy was grossly inefficient—according to the most recent figures, China consumes more than 16 percent of the world's energy while producing only 7.6 percent of its total gross domestic product (GDP). We knew that demand-side management and energy efficiency had tremendous potential here. One study found that by switching to energy-efficient technologies for industrial production and commercial and residential electricity use, China could meet as much as half of its projected new energy demand by 2014. This would obviate the need for six hundred or more new coal-fired powered plants, leading in turn to the eventual prevention of two billion tons a year of CO_2 emissions.

We began working directly with the central government, academics, regulators, grid managers, and power plant operators to help them develop the tools they needed to encourage an upgrade to more efficient technologies for things like commercial lighting, industrial motors, and air-conditioning systems. No outsiders had talked to China in these terms before, and our advice turned out to be hugely influential, not just in Jiangsu but increasingly at the national level.

However, the economics of efficiency are complicated, involving questions like energy audits, consumer rebates, and, above all, investment incentives. There is no getting around the fact that efficiency requires large up-front investments and that the market presents all kinds of barriers that must be overcome. We recognized that China would be reluctant to make these big investments unless it was convinced by hands-on practical experience that measurable and verifiable savings would result. This is why the pilot project in Jiangsu was so important.

Jiangsu province is an industrial powerhouse. With a population of seventy-six million, it produces more than 12 percent of China's total GDP and leads the country in economic growth, energy usage—and environmental pollution. Developing a strategic blueprint for demand-side management for the whole province, as we did in cooperation with Southeast University, the State Grid Corporation, and the Jiangsu Economic and Trade Commission, was a monumental challenge. Six main industrial sectors were involved—chemicals, metallurgy, building materials, textiles, machinery, and electronics—and the eight-month study entailed an analysis of more than fifteen thousand factories and commercial facilities, many of which appeared on the central government's list of the thousand most energy-intensive plants in China.

The study showed that for every *yuan* invested in DSM, seven would be returned to the Jiangsu economy. In ten years, a comprehensive DSM program would bring in the equivalent of $21 billion. We also found that it would reduce China's coal consumption by 167 million metric tons by 2015, with correspondingly huge reductions in CO_2 and SO_x and NO_x emissions.

The Jiangsu experiment quickly attracted the attention of the central government. Chinese Premier Wen Jiabao and Vice Premier Zeng Peiyan praised the initiative and told the State Energy Office that it should be promoted as a national model. The Five-Year Plan unveiled in 2005 called for China's "energy intensity"—the amount of energy consumed per unit of GDP—to be cut by 20 percent by 2010. It was the most aggressive energy efficiency program in the world.

Then, in 2007, the government invited NRDC to join China's two largest utilities in cosponsoring an international forum on demand-side management, which would serve to showcase what was happening in Jiangsu and educate provincial governments and utilities about the economic and environmental benefits. The following year, the central government identified Suzhou, China's largest industrial city and Jiangsu's biggest energy user, as the site of the first citywide experiment in energy efficiency to be led by the central government. We were asked to work with other provincial governments, starting with Hebei, the province that surrounds metropolitan Beijing. We even worked with China Central Television on a seven-part documentary on energy efficiency that aired in prime time.

By this point California had entered the picture very directly, proving that its advances in clean technology and efficiency could serve as a model not just for the rest of the United States but for the world's fastest-growing economy and soon-to-be number one carbon emitter. In September 2005, we arranged for a high-level California delegation to visit Jiangsu, headed by public utility commissioner Susan Kennedy (who would later become Governor Schwarzenegger's chief of staff) and David Goldstein's old mentor, Art Rosenfeld, who was now, at the age of almost eighty, a member of the California Energy Commission. Jiangsu and California declared themselves "friendship states/provinces" and agreed to cooperate closely on removing market barriers to energy efficiency and on promoting clean, efficient technologies and products. NRDC was invited to become a cosignatory to the agreement. Like our original memorandum of understanding with Jiangsu, the agreement was without precedent in China's history. Market barriers cannot be removed without the active involvement of the private sector, so the fourth signatory to the agreement was the China-U.S. Energy Efficiency Alliance, a public-private group that was created by NRDC and included among its founding members California's two utility giants, Southern California Edison and Pacific Gas and Electric.

Once the agreement was signed, things moved rapidly, with delegations of government officials and utility executives flying back and forth between the two countries to discuss how China could emulate California's amazing achievement in holding per capita energy consumption flat since 1970, even though it had increased by 50 percent in the rest of the United States during that period.

Only one thing was missing on the Chinese side: the word *climate*. China was quite willing to talk about problems like acid rain, polluted water supplies, deforestation, and the airborne pollution that led to four hundred thousand premature deaths each year. But mention of climate change still triggered the sensitivities that had been on display in Kyoto. To many Chinese leaders the phrase still smacked of foreign interference with their country's sovereign right to economic development and prosperity.

The big breakthrough came in 2006, when China issued its first National Assessment Report on Climate Change. The result of a four-year study by ten government departments, in collaboration with the Chinese Academy of Sciences, it brought China's view of the climate crisis closely in line with the consensus of scientists around the world. The report predicted dramatic changes in temperature and weather patterns that would lead to severe food and water shortages, and recommended that China take urgent steps to combat the threat, including making major investments in green energy technologies.

The door was open for what the Chinese called "enhanced international cooperation" on climate and CO_2. California and Jiangsu remained in the vanguard, but the central government had given its blessing to forms of collaboration that extended well beyond demand-side management. Fran Pavley's AB 32, to take just one example, could include China on its list of potential partners in a future carbon market.

The culmination of the decade of work that had begun with a chance encounter with a Jiangsu official came late in 2009, just as I was completing this book. Building on the 2005 "friendship states" agreement,

Barbara and her colleagues had been deeply involved in drafting a broader cooperation agreement between California and Jiangsu. This one would be at the gubernatorial level—another first. We put climate at the top of our list of seven areas of cooperation and then waited rather nervously to see how the Chinese side would react.

In September 2009, just days before the California-Jiangsu agreement was to be signed, President Hu Jintao was scheduled to address the UN Summit on Climate Change in New York. Among the topics he spoke about was China's upcoming twelfth Five-Year Plan. The plan that would run through 2010 had called for a major cut in *energy* intensity. The next one would set targets for reductions in *carbon* intensity. It was a one-word change, but with huge implications. Without batting an eyelid, the governor of Jiangsu signed the agreement—with climate at the top of the list.

Six weeks later, President Obama made his first visit to China, where he and Hu Jintao announced a package of joint clean energy initiatives including the development of renewables, electric vehicles, advanced technologies for carbon sequestration, and efficiency. In conjunction with the president's visit, Barbara was invited to address a high-level Clean Energy Roundtable in Beijing. Her audience of a hundred experts included U.S. Energy Secretary Steven Chu, Commerce Secretary Gary Locke, and the heads of some of the world's most successful technology companies, such as GE Energy and the Chinese solar giant Suntech (based, appropriately enough, in Jiangsu). Barbara wrote in her regular blog, "It's hard to describe the excitement that filled the meeting room at China's official state guesthouse, Daoyutai, where Nixon stayed in 1972 when he first opened U.S.-China relations." The debate about cooperation on cutting-edge energy technologies, she said, reminded her of the meetings that took place among Thomas Edison, Henry Ford, and Harvey Firestone during the birth of the automobile industry.

"I hope," she concluded, "that fifty years from now, this meeting will be remembered as an important benchmark in a concerted, global movement toward clean energy that helped to reverse the tide of climate change."

———————

Our China team has grown to more than twenty people, led by Barbara and her deputy, Jingjing Qian, an expert on advanced energy technologies and urban smart growth. Our Beijing office, in the city's "embassy district," officially opened for business in January 2008. Needless to say, it meets the most exacting building efficiency standards.

Barbara's original vision of creating a Chinese equivalent of NRDC included supporting local environmental advocates. One essential element of this is the work of Alex Wang, a Chinese-American attorney who is working to promote public interest law in China. As Director of our China Environmental Law Project, he works to ensure that environmental laws are enforced and people have a say in decisions affecting the environment and human health. His work mirrors NRDC's early work with the EPA and communities, monitoring compliance with new environmental laws so that they are more than just words on the page.

Robert Ferguson, our Director of Foundation Relations was innovative in finding ways to fund our China office. His job is to match programs with funding, and he saw Alex Wang's Public Participation Project as the perfect match for funding through George Soros's Open Society Institute. It took a year, but Robert was able to convince them that working on the legal framework in China to get environmental benefits was part of OSI's mission to advance democracy.

Our China program has been enlarged to include NRDC's Health Program. Linda Greer chose the textile industry in China because it covers a number of sectors: air, water and chemicals. Rather than try to enforce codes and new regulations on the people in China, Linda decided to work with the corporate purchasers including Walmart, Gap, and Levi. She was convinced that if these companies knew the squalid conditions and environmental disasters at the factories in China which produced the textiles they purchased, they would find a way to curb pollution along the supply chain.

Their success has been astounding; 100 factories are being built by these companies that will save more than 16 million tons of water (the annual drinking water for 12 million) and will cut 74,000 tons of CO_2 emissions. And this program is economical: in one factory a $72,000 investment in efficiency has resulted in $850,000 savings per year.

A partial list of NRDC's other activities include advice to Chinese researchers on fuel-cell vehicles, hybrids, and biofuels; technical research on carbon capture and storage; a reduction of the use of mercury in manufacturing; public health promotion in the province of Yunnan; advice from NRDC founder Dick Ayres on clean air legislation and public interest litigation; and advice on the use of safe and environmentally friendly building techniques after the devastating 2008 earthquake in Sichuan province. Any one of these things could merit a chapter of its own.

At the heart of Barbara's original vision of supporting local environmental advocates was Professor Wang Canfa, who was one of her first encounters in China. Canfa was a professor at the China University of Politics and Law who established the Center for Legal Assistance to Pollution Victims in 1998. CLAPV set up China's first hotline, which people could call from anywhere in the country to report an environmental violation. Professor Wang built a cadre of volunteer lawyers who would take their case to court, the first time this had been done in China.

In December 2005, Barbara and her colleagues set up the China Environmental Law and Public Participation Project, with CLAPV as our main partner. The idea is to increase public involvement in environmental decision making and to strengthen the legal tools for enforcement and protection. Our partnership with Professor Wang's team works at many levels, from outreach to communities in remote rural areas to high-level seminars for judges on public interest litigation.

I met Wang Canfa on one of my visits to Beijing, and as Barbara says, we immediately bonded. As I listened to him talk about CLAPV's work I could not help feeling as if I was reliving the early days of NRDC in New York. To convey the essence of the man, Barbara tells this story: "When Professor Wang studied for the law exam in college, the authorities wouldn't let him take it. They said there was a rule in China that to be a lawyer you had to be at least five feet tall—he was too short. So what did he do about it? He sued, won, and changed the law. He has that NRDC mentality: even if you don't win, you're still advancing the ball, you're getting publicity, you're showing people how to participate, and when the time comes to revise the law you'll be in a position to strengthen it."

Barbara's newest staff attorney, Gao Jie, is cut from the same cloth. She grew up in Gansu, the poorest province in China. When she was in school, she was told that she had to study physics. She refused; she wanted to be a lawyer. Eventually she went to the University of Michigan for her LLM and started looking at environmental case law. "Everywhere she looked," Barbara says, "it was *NRDC v. this, NRDC v. that*. And she said, 'That's where I want to work.'" Gao Jie is now working with China's three newly established environmental courts, where Wang Canfa also practices.

Frances Beinecke visited our Beijing office in September 2009. She had a very crowded schedule, but she particularly wanted to meet China's top climate negotiator, Minister Xie Zhenhua. We had been trying to get on his radar for a while. When Frances was finally introduced to him, he said, "Oh yes, we know about NRDC. You are old friends. And you are very influential. You have made the U.S. government regulate greenhouse gas emissions as a pollutant. That is something no other country has been able to do. That must mean NRDC is capable of anything."

A New Energy Economy

CHAPTER

24

What Minister Xie was referring to was the recent announcement by the Obama administration that carbon dioxide should be classified as an air pollutant and as such should be regulated by the EPA under the Clean Air Act. For NRDC, this was the culmination of a six-year-long legal campaign highlighted by one of the most significant environmental decisions ever made by the U.S. Supreme Court.

The origins of *Massachusetts v. EPA*, in which NRDC played a central role from start to finish, had come three years earlier, when President Bush's EPA announced that it did not have the authority to regulate global warming pollution from automobiles—and that even if it did, it wouldn't use it. The next year, the EPA took the same position on CO_2 emissions from power plants. By the time the case reached the Supreme Court, we were part of a grand coalition that included twelve states, several major cities, and more than a dozen environmental and public interest groups. Ranged against us were the EPA, the national trade associations of auto manufacturers and dealers, engine and truck manufacturers, several utility groups, and ten western and midwestern states.

The Supreme Court announced its landmark ruling on April 2, 2007. Chief Justice John Roberts and Justice Antonin Scalia both argued that the case should never have come before the court in the first place, since none of the plaintiffs had standing to bring the suit—an echo of battles we had fought in the earliest days of the environmental movement in the 1970s. But they were in a minority. Writing for the 5-to-4 majority, Justice John Paul Stevens found that the petitioners *did* have standing (Massachusetts in particular was directly affected by the threat to its coastline as a result of sea-level rise), and that "greenhouse gases fit well within the Clean Air Act's capacious definition of air pollutant." Stevens ruled that the EPA was indeed authorized to curb greenhouse gases under the act, and that its decision had to be based on the science—and the science only.

The Bush administration continued to drag its feet right to the end, coming close to open defiance of the Supreme Court's ruling. But less than three months after President Obama took office, the EPA proposed an "endangerment determination"—a finding that carbon dioxide and other heat-trapping air pollutants "may reasonably be anticipated to endanger public health or welfare." As David Doniger says, the "little ice age in Washington"—eight years of scientific and legal denial—were finally over. After weighing hundreds of thousands of public comments, the EPA adopted the final endangerment determination in December 2009.

I sometimes think of NRDC as an orchestra, and the CO_2-as-pollutant campaign was a great example of several sections of that orchestra playing at the peak of their abilities. The campaign brought together three important elements of our work—litigation, regulation, and state-level initiatives. Even so, the case was only one facet of the "encirclement" strategy that we were now pursuing. To ratchet up the pressure on Congress to pass comprehensive climate legislation, we needed above all to build momentum among the business and financial communities, and they needed to be motivated by more than the threat of the new wave of litigation that would surely result from the Supreme Court decision.

We believed that what was at stake here was nothing less than the market-driven remaking of the twenty-first-century U.S. economy

NRDC PRESIDENT FRANCES BEINECKE (SIXTH FROM LEFT) AT A MEETING BETWEEN
PRESIDENT OBAMA AND BUSINESS AND ENVIRONMENTAL LEADERS, DECEMBER 2009.

based on clean energy. Once corporations and banks recognized that
an eventual cap on carbon emissions was inevitable—and that it was
not incompatible with profitability—they would begin to make smarter
long-term investment decisions. And if market forces shifted in the
direction of a clean energy economy, Congress would be given more
and more incentive to act. To make all this happen, we would need to
expand the size of our orchestra. We already had the Climate Center and
the energy team. In 2006 we added the Center for Market Innovation,
which was headed for its first three years by Rick Duke, who joined
NRDC from the global consulting firm McKinsey and Company.

By the middle of the decade, the U.S. energy economy had reached a
watershed moment. Hundreds of high-polluting coal-fired power plants,
built in the 1950s and 1960s, were nearing the end of their useful lives,

and utilities were gearing up to build more than 150 new plants over the next ten to fifteen years. The largest of these would cost more than $2 billion apiece, and each one that relied on old-fashioned, dirty "pulverized coal" technologies would lock us into six million tons of CO_2 emissions every year (the amount produced by two million cars) during its sixty-year lifespan. We could not afford to let this happen.

Coal is the cheapest and most abundant of all fossil fuels, and NRDC had been fighting dirty coal plants and destructive mining techniques ever since 1971, when we mounted our first lawsuit against the Tennessee Valley Authority, the pioneer of strip-mining. While that case was being argued, I had traveled to Kentucky to see Harry Caudill, whose celebrated book, *Night Comes to the Cumberlands,* had inspired presidents John F. Kennedy and Lyndon B. Johnson to launch their drive against poverty in the Appalachians. Caudill invited me to stay in his home, and after a breakfast of biscuits and white gravy, he took me out to see the strip mines. I was outraged when I saw the landscape torn up for miles in every direction. How could they get away with this? I wondered.

Yet when Patricia and I visited West Virginia in the fall of 2008 and flew over the coal-mining district with a pilot from the conservation group SouthWings, we saw that conditions had only gotten worse. In the years since I visited Harry Caudill, strip-mining had evolved into mountaintop removal, the most ruthless method yet devised to extract coal quickly and cheaply. The thin seams of Appalachian coal are hard to mine because they are buried under layers of shale and limestone hundreds of feet thick. Strip miners used to auger their way in horizontally along the edge of a ridge; now gargantuan earthmoving machines simply rip off the entire mountaintop. About five hundred mountains in the Appalachians have now been decapitated in this way. Early in the George W. Bush administration, after the appointment of former coal industry lobbyist Steven Griles as deputy secretary of the interior, officials changed a provision of Clean Water Act to designate the mining waste from the mountaintops as exempt "fill" that could be dumped into the river valleys below. According to the EPA, more than seven hundred miles of pristine streams have been buried in this way, with thousands more miles contaminated with toxic orange acid mine drainage. The valleys have been turned into huge, treeless funnels that allow rain and mud to wash over downstream communities without impediment.

The people who have lived for generations in these narrow "hollers" get little benefit from the mining operations; 85 percent of West Virginia's landowners are based outside the state and have no stake in the local communities. King Coal has been one of the mainstays of the local economy for over a hundred years, but with the increasing reliance on heavy machinery, mining jobs have been reduced by 90 percent. Communities are left to struggle with poverty and the health effects of coal dust and polluted drinking water. Appalachia remains a sacrifice zone, so that the rest of us can get cheap coal.

No one has battled the coal industry longer and on more fronts than NRDC's David Hawkins. David believes that it is essential to focus simultaneously on both the "upstream" and the "downstream" impacts of the industry—how it is mined and how it is burned—but he also understands that this is a huge challenge. Because coal is such a big (and dirty) part of the world's current energy mix, it is vital that the United States and other countries both increase their use of alternatives and—to the degree that we go on using coal—do so more cleanly. But precisely because coal is so abundant and so cheap, and enjoys such powerful political backing, getting these policies adopted presents a real dilemma. Like it or not, coal is a cornerstone of the world economy, and the two emerging giants, China and India, as well as the United States, have vast reserves that they are certain to go on exploiting to fuel their economic growth. No one at NRDC likes coal; we just recognize that it's not going away anytime soon. Our view is that we can make more rapid progress in the huge battle over global warming if we don't first have to take on and win a frontal assault against the use (as opposed to the abuse) of coal. Fighting that battle would mean either going down in a blaze of glorious defeat or getting bogged down in endless trench warfare, taking heavy casualties in the process.

Of course, where the abuse is egregious we will fight it in our time-honored way, with litigation. John Walke, who succeeded David Hawkins as head of our clean air program, says, "We have to limit pollution by forcing the utilities to find a better way to produce energy. My job is to be the tough guy and, where necessary, take them to court."

The political opposition to phasing out coal is not limited to the coal industry. "The railroads are even more dependent on coal than the utilities," David points out. "They make more than $6 billion a year hauling six hundred million tons of coal." You can't "decouple" volume and profits as you can with electric utilities. "Ralph Cavanagh and David Goldstein can convince the power companies that they can make money by selling efficiency," he adds. "But you can't make that argument to the rail companies."

Given that some significant use of coal for the next few decades is an inescapable political reality, David began in the 1990s to explore technologies that may allow the stuff to be burned without wrecking the planet. He became especially interested in the potential of a technique called carbon capture and storage, in which CO_2 is buried or "sequestered" deep underground. One approach starts with "gasification," a process that turns coal into a gas that can be burned.

To gasify coal, it is heated to about 2,000 degrees Fahrenheit in a sealed chamber and injected with oxygen and steam, which breaks the coal down into its chemical building blocks. Impurities are removed from the gas stream, and when it is burned, the leftover heat is captured to make steam. This system is very efficient, and it has been around for decades (Germany used it during World War II to fuel the Luftwaffe). However, whether coal is burned outright or turned into a gas, it still produces carbon dioxide. To prevent that, the CO_2 from the power plant must be captured so that it is never released into the air. Gasification has a number of advantages in this respect, although advances are being made rapidly in both systems. The CO_2 that is captured can then be sequestered in stable geologic formations such as porous rock layers, which in theory could permanently store all of the world's projected CO_2 emissions from power plants over the next two hundred years.

In a 2005 article in our prize-winning magazine, *OnEarth*, journalist Craig Canine described the process he observed in a state-of-the-art gasification plant in Florida: "I realized I was witnessing a burial of sorts. Fossil carbon, which had been extracted from the ground as coal and wrung of its energy value at the gasification plant, was here being recommitted to the earth. Ashes to ashes, dust to dust, carbon cradle to carbon grave. If coal is to have a future as a major fuel in the twenty-first century and beyond, this is what it might look like; smokestacks effectively turned upside down, shooting CO_2 into subterranean rock formations rather than up into the sky."

Canine's article and David Hawkins's work on carbon capture and storage caused a stir among our allies in Appalachia, who are understandably skeptical of any suggestion that coal can be used in less polluting ways. We told them that while we saw carbon sequestration as part of the mix that would eventually turn the tide against climate change, we were also committed to redoubling our efforts against the horrors of mountaintop removal. The relationships that we have built in the entertainment industry have been a vital source of support for this campaign. The legendary country and western singer Emmylou Harris has been a dedicated NRDC supporter for years, and many of the biggest stars in Nashville have now joined the fight. On that flight in 2008 over the coalfields of West Virginia, our companions were John Esposito, CEO of the Warner Music Group, and singer Big Kenny Alphin, of Big and Rich.

At the time the *OnEarth* story appeared, King Coal seemed to be in the ascendancy, with new coal-fired power plants cropping up faster than NRDC, the Sierra Club, and other opponents could intervene with legal challenges to stop them. The single most egregious plan for new coal-fired power plants came from the giant Texas Utilities

(TXU), which had the audacity to propose building eleven all at once. NRDC, the Environmental Defense Fund, and other groups immediately organized a campaign to brand TXU as "the new Exxon"—the petroleum industry giant that was reaping the largest profits of any corporation in history and was pouring millions into the work of global warming "skeptics" trying to undermine the now overwhelming scientific consensus on climate change. We worked with a number of Texas mayors, notably Laura Miller of Dallas, who organized a coalition to fight the TXU plants. Robert Redford produced a documentary on the issue, and Laurie David barnstormed the state with singer Sheryl Crow.

"We worked as hard as we could to stop coal plants that don't capture their emissions from ever being built, boxing in coal and leaving them only one door to go through—climate technology," says John Steelman, program manager of the NRDC Climate Center. "We got a lot of media attention, but it wasn't until David Hawkins got the phone call that things really changed."

"The phone call" came on February 12, 2007. On the end of the line was Bill Reilly, a longtime friend of David's who had been the head of the EPA during the administration of George H. W. Bush and was now with a private equity firm, the Texas Pacific Group. David remembers the conversation clearly.

"What do you think about TXU's proposal?" Reilly asked.

"I think it's a terrible idea."

"Well, I may be in a position to do something."

Reilly explained that his firm was interested in a leveraged buyout of TXU but didn't want to inherit what he called "an environmental hornets' nest." He asked, "How about if we cancel out a couple of the power plants and get a green seal for the others?"

"No, some of those power plants will be canceled anyway," David answered. "This TXU plan is the *Mein Kampf* of energy investment. TXU's business plan is to build coal-fired power plants all over the world. They must abandon all of them if you want us to get off your back."

"I'll see what's possible," Reilly promised.

By this time, the larger political winds on global warming had begun to shift in our favor, and in two weeks of talks, NRDC and the Environmental Defense Fund persuaded TXU to scrap eight of its eleven proposed plants. "We were not interested in a shell game, where TXU would withdraw from Texas and then build the same kind of plants somewhere else," David says. In the end, TXU pledged not to build any new coal-fired power plants anywhere in the country unless they included new technology to curb CO_2 and other pollutants. The deal would also include a $400 million investment in energy efficiency measures to meet a portion of anticipated new demand.

From the point of view of those financing the buyout, which included Wall Street giants Goldman Sachs, Morgan Stanley, and Lehman Brothers, the agreement was part damage control, part good stewardship, and part smart business decision. "These are savvy investors," David says. "They believed, as we do, that having a strong environmental profile is actually a better business proposition." Essentially, the banks were expressing the same doubts about new coal plants that an earlier generation of investors had felt about new nuclear plants in the 1970s and 1980s. It takes ten years to finance and build a coal-fired power plant and another fifteen to twenty to pay off the initial investment. With a carbon cap on the way, sooner or later the economics of coal were going to be transformed, and investors knew it. "This was the moment Wall Street opened its eyes on global warming," says John Steelman. The banks had seen the writing on the wall—and added their own signature to it.

Doors in the financial sector that we had been knocking against for years now began to open. The TXU deal led to a much broader consultation over the next nine months between NRDC, the Environmental Defense Fund, and a host of banks and utilities—Citigroup, J. P. Morgan, Chase-Morgan Stanley, Bank of America, Credit Suisse, Wells Fargo, American Electric Power, CMS Energy, DTE Energy, NRG Energy, PSEG, Sempra, and the Southern Company. Investors hate risk and uncertainty, and with regional and national climate policy in such flux, the participants were keen to work out secure long-range plans for the future financing of the energy sector. The outcome of this process was the "Carbon Principles," which require participating banks to be sure, before making a loan, that any new coal-fired power plant will prioritize investment in efficiency and renewable energy sources and factor in the *inevitable* cost of the future capture of CO_2 emissions.

By now many of the nation's biggest corporations had begun moving in the same direction on climate change and the new energy economy, recognizing, as John Steelman puts it, that, "If you're not at the table, you're on the menu." In January 2007 nine major corporations and four environmental organizations—NRDC, the Environmental Defense Fund, the World Resources Institute, and the Pew Center on Global Climate Change—came together to form the U.S. Climate Action Partnership (USCAP). Since then, the number of corporate members has swelled to twenty-six, virtually all of them household names such as General Electric, PepsiCo, Shell, Johnson and Johnson, DuPont, Dow Chemical, Honeywell, and Ford Motor Company. What made USCAP so significant was that these corporate giants were calling directly for federal legislation to cap greenhouse gas emissions, urging a reduction of between 60 and 80 percent by 2050.

In just a few hectic years, we had been centrally involved in one game-changing development after another: California's landmark global warming laws, AB 32 and SB 1368; the Supreme Court's decision on CO_2 as an air pollutant; the TXU deal; the banks' Carbon Principles; the formation of USCAP. Together, they produced a kind of chain reaction: each advance helped create momentum for the next, and together they made a stronger and stronger case for Congress to act.

We had learned many important lessons from earlier attempts to pass climate legislation. Starting in 2003, Dan Lashof, David Doniger, and their colleagues had worked closely with staffers for Senator

John McCain, Republican from Arizona, and Joe Lieberman, Democrat (and later Independent) from Connecticut, on what came to be known as the McCain-Lieberman Climate Stewardship Act. When this came before the Senate in October 2003, as an amendment to a pending energy bill, it lost by a vote of fifty-five to forty-three—but forty-three was still an encouraging number, suggesting that bipartisan support for a genuine climate change policy was on the upswing. But in June 2005, the senators offered a revised version of their bill, with an added provision for lavish subsidies for the construction of new nuclear power plants. Several senators defected over this issue, and this time the McCain-Lieberman bill received only thirty-eight votes, while a watered-down Energy Policy Act passed the Senate comfortably.

This marked the low point of our fortunes in Congress, but it was also, thanks to David Doniger, the turning point. David understood that we had to respond quickly, and within twenty-four hours he had worked with staff to Senator Jeff Bingaman, Democrat from New Mexico, to draft a "Sense of the Senate" resolution intended to reaffirm bipartisan support for eventual climate legislation. The resolution read: "It is the Sense of the Senate that Congress should enact a comprehensive and effective national program of mandatory, market-based limits and incentives on emissions of greenhouse gases that slow, stop, and reverse the growth of such emissions at a rate and in a manner that will not significantly harm the United States economy, and will encourage comparable action by other nations that are major trading partners and key contributors to global emissions." This resolution passed with fifty-four votes; we had succeeded in reversing the momentum.

We also saw that it was essential to look much farther into the future than these early initiatives in Congress had. They had concentrated on setting emissions reduction targets for 2010 and 2020; the assumption was that legislators would come back to take care of the next phase later. By this time, however, the scientific findings on the speed of climate change were making it abundantly clear that we no longer had time for half measures, and thanks to the Bush administration, vital years had already slipped away from us. We had to commit to much deeper, long-term cuts in emissions, and we had to get started as quickly as possible.

We presented the elements of what was required in a groundbreaking article in *Science* magazine in November 2006, coauthored by Dan Lashof, David Doniger, and their colleague Antonia Herzog, a senior advocate in the NRDC Climate Center. We called our new approach to climate legislation "ambitious centrism." Dan, David, and Antonia laid out a plan for reducing emissions by 2050, and while it was still based on the principle of "cap and trade," this time it was cap and trade with a difference. We called our strategy "cap and invest," a term coined by E2's Bob Epstein.

There has always been (and still is) a spirited debate within the environmental movement about the relative merits of a carbon tax versus a cap-and-trade system. NRDC favors cap and trade. While a tax fixes the price of emissions, it cannot guarantee a ceiling on the total quantity. A cap does that, and we believe it also creates more reliable long-term incentives for investment, responds better to ups and downs in the economy, is more immune to later political challenges, and is more likely to get buy-in from consumers.

Earlier attempts at emissions trading were very instructive. The 1990 amendments to the Clean Air Act, for instance, included a cap-and-trade program for the sulfur dioxide emissions that caused acid rain. Although this was a much smaller program than the carbon market would be, it proved to be highly effective. At the time, industry protested that compliance would be prohibitively expensive, but the cap in fact led to unanticipated technological innovations that reduced the costs to a quarter of those originally projected. However, one feature of the acid rain cap-and-trade system—giving out allowances for free—would be a big mistake for the much larger carbon market because it would allow industry to reap windfall profits and starve investment opportunities for clean energy. Europe's cap-and-trade system for carbon emissions, adopted in 2005, made that mistake, and again power producers raised their prices to reflect the resale value of their allowances, despite getting them for free.

There are two parts to NRDC's blueprint. The first is a multi-decade declining cap on carbon emissions, starting with meaningful reductions in the first decade and leading eventually to at least an 80 percent cut by the year 2050. This gives businesses a clear market signal to make large investments in new, clean technologies. One way to visualize this—suggested to me by our son-in-law, Forwood Wiser—is as a parking lot, which represents the overall limit on emissions. Let's say the parking lot has one hundred spaces and everyone has one space (one emissions allowance). If you have a big SUV, you use up the whole space, but if you have a small car, you can use half the space and sell the other half. Next year there will only be ninety spaces, giving automakers a strong incentive to design smaller cars, and so on until eventually only twenty spaces remain.

The second part of cap and invest, as the name implies, is to use the value of allowances created under the cap to drive investments in the future low-carbon economy. Rather than giving away the allowances with no strings attached, as the Europeans did, we think it makes more sense for them to be auctioned off or otherwise used for the benefit of the public, as happens with frequencies for radio stations. This could create an enormous fund for investment, as much as $200 billion a year, to accelerate the transition to a new energy economy. Some of that money would be invested in consumer and business efficiency; some in developing cleaner technologies such as wind and solar power, biofuels, carbon capture and storage, and advanced vehicles; and some in tax credits and other forms of financial support for low-income families facing higher utility rates in the short term. We think of it as using pollution to pay for the solution.

Calibrating the cap and invest strategy is very complicated, especially since opponents of climate legislation immediately point to the short-term cost to the consumer. So the auction revenues have to be synchronized with new investments so that you constantly stay ahead of the curve of the most expensive costs. This has involved the most sophisticated financial analysis and policy design NRDC has attempted, calling on the combined expertise of the Center for Market Innovation, the Climate Center, the energy team, and our friends in E2.

NRDC had done more than anyone to create the paradigm for the next wave of climate bills to come before Congress, which embraced most of our ideas for a long-term, steadily tightening cap on emissions and a time horizon of 2050. The next important piece of proposed legislation was the Lieberman-Warner Climate Security Act of 2007. This time Senator Lieberman's Republican cosponsor was Senator John Warner of Virginia, and the two were joined the following year by Democrat Barbara Boxer of California, chair of the Senate's Environment and Public Works Committee. The addition of the word *security* in the title of the bill was significant, because it drew attention to a number of new considerations that had entered the debate: our dangerous dependency on Middle East oil; the likelihood of new national security threats emerging from the social disruption caused by a warming planet; and the fact that U.S. industry risked losing its competitive edge unless it made the same kind of smart investments in new energy technologies that were already happening in Europe, Japan, and China.

In supporting the Senate bill, the first major challenge was to get the most positive language we could into the legislation. Much of the drafting was done by two NRDC alumni, David McIntosh, who had become Senator Lieberman's top environmental aide, and Erik Olson, who had been appointed as general counsel to Senator Boxer. David Hawkins, Dan Lashof, and David Doniger worked hard to broker agreement between industry and important Senate offices on major provisions of the bill, and Hawkins and Frances Beinecke testified at key committee hearings. Finally, in December 2007, the bill was approved by Senator Boxer's committee—an historic accomplishment in which NRDC was centrally involved.

The bill proposed to auction a much smaller proportion of carbon allowances than we would have liked, and set a target for total emissions reductions by 2050 that was somewhat lower than the 80 percent that the Intergovernmental Panel on Climate Change says is necessary to stave off the worst effects of global warming. Our second challenge, then, was to forge a consensus within the Green Group in Washington behind an admittedly imperfect bill. From its modest beginnings, the Green Group had become a powerhouse with a robust field presence in twenty-five target states and a combined database of 4.5 million names who could be called on to create public pressure. Within such a huge community, it's hardly surprising that there is sometimes serious disagreement about the best way to achieve our common goals. "Some of the other environmental groups wanted more than the Lieberman-Warner bill provided and said we should wait for the next Congress," Dan Lashof recalls. "But we said, no, there would be other things competing for the agenda, and it wouldn't be that much easier."

Even though several organizations ended up opposing the bill, Frances did a masterful job of holding most of the Green Group together to support and strengthen it. "The Green Group is a very ideologically diverse body," she says, "and you have to realize that different organizations have different roles to play. Some are idealists who set the bar very high; our view is, let's get something done—because climate is different from all other issues. The science is such that we can't afford to wait for ideal solutions."

The bill went to the Senate floor in June 2008, and for the first time the nation's highest legislative body spent several days debating a full-blown climate change bill—not an amendment to an energy bill, as McCain-Lieberman had been. Frances and Senator Boxer were on the phone with one another several times a day as the senator tried to steer the bill past the obstructive tactics of a handful of Republican senators. But after a week, the Senate had to decide whether to end these delaying tactics and move to a final vote. Fifty-four voted in favor, six short of the number needed to avoid a filibuster, and the bill was withdrawn.

No one had ever said that getting climate change legislation through Congress would be easy. After all, we remembered, it had taken a decade to pass legislation on acid rain, and this was much more complex and far-reaching. Although the debate over the Climate Security Act had been frustrating, we didn't see it as a defeat—merely as a dress rehearsal for the battle that would be renewed the following year, with a new Congress and a new president in the White House.

The inauguration of Barack Obama marked a sea change in federal policy on the environment. With a slew of new appointments to key positions—including Lisa Jackson as EPA administrator, Steven Chu as energy secretary, Carol Browner as the president's special assistant on climate and energy issues, all of them well known to NRDC—the administration signaled its strong commitment to a low-carbon, energy-efficient future that would slash greenhouse gas emissions, make the United States more globally competitive, and create new jobs. Climate change was not the only thing on the administration's agenda. It also promised to take tough action on many of the issues that had been at the heart of NRDC's mission for forty years: new rules to clean up coal-fired power plants, thorough reform of the outdated and ineffectual Toxic Substances Control Act, a substantial increase in fleetwide mileage standards for automobiles, initiatives to guarantee the safety of our food supply, a sweeping transportation bill.

In January 2009, on the eve of the inauguration, USCAP released a detailed blueprint for climate legislation, which we had been working on for the two years since the group was formed. This alliance of major corporations and leading environmental groups, now numbering more than two dozen, reiterated that the science on global warming was clear and unequivocal; insisted that the United States had to make a fundamental change in how energy was produced; and stressed that it was urgent for Congress to act, since "each year of delayed action to control emissions increases the risk of unavoidable consequences."

The 111th Congress responded swiftly at first. The American Recovery and Reinvestment Act (better known as the "stimulus bill") included the largest ever government investment in clean energy, a significant down payment toward comprehensive climate and energy legislation. In the House of Representatives, Congressmen Henry Waxman, Democrat from California, and Ed Markey, Democrat from Massachusetts, introduced the American Clean Energy and Security Act (ACES). Waxman had long been one of NRDC's best friends on Capitol Hill, and we worked closely with his staff, as well as with wavering members of both parties, as the bill worked its way through the various committees. In the wake of the economic meltdown in 2009 and in the new, intensely partisan atmosphere in Washington, it was a tough summer for major new legislative initiatives, but the economic arguments for ACES were very powerful. In supporting it, we emphasized the boost it would give to the weakened economy. Our analysis showed that the bill would lead to public and private investment of $300 billion a year in clean energy and efficiency. It would reward smart companies and create about 1.9 million new jobs. It was just what the country needed, in other words, and in June it passed the House. Now it was the turn of the Senate—and of the international community.

The UN Climate Change Conference in Copenhagen in December 2009 was a momentous event. We had hoped that the Senate would have passed its version of a climate bill by then, but it was bogged down in the protracted debate over healthcare reform. The world did not adjust its schedule to accommodate the U.S. Senate. A hundred and ninety-three countries sent delegations. There were kings, presidents, and prime ministers from 130 nations, all there to discuss how the planet was to be sustained for coming generations.

We had come a long way since our first foreign venture, the 1972 Conference on the Human Environment in Stockholm. There had been little or no awareness of climate change in those days, but the conference was the awakening of the international environmental movement, and I had been happy just to be there.

I reminisced about that day thirty-seven years earlier as Frances Beinecke and I stood on line outside the Bella Center in Copenhagen, the official site of negotiations. She described the scene in her blog:

"Maybe it's geography's gift to Copenhagen, sitting astride two great seas—the Baltic and the North—but this is a great city for fresh air. Believe me, I got plenty of it on Monday, as I stood outside for eight solid hours waiting to be admitted to the UN climate summit here. That's what happens when there are four registration desks for more than 20,000 NGOs and other outside observers registered for the summit. Little matter. After three decades at the climate change ramparts, I figured, what was another eight hours at the Danish barricades?"

NRDC had had only two representatives in Stockholm—me and Jim Marshall. In Copenhagen, our delegation was thirty-three strong. All the veterans of our climate team were there—David Hawkins, David Doniger, and Dan Lashof. They were accompanied by some important recent arrivals, including Jake Schmidt, our international climate policy director; our international advocate Heather Allen, who worked closely in Copenhagen with Jacob Scherr; and our senior press secretary for climate, Eric Young, who spent most of the conference glued to his Blackberry. Apollo Gonzales, our netroots campaign manager, was on call around the clock, sending back on-the-spot information to our millions of website visitors. In 1972 there had been no talk of China— Chairman Mao was still in charge then. But Barbara Finamore came to Copenhagen from Beijing with a team of five.

At first our hopes had been high that Copenhagen would succeed where Kyoto had failed, that it would finally produce a binding global treaty to reduce greenhouse gas emissions. But as December approached, it became clear that this wasn't going to happen. The divisions were too deep, and the UN machinery too cumbersome; the negotiations proceeded at a snail's pace until the conference appeared to be on the verge of collapse. But President Obama's personal eleventh-hour intervention secured an agreement—historic in its own modest way—in which the

NRDC Staff Retreat, Stowe, Vermont, Fall 2008

most important participants, including China and India, promised to make substantial voluntary cuts in their emissions.

This was far short of what we had hoped for, but we recognized that the president's hands were tied by the political realities in Washington. He could not promise anything that he could not deliver back home, and nothing in Congress was going to be easy. After the conference ended, conservative Republicans, climate "skeptics," and lobbyists for the fossil fuel industry all redoubled their efforts to oppose legislation, even reviving their long-discredited attacks on the scientific consensus about the severity of climate change by seizing on a handful of minor errors in the IPCC's most recent 2,000-page report.

Some of our friends in the environmental movement were demoralized by what they saw as the failure of Copenhagen, but while we shared their sense of urgency, we continued to take the long view. Having experienced the worst of the Reagan years, the 104th Congress, and the eight-year onslaught on the environment under George W. Bush, we saw the latest attacks from the opponents of climate legislation as a desperate rearguard action by forces we had confronted before and whose influence had steadily eroded. An indication of this came when Senator Lisa Murkowski, Republican from Alaska, failed to rally the votes to overturn the EPA's "endangerment finding" that CO_2 could be regulated under the Clean Air Act. The Supreme Court decision that led to this had originated with a petition to regulate greenhouse gas

emissions from automobiles and resulted in an historic agreement between California, the EPA, and the Department of Transportation on a unified set of standards. And who opposed Murkowski's attempt to reverse that decision? Not only the unified environmental movement, but the United Autoworkers and the Alliance of Automobile Manufacturers, with whom we had been consulting closely, and who wanted the certainty that only national standards could deliver.

The new bill being prepared in the Senate was sponsored by a bipartisan group that included Senators John Kerry, Democrat from Massachusetts; Joe Lieberman, Independent from Connecticut; and Lindsey Graham, Republican from South Carolina. We knew that it would involve some inevitable compromises, and some overheated rhetoric even began to declare that "cap and trade is dead." Instead there was talk in the air of "cap and dividend," or "cap and refund" (and not to mention our own formulation, "cap and invest"). But the first word in this phrase was more important than the last. We were as confident as ever that there would be a carbon cap; the question was no longer whether, but how and when.

Through the tumultuous first year of the Obama administration, the broad coalitions we had built remained rock solid. To me, this vindicated NRDC's core philosophy. You have to be patient and systematic; you have to fight on many fronts at once; you have to develop a full menu of skills, starting with litigation and legislation and moving through science, economics, and communications; you have be equally adept at working inside the Beltway and out at the grass roots, with your members; and you have to dig in for as long as it takes. While climate change remains the overriding threat to the future of the planet, these same principles apply to our fight for all the things we want to hand down to our children: clean air, clean water, wild places, wild creatures.

That's the kind of organization we have built at NRDC. We've been going for forty years already, and we're ready to roll up our sleeves for forty more.

Epilogue:
Back to the Future

In the summer of 2009, Patricia and I hosted a trip to the Tongass National Forest with a group of NRDC supporters and staff members. Standing on the deck of the boat, looking out at the mountains reflected in the deep fjords of Southeast Alaska, we thought of how much has changed since our first trip in the 1970s and how much has stayed the same, both in Alaska and at NRDC.

This trip was emblematic, in a way, of our history. First of all, the primary environmental issues we addressed in the 1970s—clean water, clean air, a sustainable environment, and the preservation of America's unique wilderness—are the same issues we fight for today. Although litigation is still the bedrock of NRDC, we have enormously expanded the methods we use to win our battles. The people with us on the boat represented both the traditional and the new ways in which we conduct our business.

Take communications. In the 1970s, Patricia and Winsome McIntosh put together two hardcover journals about our trips to Alaska, complete with snapshots of bears, glaciers, and games of Frisbee on rocky beaches. It was the only record we kept. Today NRDC's trips to Alaska are recorded on our website, in our publication *Nature's Voice*, which goes out to more than a million members and online activists, and in multiple blogs and electronic images.

Like those early journals, our first letters and press releases were typewritten and sent out in what is now called "snail mail." Through the 1980s and 1990s, we made modest investments in communication, but it was the BioGems program, starting in 2000, that got us online in a way that could reach multitudes. Since then, BioGems Defenders have sent more than ten million messages in defense of wildlands in the Americas.

As part of our rapidly developing strategic plan, in 2005 we hired communications expert Phil Gutis. He was challenged by NRDC's long tradition of getting the job done first and foremost without much focus on publicity.

"I was with the ACLU before I came to NRDC," Phil says, "and there, anything that is newsworthy is immediately published. Here I rarely hear from lawyers wanting publicity. They are used to fighting in a court of law, but we need to fight in the court of public opinion. And most important, we have to make our message simple—which is not easy to do."

Vanity Fair cosponsored our Forces for Nature event in 2007, honoring the magazine's editor, Graydon Carter. When Phil talked to *Vanity Fair* executive Sarah Marks about what we wanted said in the evening's presentation, she shook her head, held up her Blackberry, and said, "If the information doesn't fit on the first screen, it doesn't work."

Like many people of my generation, I find that my head swims with the language of new media—blogs, Twitter, Facebook, YouTube, iTunes, Blackberry, Google. Even some of our younger staff have found the rapid changes challenging. When we talked with Ronnie Cohen in our San Francisco office for this book, she was just posting something on her blog. Ronnie, who is an expert on water efficiency, explained:

"I had never even read a blog until Phil convinced me that this is where it's at, and now I find blogging essential. It is a challenge, however; I have to be very careful. For instance, right now I'm responding to a *New York Times* article that says drip irrigation is not as efficient as flood irrigation. I disagree, but I can't respond until I read the underlying study. However, I can get the study online, which is another benefit of the Internet, so perhaps I can get my response out this morning."

Apollo Gonzales, our first Netroots campaign manager, is a master at finding online communities that may be interested in the environment and then messaging them to get behind issues they care about, using Facebook and MySpace. NRDC has also built a new online community of its own, Switchboard. Here staff as well as ordinary citizens can contribute thoughts and ideas. It was named one of the Internet's best green websites by *Time* magazine.

Our lawyers and scientists are learning to simplify and use everyday language to talk about even the most complex issues. For instance, in the spring of 2008, when Alan Horn arranged a meeting for NRDC scientists with Warner Brothers executives, our oceans specialist Lisa Suatoni gave a presentation on the growing acidification of the oceans. As a result, she was invited to appear on the *Ellen DeGeneres Show*. Since talking about ocean acidification was too complicated and too negative to be entertaining, Lisa talked about creating national parks in the oceans. It was a positive message about an NRDC program that also created public awareness about the threats to the ocean. The highlight of Lisa's appearance was when she handed a live sea cucumber to DeGeneres, who held it squeamishly but with good humor, and the message was clear.

To win hearts and minds for the battle against climate change, Phil insists that we change our message. He maintains that the environmental movement has been branded for years as negative and more concerned with "critters" than with people. We need to talk about solutions. For instance, energy efficiency solves two problems at once: it will create new, green jobs, and it will significantly reduce carbon emissions. Like many of the things we have been promoting for years, it can be shown to be good not just for the environment but also for the economy.

Board member Michel Gelobter agrees and says his goal is to "connect every consumer purchase to a solution for global warming." Until 2007, he was executive director of Redefining Progress, an organization dedicated to finding a sustainable environment in a just society through changing public policy. He maintains that people can change the world in two ways—they vote and they shop.

"I told Frances," he said, "every time you speak, envision the CEO of GM. We cannot beat oil and coal and the huge profits they reap without having a real economic alternative. Independent of how much people care about the environment, they still care about their pocketbooks more. We need to show people we are about sustainable livelihood. Green jobs are an important piece of it."

Another of our companions in Alaska was board member Bob Epstein, a major player in this computer world that was just beginning in the 1970s, when, on our first trip to Alaska, we were joined by Jay Last, a Silicon Valley pioneer and one of the creators of the Fairchild Semiconductor corporation.

As well as bringing NRDC into the world of the Internet, Bob helped form Environmental Entrepreneurs (E2), establishing an organizational pattern that we have followed with our new Global Leadership Council, which I chair with Wendy Gordon. Three members of the council were also on the boat with us in Alaska: Michael Wolfe, David Welch, and Dayna Bochco. David works with an optical networks company, and Dayna, a lawyer, is president, with her husband, of Steven Bochco Productions, which has received Emmy awards for *LA Law* and *Hill Street Blues*.

The Global Leadership Council brings important friends from a wide circle of business leaders, philanthropists, and political activists to meet with elected officials and members of the administration to help shape their environmental policies, particularly on climate. This requires professional staffing, and Julie Truax, a senior member of our administrative team, manages this and the many other coalitions that we work with.

Standing on the deck of the *Mist Cove*, Patricia and I saw firsthand the unrelenting effects of climate change. It was the driest summer Southeast Alaska has seen in recorded history. Salmon flailed about at the mouths of streams, unable to get back to their spawning grounds because the water was so low. Starving grizzly bears with cubs roamed around Sitka, searching for food.

Climate change is NRDC's major focus now and will be for years to come. Luckily, under Frances Beinecke, who was also with us on that first trip to Alaska, we are in good hands. When I thought about the need for succession, I was convinced that she was the person to take over. To prepare for the change, I first spoke with Fritz Schwarz about a timetable and told him that Frances was my candidate for successor. Then I met with the senior staff, and we agreed that we didn't need to change or fix anything; we just wanted to continue our success. Frances was the clear choice to become our next leader.

Fritz saw the importance of keeping the traditions, the trust between the board and staff, and the feeling of family—all the things that have made NRDC a special place to work. He handled the transition expertly, and the board chose Frances as our next president, to take over in 2006. Philip Korsant developed a transition plan; my title would be founding director, and I would continue to help on fundraising, climate, and a range of other issues. I would be available as a resource for Frances and other staff as they needed me. I was elected to the board. It was complicated to leave a place after thirty-five years, but having my good friend Ann Roach continue as my assistant made the transition much easier. There was a wonderful series of parties in each of our offices, and I was given the NRDC "Forces for Nature" award in the spring of 2006, which included a check to the organization from the board for $11 million.

After a three-month sabbatical in early 2006, I returned to the office and immediately realized my role had changed. Although I was still a close friend and advisor to Frances, she was now in charge. From all reports, both looking back three years and talking to people for this book, the transition was miraculously smooth. Christine Russell, who joined our board in 1985, after working for several years at NRDC with Eric Goldstein, ascribes this to the special atmosphere of NRDC: "We didn't skip a beat going from John to Frances. We always felt we were in good hands. I wouldn't have had such a long tenure without the personalities in this organization. NRDC attracts people with good values who care about the issues and are enthusiastic. It's a culture that is very embracing."

As good fortune would have it, when Fritz stepped down one year after I did, we found a capable young business leader, Dan Tishman, to take his place. Paul Elston, Frances's husband, then president of the New York League of Conservation Voters, first introduced me to Dan at an event where the league was honoring Dan for his work on green buildings. When Dan and his wife, Sheryl, moved to New York from Maine, Patricia and I spent time with them and their two young sons, who are both superb athletes. Sheryl is a Maine guide and has hiked the Appalachian Trail, and she and Dan met when they both worked for the National Audubon Society. This love for the wilderness, coupled with sharp business acumen and a commitment to showing that a green economy is a strong economy, makes Dan the perfect leader for our time. He and Frances are a great team.

One of Frances's first goals was to find the right person to take her place as executive director. She chose Peter Lehner, who had worked with Eric Goldstein and Sarah Chasis on water issues and then was the assistant attorney general in charge of environmental protection for Attorney General Eliot Spitzer of New York. Fritz was very supportive of this choice. During his tenure as New York City Corporation Counsel, he had worked with Peter; he was also a family friend.

Having worked "in house" and also dealt with NRDC as a state official, Peter observed, "Sometimes people feel they should win a case just because they are 'morally right,' but at NRDC no one thinks that. They know they must do the hard work of law and science and that our brief must be not just as good as the other brief, but better. People at NRDC know that and work that way. This is why we have been so successful."

At the same time, as Peter talked with Frances, he saw challenges. NRDC has grown by leaps and bounds—from three hundred to four hundred employees in just a couple years—and Peter has looked for ways to integrate staff who have been here for decades with the influx of new professionals. The way to do this, he maintains, is through "cross-programming." This means that the scientists and lawyers who have been developing programs for years now use the expertise of a whole new generation who are building new ones. This gives younger people added responsibility and a say in NRDC's future.

"Climate change has forced us to do that," Peter says. "For example, the oceans program is looking into ocean acidification because of fossil-fuel emissions, which ties the oceans and energy programs together. What we are doing in China is tied to our climate program. Allen Hershkowitz's urban work with recycling led to the greening of our sports arenas, and that has crossed over into sustainable development. Linda Greer's work on toxics with our health program has led to cross-programming with air and energy. This approach marks a conscious change for the organization. We have to use every tool we have because NRDC is one of the largest and most influential environmental groups in the world, and that means we have to tackle the biggest problems."

Prior to my departure, Frances and the board began a strategic planning process, in which board member Patricia Bauman played a central role by showing how toxic chemicals and public health are intrinsically tied to the issue of global warming. She was supported in this argument by Ricky Perera, a fellow board member who was instrumental in building our toxics program in the 1980s. The strategic plan identified six future priorities for the organization: curb global warming, create a clean energy future, revive the world's oceans, save endangered wildlife and wild places, stem the tide of toxic chemicals, and accelerate the greening of China.

Guided by development director Jack Murray, NRDC launched its Partnership for the Earth Campaign with the goal of raising $500 million to execute this strategic plan. Board members Philip

Korsant, Wendy Neu, and Wendy Schmidt cochair this campaign with me, and in spite of the economic downturn of 2008, we are well on the way to our goal. (As I write, we have raised about $450 million.) The campaign has allowed us to create our Science Center, under Gabriela Chavarria; triple our China program staff; and establish the Center for Market Innovation, which was funded by trustee Shelly Malkin and her husband, Tony. The center's expertise has played a key role in our climate negotiations, particularly with the Senate. (Its first director, Rick Duke, joined the Obama administration's Energy Department in 2009 and was replaced by Peter Malik.) These are only a few examples of how NRDC has grown since Frances Beinecke took over the leadership.

Patricia and I look forward to many years of continued participation with NRDC and others who care about the environment. We are proud of and grateful to all the people who have made this the strongest environmental organization in the world. It is a great gift for all of us to leave those who come after.

The main reason we continue to work so hard to protect our global environment was also with us in Alaska: our granddaughter, Lulu; the Welch children, Tom, John, and Alex; and Michael Wolfe's son, Sam. To see them kayaking through the deep water, sloshing through the tidal flats looking for smooth rocks, spending hours fishing for halibut or salmon (this sure takes patience, Lulu would say with a sigh), or collecting moss from the rain forest is to see our future. We hope not only that they will inherit great wilderness areas such as the Tongass but also that their daily life will include clear, clean skies and pure water. The challenge before us is as broad and global as climate change, but it is also as close and personal as our families.

Time Line of NRDC and the Modern Environmental Movement

1962
Rachel Carson's *Silent Spring* is published.

1964
Wilderness Act.

1965
Scenic Hudson Preservation Conference v. Federal Power Commission.

1970
National Environmental Policy Act. Environmental Protection Agency (EPA) is created.

Natural Resources Defense Council is incorporated.

Clean Air Act.

First Earth Day.

1971
First NRDC lawsuit, challenging strip-mining by the Tennessee Valley Authority.

1972
Clean Water Act is enacted, with major input from NRDC.

Federal Insecticide, Fungicide, and Rodenticide Act amendments.

United Nations Conference on the Human Environment in Stockholm.

NRDC opens western office in Palo Alto, California.

Court rules in *NRDC v. Morton* that Interior Department must consider energy conservation as an alternative to proposed offshore oil drilling.

Court rules in *NRDC v. Grant* that the federal Soil Conservation Service must study environmental impacts before channelizing streams.

1973
Endangered Species Act.

NRDC wins landmark lawsuit requiring the Atomic Energy Commission to study environmental effects of the Liquid Metal Fast Breeder Reactor Program.

1974
Safe Drinking Water Act.

Bureau of Land Management is required to assess environmental impacts of livestock grazing on public lands.

NRDC forces EPA to regulate dredge and fill materials used in wetlands.

NRDC wins the nation's first lawsuit to curb acid rain.

Federal courts rule for NRDC and against "tall stacks" that disperse pollution.

1976
Resource Conservation and Recovery Act; Toxic Substances Control Act

NRDC negotiates federal agreement regulating industrial water pollution.

NRDC-supported provisions are incorporated into National Forest Management Act.

Federal Land Policy and Management Act passes with NRDC-supported provisions protecting publicly owned lands throughout the West.

1977
Clean Air Act amendments protecting wilderness areas.

NRDC publishes blueprint for replacing all new Pacific Northwest power plants with conservation and renewable energy.

Clean Water Act is revised, including key recommendations from NRDC.

NRDC prevents Nuclear Regulatory Commission from licensing plutonium fuel use and processing facilities without environmental review.

1978
Love Canal disaster gives birth to the environmental justice movement.

NRDC wins a ban on ozone-depleting CFCs in aerosol cans.

NRDC lawsuit cuts sulfur dioxide emissions by a million tons annually.

New York City adopts NRDC blueprint for reform of public transportation.

NRDC forces EPA to establish a national health standard for airborne lead.

Nuclear Non-Proliferation Act incorporates NRDC-supported provisions for more stringent controls of nuclear sales abroad.

President Jimmy Carter prohibits the licensing of plutonium recycling activities.

1979
Three Mile Island nuclear accident.

First issue of NRDC's *Amicus Journal.*

NRDC shapes EPA rules for pollution controls on all new coal-fired power plants.

1980
Congress establishes Superfund to finance cleanup of hazardous waste sites.

NRDC helps win federal protection for 100 million acres in Alaska.

NRDC forces EPA to establish a program under TSCA for testing chemicals.

Landmark settlement of 17-year dispute over Hudson River power plants.

1981
NRDC litigation protects millions of acres of wilderness areas in national forests.

NRDC convinces Congress to enact the first of eight annual prohibitions on oil and gas leasing in sensitive coastal areas off California and other states.

1982
NRDC files first successful citizen lawsuit against industrial water polluters.

1983
NRDC lawsuit wins first public access to EPA health and safety data on pesticides.

NRDC wins the first in a series of victories forcing federal nuclear weapons facilities to obey the same environmental laws as private industry.

Congress cancels Clinch River breeder reactor project.

NRDC launches Hood River Conservation Project in Oregon.

1984
Explosion at a Union Carbide plant in Bhopal, India, kills 3,000 people.

NRDC wins challenge to below-cost logging plans in the Colorado Rockies.

NRDC forces EPA to issue standards for diesel truck and bus emissions.

In response to NRDC petition, California adopts standards to slash energy consumption by air conditioners and refrigerators.

NRDC lawsuit forces EPA to require safety testing on 20 potentially dangerous chemicals widely used in industry.

NRDC publishes first volume in its *Nuclear Weapons Databook* series.

1985
NRDC helps win adoption of national efficiency standards for appliances.

1986
Chernobyl nuclear accident.

NRDC negotiates agreement with major oil companies on offshore oil leasing in Alaska's Bering Sea.

NRDC-supported Proposition 65, the Safe Drinking Water and Toxics Enforcement Act, passes in California.

Superfund law is reauthorized with NRDC-supported strengthening amendments.

NRDC and the Soviet Academy of Sciences reach historic agreement to set up seismic monitoring stations in the U.S. and USSR to monitor underground tests.

1987
NRDC negotiates an energy conservation agreement with the Pacific Northwest's largest utility, Pacific Power and Light Co.

National Appliances Energy Conservation Act.

NRDC and Soviet Academy of Sciences conduct chemical explosive experiments to test the sensitivity of their joint stations around Soviet nuclear test sites.

NRDC initiative leads to a 30-nation agreement to reduce chlorofluorocarbon (CFC) production by 50 percent by 1998.

NRDC wins $1.5 million settlement against Bethlehem Steel for water pollution.

1988

Congress enacts an NRDC-initiated reform bill mandating complete health and safety testing of pesticides used in the U.S.

Joint U.S./Soviet nuclear test ban verification experiments in Nevada.

NASA scientist James Hansen warns Congress about possible consequences of global warming; Intergovernmental Panel on Climate Change (IPCC) is established.

1989

Exxon Valdez oil spill off Alaska.

New NRDC offices in New York City, a national model of energy efficiency.

EPA issues a comprehensive ban on asbestos sought by NRDC.

After NRDC campaign, Uniroyal withdraws Alar from use on food worldwide.

NRDC campaign leads to landmark New York City mandatory recycling law.

California refrigerator efficiency standards are extended nationwide.

1990

NRDC litigation establishes model program in Los Angeles to protect children from lead poisoning.

NRDC leads successful fight for passage of Clean Air Act Amendments.

1991

Defeat of Senate bill to open Arctic National Wildlife Refuge to oil drilling.

1992

NRDC convinces Forest Service to end clear-cutting in national forests in the Sierra Nevada.

NRDC achieves passage of the most significant lead-poisoning law since the phaseout of leaded gasoline.

NRDC helps win Congressional passage of the Energy Policy Act, the most important energy-efficient legislation in over a decade.

Earth Summit in Rio de Janeiro, Brazil.

1993

NRDC wins landmark case banning cancer-causing pesticides in foods.

"Golden Carrot" project produces a super-refrigerator that cuts energy use and operates without CFCs.

1994

NRDC helps the Cree defeat the James Bay hydroelectric project in Quebec.

NRDC secures far-reaching EPA regulation to reduce toxic emissions from chemical plants by one billion pounds per year.

1995

Sweeping attack on environmental laws is launched by 104th Congress.

1996

NRDC plays central role in defeating environmental rollbacks proposed by 104th Congress.

1997

Kyoto Protocol adopted by the U.S. and 121 other nations but not ratified by Congress.

1999

NRDC helps win commitments from over 200 companies to phase out the use and sale of old-growth wood products.

NRDC launches membership bulletin, *Nature's Voice.*

NRDC sponsors Marine Life Protection Act in California.

2000

Mitsubishi abandons plan for salt factory in Laguna San Ignacio, Mexico.

NRDC victory against Texaco for Clean Water Act violations in Delaware River.

Congress requires consistent national health standards for testing waters off beaches.

NRDC and Dow Chemical Company produce a comprehensive joint plan to reduce waste and emissions at Dow's plant in Midland, Michigan.

Major NRDC victory when Governor George E. Pataki announces plan to clean up New York City's entire diesel bus fleet.

NRDC reaches settlements with California's largest grocery chains, which agree to add more than 150 clean alternative-fuel trucks to their fleets.

EPA forces GE to pay for the dredging of toxic PCBs from Hudson River.

2001

NRDC launches BioGems initiative.

Clinton administration adopts the "roadless rule," the largest land-conservation measure in U.S. history.

Following NRDC's decade-long campaign, EPA announces a stricter standard for limiting public exposure to arsenic in tap water.

NRDC helps secure agreement protecting millions of acres of the Great Bear Rainforest in British Columbia.

NRDC launches Climate Center to focus on global warming.

2002
NRDC lawsuit compels Bush administration to turn over records of meetings with industry lobbyists involved in writing the nation's energy plan.

Senate again rejects attempt to open Arctic National Wildlife Refuge to oil drilling.

California establishes 12 marine reserves in waters around the Channel Islands.

California passes historic AB1493 law to cut global warming pollution from cars and trucks sold in the state.

NRDC successfully opposes cuts in New York City recycling program.

2003
New York Governor George E. Pataki draws on an NRDC blueprint for the Maine-to-Maryland carbon cap initiative, the first such regional effort.

EPA proposal to cut diesel pollution from farm and construction equipment.

John Adams invited to join the Pew Oceans Commission.

Federal judges side with an NRDC-led coalition to limit U.S. Navy's use of low-frequency sonar in the Hawaiian Islands Whale Sanctuary.

NRDC forces the city of Los Angeles to clean up its enormous shipping port.

NRDC opens the Robert Redford Building in Santa Monica, California.

NRDC blocks administration efforts to weaken Clean Air Act requirement that power plants and factories install modern pollution controls when upgrading.

McCain-Lieberman Climate Stewardship Act, supported by NRDC.

2004
NRDC opens a new, energy-efficient San Francisco office.

NRDC helps develop national energy-efficiency plan for China.

2005

NRDC negotiates a pact with leading paper producer, Bowater, to stop clear-cutting hardwood forests on the Cumberland Plateau.

U.S. Senate again blocks drilling in Arctic National Wildlife Refuge.

Federal appeals court panel strikes down Forest Service program of logging in pristine areas of Alaska's Tongass National Forest.

NRDC opens Science Center.

Landmark agreement to restore California's San Joaquin River.

2006

Coalition including NRDC sues the EPA to prevent unethical testing of pesticides on human subjects.

Former U.S. Vice President Al Gore releases documentary, *An Inconvenient Truth.*

California imposes a cap on greenhouse gas emissions, the first state to do so.

NRDC opens its first international office, in Beijing.

NRDC leadership helps eight eastern states develop the Regional Greenhouse Gas Initiative, which uses market-based strategies to cut global warming pollution.

NRDC leads efforts to win a landmark United Nations agreement restricting bottom trawling in 20 million square miles of the South Pacific.

2007

NRDC members and online activists numbering 370,000 send comments urging the U.S. Fish and Wildlife Service to protect polar bears under the Endangered Species Act.

NRDC partners with the Academy of Motion Picture Arts and Sciences to green the 79th Annual Academy Awards.

NRDC launches Center for Market Innovation.

Al Gore and the Intergovernmental Panel on Climate Change win the Nobel Peace Prize.

2008

NRDC prompts major banks to adopt new lending principles that steer investments away from dirty coal plants and toward energy efficiency and renewables.

NRDC efforts in Congress and the European Union lead to policies that will remove one-third of the world's supply of mercury from circulation.

2009

NRDC establishes Growing Green Awards for pioneers in sustainable food.

President Barack Obama calls for a National Oceans Policy.

NRDC plays a central role in historic agreement on greenhouse gas emissions and energy efficiency between California and the province of Jiangsu, China.

In response to an NRDC lawsuit, a federal judge rules that all children's toys and childcare products containing toxic phthalates must be removed from stores.

NRDC members and online activists pass the 1.3 million mark.

House of Representatives passes NRDC-supported American Clean Energy and Security Act.

UN Climate Change Conference in Copenhagen.

386

THE NEW YORK ALUMNI PARTY CELEBRATING JOHN ADAMS'S RETIREMENT, 2006
Left to right: Edward Strohbehn, Founding Staff, NRDC; Patricia Sullivan, Deputy Director, NRDC; Cardboard cut-out of John Adams, Founding Director and Trustee, NRDC; David Hawkins, Founding Staff and Director, Climate Programs, NRDC

Index

Page numbers in italics indicate photographs